A Treasury of Old
SILVER

Courtesy of the Philadelphia Museum of Art

Colonial silver coffeepot made by David Hall of Philadelphia, circa, 1766. Standing thirteen inches high and distinguished by the shell-like Chippendale scroll at the base of its spout, this handsome piece embodies an extreme simplicity of design in keeping with Quaker tastes.

A Treasury of Old
SILVER

Edited by KURT M. SEMON

PUBLISHER OF AMERICAN COLLECTOR

ROBERT M. McBRIDE & COMPANY

NEW YORK

A TREASURY OF OLD SILVER
COPYRIGHT, 1947, BY
AMERICAN COLLECTOR

PRINTED IN THE UNITED STATES OF AMERICA

In Canada
GEORGE J. MC LEOD, LIMITED
TORONTO

CONTENTS

FOREWORD	7
THE FOUR GEORGES	
NOTES ON ENGLISH DOMESTIC SILVER 1714-1760	9
GEORGE III AND GEORGE IV—1760-1830	13
POMANDER AND VINAIGRETTE	17
TEA DRINKING MADE TRADE FOR SILVERSMITHS	20
HUGUENOT SILVERSMITHS: THE COURTAULDS	22
OLD ENGLISH SILVER-IN-THE-LITTLE	26
ENGLISH STANDING-CUPS	28
SHEFFIELD PLATE: AN ACCIDENT	32
MAKING SHEFFIELD PLATE WAS BIG BUSINESS	33
SILVER PLATE OF GEORGIAN ENGLAND	37
THE LONDON COMPANIES AND THEIR PLATE	39
HOW TO READ ENGLISH HALL MARKS	40
THE SCOTTISH SILVERSMITHS	42
IRISH PLATE WAS WIDELY MADE	43
AMERICAN SILVER STYLES AND THEIR ENGLISH BACKGROUND	45
17TH CENTURY NEW YORK SILVER WAS BOTH DUTCH AND ENGLISH	48
THE DROWNE SILVERSMITHS OF PORTSMOUTH	53
PHILADELPHIA SILVER BY GHISELIN AND SYNG	55
WILLIAM GILBERT, SILVERSMITH OF NEW YORK	61
WILLIAM CARIO, FATHER AND SON, SILVERSMITHS	64
PAUL REVERE, HIS CRAFTSMANSHIP AND TIME	67
EPHRAIM BRASHER, SILVERSMITH OF NEW YORK	69
ALBANY WAS A COLONIAL SILVERMAKING CENTER	71
STANDISH BARRY, BALTIMORE CRAFTSMAN	73
SMALL BUT USEFUL AMERICAN SILVER	76
VIRGINIA FAMILIES AND THEIR SILVER	79
AN IMPORTANT SILVER MUG BY JACOB HURD	81
HISTORY IN AMERICAN SILVER	
18TH CENTURY	82
19TH CENTURY	86
WASHINGTON'S CAMP SILVER, PEWTER AND TIN	90
NICHOLAS SEVER'S PLATE RETURNS TO HARVARD	92
THE SILVER OF CAPTAIN TOBIAS LEAR OF PORTSMOUTH	96
OLD CANADIAN SILVER	99
THREE CENTURIES OF FRENCH DOMESTIC SILVER	102
FRENCH SILVERSMITHS EXCELLED BUT GERMANS MORE PROLIFIC	104
FINE SILVER MADE EVERYWHERE IN NORTHERN EUROPE	107
ITALY, SPAIN AND PORTUGAL MADE ELABORATE SILVER	110

FOREWORD

There is great fascination in collecting fine old silver with its graceful pattern and satin smoothness. Ever since man found expression in works of art this gleaming metal has been used in the creation of precious vessels and rare ornaments. Long before the Christian era it was a favorite metal with the Mesopotanians, Egyptians, Chinese, Persians and Greeks. As a collector's item early silver enjoys the advantage of being both useful and ornamental; it has permanence and lasting worth as a precious document of bygone culture.

Our own silver heritage dates from the time of the early American colonists who brought with them to the new world the fine art of silversmithing. Its craftsmen were mostly English and Dutch, with a sprinkling of Huguenots. Naturally, from these sources, especially from the English, America took its form and pattern. Strangely enough the appreciation of our native silver is of comparatively recent origin for it was less than seventy years ago that the simple beauty of American silver secured recognition. Increasingly since then it has taken its rightful place among the fine arts of our country.

A Treasury of Old Silver attempts to give a broad panorama of the subject under the authorship of many authorities. There are chapters on silver in a wide variety of forms as well as on some of the early craftsmen who made it. This material has been drawn from numerous issues of the American Collector in which it appeared over a period of years. To its distinguished authors for their gracious permissions I wish to express my gratitude for making this volume possible.

So this book is dedicated to the beginner and to the seasoned collector in the hope that it may prove a source of inspiration and help in one of the most delightful of occupations—the discovery and collecting of old silver.

K. M. S.

Private collection

GEORGIAN OCTAGONAL COFFEEPOT AND MUFFINEERS

George I silver coffeepot and plain octagonal lighthouse form, hinged cover with finial, the spout wrought to simulate a duck's head, was made by Anthony Nelme of London in 1716. Nelme was one of the most famous silversmiths of his time and worked in a period notable for its silver craftsmenship.

The Four Georges

NOTES ON ENGLISH DOMESTIC SILVER
1714-1760

By Kurt M. Semon

(*Illustrations Courtesy Metropolitan Museum of Art*)

Possession of silver articles has always been considered as a step up on the social ladder; something to be proud of and something to bolster self-respect. Even today we see people, making more money and making it faster than ever before, acquiring silver objects of all kinds. The market seems to be definitely a seller's market.

Probably in no other country has so much fine silverware been produced as in England, and nowhere has the collecting of it been keener and its use more widespread. For several reasons this may seem strange, with no adequate source of raw material on the British Isles. But with the growth of the nation, the war against competitors, such as Holland and Spain, for the domination of foreign territories and riches, more silver came to victorious Albion. And so we witness an evolution that not only brought to the churches gifts from the faithful parishioners, silver for the official use of kings and nobility, the plate of the liveried companies, but also an ever-growing quantity of so-called household and decorative silver.

Of the fifteenth and sixteenth centuries fine examples of church silver and representative silver of the kings, the nobility and prominent institutions have survived, but pieces of household silver earlier than the sixteenth century are extremely rare, much of it probably perished in the long years of internal struggle, though a few pieces grace the collections of museums and private collectors.

The history of the guilds of the goldsmiths, their standing and responsibility, the history of the acts to protect the quality of the silver, or the coin of the realm, the history of the system of hallmarks and date letters, of makers' marks and of assaying have been exhaustively explored and ably described. The profession of the goldsmith always was held in high esteem in England, well organized and watchful to keep up the quality of the work and the honesty and integrity of its members. It was obvious that such diligence and precaution guaranteed a high level of work and protected the public as well as the guilds themselves from any attempt at counterfeiting or other fraud. The trustworthiness of the goldsmiths was of course reflected in the ever growing spread of the use of fine silver and it attracted many able artists and craftsmen to this honorable and lucrative profession.

Silver as an easily workable precious metal always has fascinated the artist, but there were very few in England during the fifteenth and sixteenth centuries. The fine early English plate as far as its style and form goes owes much, if not everything to foreign influence. Of these early times, the Tudor-Gothic and the Renaissance, we will remember the drinking horns, remnants of a more ancient past, and other kinds of drinking vessels as the mazer, a bowl mostly of wood mounted with a band of silver to protect the edges, developing into the cup, and we have the tankard and the beaker. Practically in the same class are the porringers or caudle-cups introduced into common use in the early seventeenth century for possets and hot drinks, very much in vogue at that time. The posset, a kind of hot sack with spices, milk and eggs was practically universal as a beverage; of course it was somewhat thicker than mere spiced ale or hot wine.

We can quote Shakespeare from the Merry Wives of Wind-

George I tankard engraved with the Newland arms, Petley Ley, ent. 1715, London.

George I cream jug, 1721-1723, Anthony Nelme, London.

A TREASURY OF OLD SILVER

George I caster with repousse decoration, John Bignell, ent. 1720, London.

George II loving cup, Samuel Courtauld, ent. 1746, London.

sor, "Thou shalt drink a posset tonight in my house." And we hear the devilish Lady Macbeth saying, "I have drugged their possets that death and nature do contend about them, whether they will live or die."

At the time of King George I, 1714-1724, a great variety of household silver was already fashioned and used; forks, spoons and knives, candlesticks, snuffers and snuffer trays, casters, cruets, soup tureens, wine tasters, bread or fruit baskets, and of course snuff boxes;—more and more was added, first as a luxury and then as a necessity.

It may be of interest to note that for the style of the early Georgian silver, England is heavily indebted to France. With the repeal of the Edict of Nantes a great number of prominent French artists and craftsmen sought refuge from religious persecution, and we have a long list with imposing names of refugee silver-and-goldsmiths coming to England as early as during the last years of Queen Anne's reign, and during the reign of the first two Georges, starting with men like Simon Pantin, Pierre Harache, John Chartier, Isaac Ribolau, Pierre Platel, Le Sage, Pileau, Courtauld, Willaume and culminating in the most famous of all, Paul Lamerie.

In the time of King George I, the dominating figure at the head of any European nation was Louis XIV of France, the Roi Soleil. The manner and style of his court were imitated in one form or another by many minor potentates and beginning in France, started the victorious spread of the Rococo style The word Rococo probably comes from "Rock-Coquille." The forms originated from Italy and were then developed in France. We know that the director of the royal factory in Paris, Meissonier, published several works about Rococo style in 1723. The motifs fundamentally were Oriental with a prevalence of shells and marine subjects. We see them together with the Gadroon or other borders, the acanthus and lanceolate leaves, together with tritons, dolphins, sea-monsters, grape-vine leaves and grotesque masks. When this style was introduced into England where a natural restraint and the gift for understatement quieted the exuberance of the French style in a very healthy manner many works of excellent taste resulted, and some of the finest silver in this style was created by Paul Lamerie.

It seems that very little is known of the life of the famous silversmiths of that period. Probably they lived uneventful, regular lives as good citizens, devoted to their profession and at times also active in some kind of civic work, but nothing was outstanding in their personalities or artistic achievement to be recorded and passed on by contemporary writers or later historians. There is the one exception of the just-mentioned Lamerie, who although not attaining high honors

George II salver, 1730-1731, Paul Lamerie, London.

George II cake basket, 1745-1746, Paul Lamerie, London

ENGLISH SILVER

George II sugar bowl with repousse decoration, Samuel Taylor, 1751, London.

second dating from the year 1732 and a third from 1739 which complied with a new law of King George II ordering all working and manufacturing goldsmiths to change the form of their maker's mark and register a new form forthwith at the goldsmith's hall. It should be noted that during this period also the old silver standard, raised since 1697 to stop the melting of coins for the use of silverware, was revised in 1719.

A few years after the establishment of his own shop Lamerie married Louise Juliott in 1716. He had six children, four daughters and two sons, but the sons and one daughter died at an early age.

In his civic career Lamerie was known as Captain from 1736 on and was later styled "Major". Probably he was a member of some private volunteer organization of military character yet not recognized officially, organized in companies, having its own equipment at its own expense, but never called upon to carry out any duties by authority and probably not considered as a body of troops for any length of time. Only by courtesy were its officers allowed to assume the title of their representative ranks. It was a private volunteer organization of this sort that Lamerie joined in a patriotic spirit.

in any official capacity became so famous for his work that much data of his family and life have been assembled and published.

On the fourteenth of April in 1688, Paul Jaques, the son of Paul Souchay de la Merie was baptised in the small town of Bois le Duc, according to the register of the Wallon church of this little town in southern Holland. When the little family left for England in March, 1689, they did not forget to take this baptismal record with them and it served them as a kind of religious passport together with attestation papers as members of the Wallon church. The head of the family, a French nobleman had been accepted in the service of the army of the united provinces of the Netherlands. In England the name of Souchay was dropped. We find the first mention of a Paule Lemurre in 1691. In 1701 this was changed to La Merie and finally in 1702 to the name Lamerie. The nobleman had the idea that any kind of craft was below his personal standing and the dignity peculiar to his class; he managed to get a small pension for a while from the crown but died a pauper in 1735. For his son the goldsmith's craft was all he would accept as becoming to a member of a noble family, and little Paul accordingly was apprenticed to another refugee, Pierre Platel, in 1704. Eight years later he became a freeman on September 4, 1712, and entered his maker's mark the next day. We have two additional marks of Lamerie, a

George II cruet frame and cruets, 1758-1759, Samuel Wood, London.

His rise in the Guild hierarchy was rather rapid. In 1738 he was appointed to a committee for "The Parliament business of the goldsmiths company" drawing up a petition and bill to be offered to Parliament.

With the rise of good business and widespread recognition, our master moved from modest quarters to a new address in 1738 where he became neighbor to many persons of high degree, and it is here, at Garard St. where he was to grow to fame and eminence in his profession, where he saw one of his daughters married and where his mother died.

It seems that the French refugees kept close together, because the husbands of Lamerie's daughter, Joseph Debaufre, the son of a watchmaker of renown also had come from abroad. At the time of this marriage in 1750 Lamerie became seriously ill, but he managed to attend a meeting of the goldsmith's company where his able and sound advice carried weight and we know that the activity, ability and power of artistic expression which had been his for forty years were not lost at that time.

George II soup turreen, 1758-1759, John Swift, London.

One would expect to find some recognition for the creator of such outstanding work in the form of an appointment as goldsmith to the crown, but in royal collections not one piece by Lamerie can be found. As during his lifetime Samuel Smithin and later Thomas Minor were crown goldsmiths it may be that Lamerie's foreign origin prejudiced against such nomination.

The master's life span came to an end in 1751. In the London Evening Post, August 3rd to August 6th, 1751, we find the following obituary notice: "Last Friday died at Daventry in North Hampshire, Mr. Humphrey Paine, formerly an eminent goldsmith at the "Hen and Chickens" at Cheapside, but having acquired a handsome fortune, he quitted trade to his son a few months ago, to whom he has left the bulk of his estate.

The same day died Paul D'Lamerie, Esq. an ancient goldsmith in Garard St.; Soho; they both were ancient members of the goldsmith's company and had each of them been upwards of fifty years in trade, wherein they would be very largely concerned. The latter was partly famous for making fine ornamental plate and has been very instrumental in bringing that branch of the trade to the perfection it is now in."

In his will Lamerie made specific provisions and left directions for the disposal of his estate, evidently in order to avoid any possibility of dispute between his wife and unmarried daughters. His business was to be closed, the goods to be put to public auction, and there were also instructions as to the disposal of his leaseholds.

No catalogue of auction sale has been found, only two announcements of forthcoming sales, one of plate, jewels and watches, the other of patterns, tools and shop fixtures.

The status of the artist and master craftsman, Paul Lamerie is known universally. We know that at the start of his career the so-called Queen Anne style, with its unadorned simplicity was still in vogue and that the Rococo style was widely favored, bringing new forms and new decorative motifs. Accordingly, Paul Lamerie's career falls practically into two parts, the first from his original registration to his second mark where he worked already in the so-called new silver standard. His pieces of this period are more delicate and less elaborate. The ornate Rococo work in the later period of the old silver standard has a different and probably not so high an artistic quality. Sometimes details are not handled with care and the pieces become really "compositions" seemingly by "chance" in silver, with a touch of genius.

When we try to find out if other artists or craftsmen of the period crossed the path of Paul Lamerie we come to the famous engraver and painter, William Hogarth who was first apprenticed in 1712 to Ellis Gamble, probably an engraver of silver. He did some work for Lamerie and also engraved Lamerie's bookplate with the three "Souches", meaning "tree stumps." These Lamerie had chosen for his own arms, probably adopted from the arms born by another branch of the Souchay family.

We have dwelt at length on this eminent master because he is the most representative and the greatest of his period, and in his case we are fortunate that family and other records have been preserved, but we must not forget that during the reign of the first two Georges other splendid silver was created by famous refugees such as Pierre Harrache, David Willaume, Augustine Cortauld, Peter Archambo, Peter Platel, just to name a few, and also by some English-born artists, such as Anthony Nelme and Benjamin Pine.

The silversmith's art, of course, was not confined to the city of London. In England proper, Norwich, Exeter, Newcastle and Chester were centers for the production of fine plate. In Scotland, Edinborough and Glasgow were prominent, and in Ireland the same held true for Dublin and Cork.

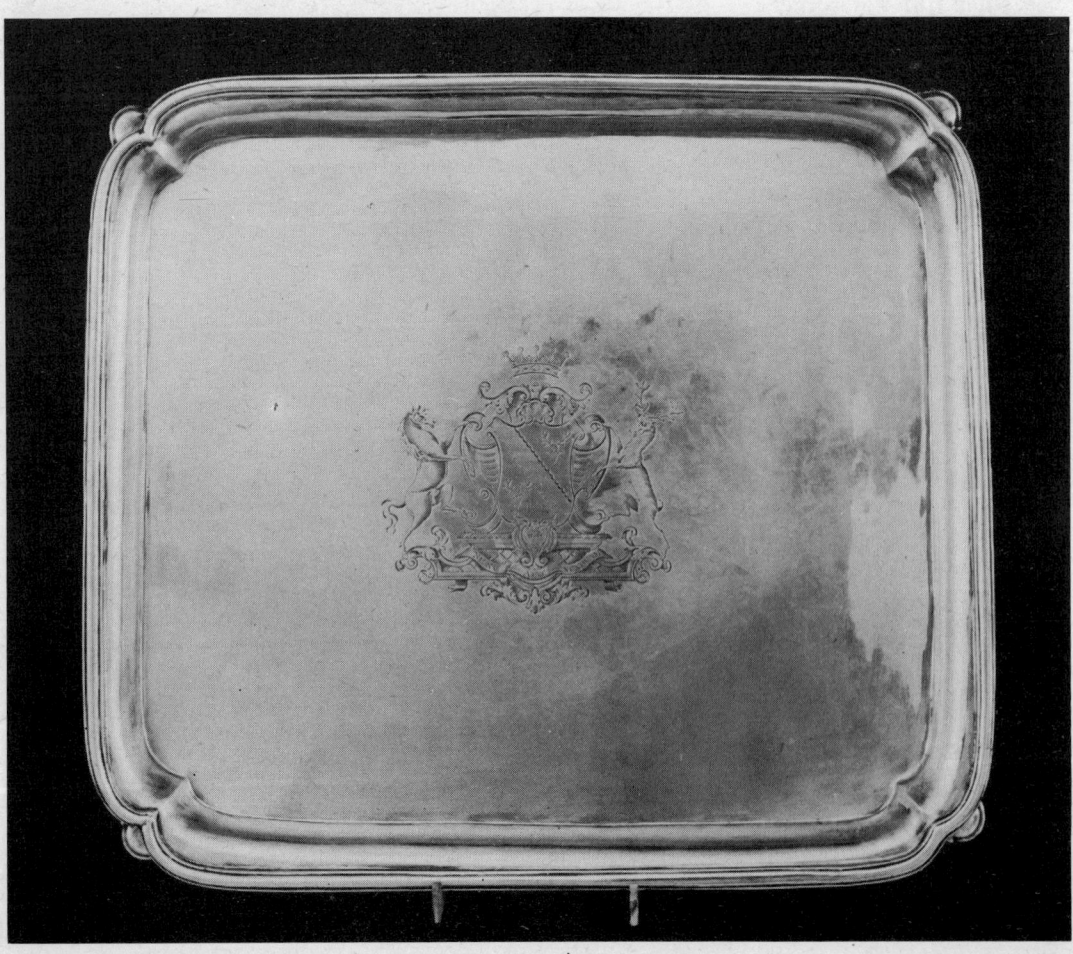

GEORGE II SILVER ARMORIAL TRAY

Oblong deep tray with invected corners and molded rim, the center engraved with the coat of arms of the Earl of Kilmorey. Made by Charles Hatfield, London, 1730.
Private collection

Part II
GEORGE III and GEORGE IV—1760-1830

It is safe to state that no other period of English history can compare with the times of George I and George II for an abundance of fine silver of excellent taste. Much of this noble quality was due, of course, to the influence of immigrant silversmiths and such quality continued to be the tradition during the years immediately following the death of George II because there were still alive such prominent artist craftsmen as John Emes, John Wakelin, William Chawner and Robert Garrard, to name only a few. But thereafter British creative genius seems to have turned away from silver to other materials, seeking and finding other outlets and modes of expression. The oncoming era was the period of the great portraitists—Joshua Reynolds, Henry Raeburn, Thomas Gainsborough, George Romney and John Hoppner. Also the famous cabinet-maker, Thomas Chippendale (1718-1779), was reaching the height of his glory, blending Gothic, Chinese and French Rococo motifs into a new style that left is impression all over the world.

Also, a new artistic ideal began to sweep over Europe—the new classicism. It was largely inspired by excavations of Herculaneum, 1738, and to a higher degree of Pompei, 1758, and Spalato, 1760. The Adam brothers, Robert and James (1728-1794), were its English protagonists. As architects, designers of interiors, of furniture and decorative objects, they molded Greek and Roman motifs into a graceful, elegant and refined new style.

Few silver articles were made in the late eighteenth century that were not for table use. Their forms were mostly undecorated and often resembled Greek or Roman vases. We see the bright-cut engraving, boat-shaped sugar bowls and salt cellars and the column candlesticks. The use of gilt was discarded.

This revival of classicism, though its antique source was similar to the one of the Renaissance, was entirely different in its interpretation of Old World art. We must remember that the age of reason had started. At this time the accent was on purity, restraint and balance; there was no Rococo exuberance and no fancifulness. Gradually the style of George II deteriorated, and in the new style, as related to silver, there was a dearth of vigor—of red blood corpuscles.

Do we know much of the silversmiths of this period of George III and George IV? The answer is "no." Memoirs and diaries are lacking, perhaps because these craftsmen never rose above the special qualifications of their profession. Even of Paul Storr, who came at the tail-end of this period, little is known although he fashioned much silver for the nobility and for the court. The same goes for Hester Bateman, famous woman silversmith working at the turn of the eighteenth century, as well as for the other members of her family—Peter, Ann, William and Jonathan, all able craftsmen.

There is one exception in Matthew Boulton of Birmingham, 1728-1809. He was known not so much as a prominent silversmith as for his part in the developing of the steam engine with his friend and partner, the inventor, James Watt. Boulton was a man of remarkable versatility, outstanding for his resourcefulness in industry and business. He possessed not only high intelligence and great driving power but also impeccable moral qualities. He was kind and dignified.

At the risk of digressing somewhat from our subject we suc-

—S. Wyler
George III Epergne
William Caldecott, 1765.

cumb to the impulse to give the reader a glimpse of this extraordinary man. At the age of fifteen he entered the toy business of his father, Matthew Boulton, Sr. Birmingham at that time was called "Europe's Toy Shop" and toy-making meant the manufacturing of all kinds of hardware including an endless variety of articles in gold, silver, steel and other metals, as well as tortoise shell. Boulton Senior's branch was steel.

The business of toy manufacturing was only the start of the son's career. Let us look at the variety of activities which engaged him across the years. Toys, ormolu, plated ware, silver, steam engines, mechanical copying of pictures, letter copying machines, buttons and buckles, medals, mint for copper coin of the Government, manufacturing of steam-driven coining machines, an iron foundry — all these felt his influence. Added thereto may be Boulton's successful efforts to have a silver assay office established in Birmingham; his introduction of a benevolent workmen's compensation in his factory and numerous other civic activities. He happened not to be

—Billy Rose
George III Wine Coolers and Hotwater Jug
Paul Storr, 1804 and 1817.

13

commercially successful in all his enterprises, especially not in those having artistic aims, such as ormolu, the copying of pictures and medals; these had to be given up after unsuccessful attempts. But the greater part of his activities proved him to be a sound, progressive businessman. At times he employed more than 1,000 workmen and he left a valuable, prosperous business to his sons.

Like a charmed cycle, Boulton's life started with metal, and following his activities in other fields, his career was climaxed by his invention of the machine to mint the coin of the realm—an invention of great importance for the quality and stability of English currency. In the first place, however, Boulton's name stands out supreme because of his connection with the steam engine, but this does not diminish the fact that in everything he touched, quality was the watchword.

A silversmith of fine taste, his plated ware became longer-lasting when he introduced silver thread borders. When occupied in the steel toy business he made fine frames for the cameos of his friend, Josiah Wedgwood. With his ormolu (from the French "or moulu," ground gold with mercury gilding ornamental brass), he embellished fine vases, and in this he was advised by James Adam, "to do some work in plate and ormolu in elegant and superior style," a suggestion he never followed. Some of Boulton's ormolu work still graces Buckingham Palace and some was purchased by Catherine, Empress of Russia.

—Billy Rose
George III Hot Water Urn
Paul Storr, 1809.

To understand Boulton's successful endeavors in 1773 to secure an assay office in Birmingham, we must have in mind that London was 112 miles away from Birmingham and that Chester, the other nearest office, was 72 miles away. Thus there always were involved, costly delay, the risk of highway robbery, damage and the possibility of designs being copied. In his most far-reaching activity, the steam engine, James Watt, his partner, 1783-1800, had the biggest share, as a remarkable inventor. In his own factory, Boulton, however, conceived the idea of using steam as power to lift water after it had gone over the water wheel, thus getting it back into the pool and using it over again. The importance of this new machine was first demonstrated in mills, coal mines and the water supplies of cities; finally the newly-harnessed power reached out into all fields of industrial activity.

After a long period of frustration in his efforts to interest the Royal Mint in the use of his newly invented steam-driven machine for coining, at last in 1797 he got a government order to execute the coinage of two-penny and one-penny copper pieces, amounting to about 500 tons, and additional orders during the next two years for half-pennies and farthings, amounting to about 1800 tons. Such coinage, oddly, was not furnished to the Mint, but was distributed by the contractor. Up to the year 1808 Boulton coined about 3,500 tons of copper coins, and a year later he was called to restamp Mexican silver dollars, making them into five shilling pieces for the Bank of England at a value of $500,000. When, in 1805, the Royal Mint finally decided to use coining by machine, Boulton was employed in the planning and building of the new Mint and also furnished machinery and steam power. It seems eloquent proof of the quality of his machine that it was not replaced until 1881.

The strain of incessant work was finally felt by Boulton and he left more and more to his son, Matthew Robinson Boulton, and to James Watt, Jr. He died peacefully in 1809. In the memoir written by his old partner, James Watt, we find these well-fitting lines. "He has conducted the whole more like a sovereign than a private manufacturer. His love of fame has been to him a greater stimulus than his love of gain."

After this disgression into the life and accomplishments of a great industrialist captain, who was, as well, a prominent silversmith, we turn again to the craftsmen who devoted all their time and effort to the fashioning of silver. We

—R. Hyman
George III Candlesticks
(Two of Four)
John Parker, 1799.

—Peter Guille
George III Silver Cup
with Cover
Daniel Smith, 1786.

reported at the start on the gradual decline of form and style. Actually the volume of silver articles increased and their use became more widespread, but the silver of the later times of George III and during the reign of George IV is not important for artistic quality. The development becomes technical rather than spiritual.

Only two names stand out at the turn of the century, Hester Bateman and Paul Storr, the former for purity and delicacy of line, the latter for strength and compact form. Today, Hester

—Peter Guille
George III Teapot on Stand
Hester Bateman, 1782.

Bateman is very much in vogue. People like the feminine charm of her work in the classical style, though we could wish for a little more strength. She was entered in 1774. We find her first mark, 1778 and her last one, 1820. We also have quite a number of marks of members of her family in different combinations: Peter and Jonathan Bateman, 1798; Peter and Ann, 1795; Peter, Ann and William, 1800; Peter and William, 1820; and William, alone, 1807. A similar variety of marks were used by the Hennell family and we find other interesting instances of continuity and combinations of marks in the Chawner and Emes families.

For strength we turn to Paul Storr. From his work we get the impression of something very substantial right away. It reminds us of the solidity and power of the British Empire.

—Metropolitan Museum
George III Chamber Candlesticks
Matthew Boulton, 1805.

There is no looseness of form, no overloading with ornament. His large dinner sets, a few pieces of one of which we show, are examples of his powerful, imposing style. His fame and the admiration for his work seem to have grown in the last twenty-five years. Paul Storr's mark first appeared in 1793. He and John Mortimer opened the silver shop "Storr and Mortimer" in 1821. His last mark is entered in 1834.

There was another London silversmith of the late George III period, a minor figure, who left us his memoirs. The title is "Fruits of Experience," or Memoirs of Joseph Brasbridge, printed for the author, sold by Simpkin & Marshall, Stationers Court and Joseph Capes, Fleet St., 1824. This book is not important for any phase of the art of the silversmith. The author seems somewhat vain, self-pitying and self-admiring, yet we get an amusing picture of the life of the London middle-class of that time, rubbing its shoulder with the higher-ups.

Brasbridge started his business in 1770. He recalls that when he was young the broad-wheeled wagon was used in Oxfordshire and that lamps for carriages "are quite a modern improvement." He also mentions, and this is of special interest to us, a wine merchant, Sir Brook Watson, "whose memory is still preserved by the fine picture of Copley's which represents the incident of Brook's leg being bitten off by a shark while he was bathing in the West Indies."

Brasbridge was a died-in-the-wool Tory, easy-going, riding to the hounds, member of numerous clubs, guest at drinking and gambling parties. He catered to the nobility as his preferred clientele. His musical taste seems rather old-fashioned. "I will defy any Italian opera to produce on the town that real feeling of delight with which 'Love in the Village' was received on its first appearance." And smoking to him "is the idlest of

—Metropolitan Museum
George III Teapot
William Plummer, 1785.

all amusements and the stupidest of all kinds of intoxication." When he neglects his business and gets into trouble, it is Mr. Boulton who urges him to look "more narrowly" into his affairs and is helpful in sending him two of his own clerks to assist him. The outcome was that he was forced to go into bankruptcy. But as a man of high honesty, he paid off his debts and with the help of the Lord Mayor of London and other friends he started anew and won back most of his old customers. He finally retired with a small fortune and lived his last years in a little cottage at Herne Hill near London.

Brasbridge was a man who really enjoyed good life, good company and a good story. We have a few examples of the latter in his memoirs. One of his friends, a night bird, when he was told, "You will ruin your constitution by sitting up in this manner at night," answered, "You don't know my constitution, I sit up at night to watch it and keep it in repair whilst you are sleeping carelessly in your bed." Another friend gave him advice on his advertising: "The art of advertising is the

—Metropolitan Museum
George III Candlesticks
John Carter, 1771.

A TREASURY OF OLD SILVER

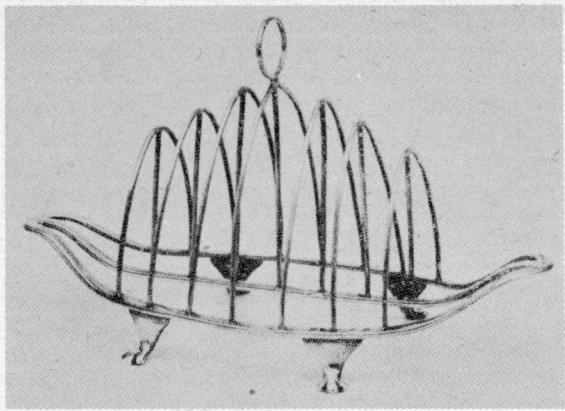

George III Toast Rack
Matthew Boulton, 1800.
—Metropolitan Museum

George III Lighthouse Pepperpot
John Emes, 1807.
—Peter Guille

same to a tradesman as the art of dressing to a beauty, the great secret of both is to expose enough to excite curiosity, and to conceal enough to leave curiosity ungratified."

Of special interest for silver collectors is the order that Brasbridge filled for the Duke of Argyle: a set of forks, plated on iron as more durable than silver. He himself had such forks in his own use for at least forty years.

We now take our leave of Brasbridge and end on a sad note, the definite decline of English silver. In the wake of Napoleon's return from Egypt, the style reverted to Empire. A certain coldness, a hard arrogance set in, an unhappy, lifeless assembling of ancient forms. It was the doom of the silver artist with his creative sense of form, balance and refinement.

GEORGE III PIERCED BASKET

This silver basket was made by a craftsman now unknown, but the arms are those of the Tucker family in Dorset and were recorded at the Heralds' visitation of Dorsetshire in 1565. The basket is dated 1771.
Alice Coutant

Vinaigrettes as They Were Made in Birmingham, England in the Early 19th Century

All of silver with pierced grille design somewhat like watch bridges of the period and finished in silver gilt. The one in the lower right-hand corner has been left closed to show elaborately engraved design of cover. From left to right and row by row, the makers of these vinaigrettes and their dates are J. Taylor, 1826; T. Shaw, 1800; J. Taylor, 1811; Nathaniel Mills, 1833; T. Taylor, 1808; T. Willmore, 1835; Francis Clark, 1839; Lea & Clark, 1825; John Bridges, 1822; J. W. C. (unidentified), 1816; Unidentified maker, 1798; and Cox & Betteridge, 1816.

Pomander and Vinaigrette
By Charles Simms

"And at parting I gave my dear Henry
A beautifull vinegrarette."—Thackeray.

THIS LINE from "The Almark's Adieu," written in 1855 shows that the little vial known as a vinaigrette was still in fashion at that time. And some of us of the older generation will remember the small smelling-salt flasks, last remnants of the scent smelling habit, which were part of the paraphernalia carried about by the fine ladies of the late 19th Century.

Although it is with charming woman that we associate the vinaigrette, originally it was used by men as well, especially doctors and clergymen visiting people suffering from infectious diseases. The little sponge soaked in vinegar was believed to counteract the obnoxious atmosphere of a more or less air tight sickroom. In fact the habit of carrying spice or perfume dates a long way back. In England, the earliest mention of a pomander, the vinaigrette's forerunner, is in 1492 during the reign of Henry VII. The word *pomander* of course is derived from the French *pomme d'ambre*. Originally it referred to a ball made of perfumes such as ambergris, musk, civet, or dried spices, but later the term was applied to the case containing such scents.

Some of these boxes had several compartments of which the one shown on upper right of page 18 is an example. Dating from 1621, it is in the form of a Bible, pure gold with black enamel. The box parts are held together by a pin on a chain. Between the eight compartments is a hinged plate or tablet inscribed in old German, *Negelken* (clove) *Annis* (anise), *Zanen, Citronen* (citron), *Slag, Muschaten* (musk), *Cimit* (cinnamon), and *Rosen* (rose). One side shows an intricate monogram and the date, the other an ornament. A precious stone in the center of one cover is missing.

In one of such compartments a sponge soaked in aromatic vinegar was often found. Later this compartment became a separate trifle, the vinaigrette, probably about the middle of the 18th Century. In 1732 Edward Pinchbeck of London is

A TREASURY OF OLD SILVER

—Owned Anonymously

An American-Made Vinaigrette
Open to show touch mark of W. G. Forbes, New York who worked 1773 to 1809 and grille. The latter is engraved with conventionalized scrolls and the background is pierced.

—F. Snyderman

Gold Pomander of 1621, Open
This shows the compartments with names of scents engraved on central divider.

said to have made them in very fancy shapes. Gradually the fad spread until the vinaigrette became an indispensable part of mi-lady's handbag. Small gold or silver containers often had engraved or embossed lids, some showing pictures of famous buildings and some grilles of charming design. Usually the form was rectangular, but later shapes became very fancy, as shells, watches, baskets, purses, etc.

Today vinaigrettes are cherished collector items. Clear hallmarks may be looked for inside the lid, in the interior of the box, and sometimes on the inner rim. The principal place of manufacture in England was Birmingham where some fine work was done by John Shaw, (1803-04), Joseph Taylor (1804-05), Joseph Wilmore (1823-24); and in Victorian times by Gervase Wheeler (1835-36), and Nathaniel Mills (1846-47). Hallmarked pieces are found as late as 1887. Other material besides gold and silver was used in fashioning the vinaigrette, such as semi-precious stones, carnelian, lapis lazuli, agate, enamel, paste, all in a variety of shapes too great to be enumerated.

In closing, a line from a 19th Century English novel emphasizes the place of the vinaigrette in its day.

"She had no resources but silence, her fan and her vinaigrette."

—S. Wyler Inc.

One French and Two English Vinaigrettes
At the left a box-shaped example by unidentified maker dated London 1801; center, French vinaigrette in watch case shape, maker unknown, date 1790; vinaigrette at right by J. Arnell, London, 1792.

ENGLISH SILVER

Museum of Fine Arts, Boston

TEA CADDY, SUGAR BASKET AND BEAKER

Handsome silver pieces made by Hester Bateman, the most famous of all women silversmiths, in London, 1785 and 1783.

GEORGE III TEA SET

Tea set marked with the dates 1790, 1791 noted for its exquisite simplicity.
Alice Coutant

Tea Drinking Made Trade for Silversmiths

By Seymour Wyler

TEA, LIKE many other things now taken for granted by the Western World, came out of the Orient. The Chinese were doubtless making a ritual of tea drinking centuries before ever the first Saxon set foot on British soil. The beverage that has since become so popular with that nation was first presented to the English people through an advertisement that appeared in a London newspaper in 1658.

Two years later Samuel Pepys wrote in his Diary, "I did send for a cup of tee (a China drink) of which I never had drank before." In 1664 the East India Tea Company presented a pound

An Early Bullet Tea Pot

A London piece, about 1730

of this new luxury to Charles II. It found instant favor with the Court and those who could afford to indulge themselves consumed as many as 20 to 25 cups daily. At this time over 40 shillings were needed to buy a pound of this fine Chinese importation. As the demand increased, more was imported and the price was lessened until about 1720 tea could be enjoyed by all classes.

As it increased in favor, dishes for serving it were naturally in demand. The earliest known teapot was fashioned in 1670 and is now in the Victoria and Albert Museum. This pot bears the arms of the East India Company and the inscription: "This Silver Tea-Pott was presented to ye Comtte of ye East India Company by Ye Honue George Lord Berkeley Castle. A member of that Honourable and Worthy Society and a True Hearty Lover of Them 1670." In shape and size it was very similar to the pots designed for coffee, a beverage that antedated tea in England by a decade.

During the reign of Queen Anne many fine teapots were made to order for the nobility. They were small, however, as tea was still expensive. Not until the reign of George II, 1727-1759, were they made in larger size or in profusion. The earliest teapots were severely simple in style. Then, as demand increased, silversmiths began to give free rein to their artistic abilities. Fine chasing appeared. There were frequent changes in shape and decoration to please the taste and purse of their clients.

The teapot did not become part of a service, however, until 1790, when a sugar bowl and creamer to match were added. During the latter part of the George III era, came matching coffee pots to be followed years later by the complete service with kettle and waste bowl of uniform size.

A few interesting notes about tea are to be found in the records carefully preserved by the guilds and handed down from generation to generation. Porringers were the first tea cups, so to speak. This may be because it was at one time believed to possess medicinal qualities. For instance, Pepys states in June, 1667, "Home and there find my wife making of tea; a drink which Mr. Pelling, the Potticary, tells her is good for her cold." Silver tea cups and saucers are among the rarest known objects. A few examples dating from 1684 to 1686 are still extant.

The Chinese method of preparing tea differed from that of the English. The Oriental merely poured hot water on the tea leaves. An infusion of tea in the pot was the English way. This greatly influenced the changing styles and shapes of pots. Those with characteristic spouts began to appear in the last quarter of the 17th Century. Tea pots of the Queen Anne and George I periods were very beautiful. As a rule they had a pear-shaped body with a domed lid. The popular type with an inverted pear-shaped body appeared about 1730.

As demand increased to the point where practically every home of good standing owned a silver tea pot, styles changed repeatedly. The Adam period was extremely prolific in designs. Typical specimens were those made with a circular, oval, or octagonal drum-shaped body, usually with a straight spout. Many and caustic domestic comments drive him to the purchase, which he finally makes, from another smith.

The tea pot so popular in Scotland for many years was of a globular shape on a tall foot. It remained purely local though and never found much favor south of the Tweed.

Oddly enough, although the English had their own ideas about brewing tea, they continued to drink it Chinese style without sugar or cream for some 50 years. The first silver sugar basins were introduced in the reign of William III, 1695 to 1702. They were originally made on a rounded base with a saucer-like cover similar to the Chinese tea cup. This was in time discarded for a type set on three feet and, many years afterward, made to match the tea pot. Sugar baskets were first made in the Queen Anne period and reappeared at the end of the 18th Century with colored glass linings. In early tea sets, the sugar bowl is decidedly out of proportion in size to the rest. This marks the era of unrefined sugar when a large and bulky loaf came to table and was broken into fragments as desired.

A taste for cream in tea appears not to have developed much before the time of Queen Anne. At least there are no earlier silver pitchers for this accessory known. Early examples were made on a simple round foot. This style changed with the varying shapes of tea pots and in later years of course resembled the general style of the pot. The popular type of helmet-shaped cream pitcher came during the George III years. The oval forms of the 19th Century were called squat creamers. These containers were also made in many eccentric forms, the shape of a cow being the best known. These are very rare and are not to be confused with the modern Dutch ones that flooded the market for years.

Because of the high cost of tea, waste was prevented by infusing the beverage at the table. Consequently the addition of a kettle with spirit lamp underneath was logical. The earliest mention of a tea kettle is in a royal warrant of 1687. The earliest example extant was the work of David Williams in 1706; the next was that of the Duke of Portland, made in 1709 by Anthony Nelme. Like the tea pots, the first kettles were of severely simple style. During the George II reign, came the richly embossed pieces. Kettles were now made with a small triangular stand to protect the tea table from the flame of the lamp. There is also mention in the latter part of the Queen Anne period of a huge stand, sometimes three feet high, which held the kettle conveniently near the tea table. Only one or two of these are extant.

Sheffield Tea Urn
Made in London, circa 1790

had stands to match. The latter protected the tops of the highly polished tea tables from the burns and scratches liable to occur when the pot was set directly on the wood surface. Many a person did not realize this at first, as is evidenced by the fact that one may find a tea pot by one maker and a stand to match by a different smith of a few years later date. One can picture a fairly prosperous individual with a few pounds to invest, ordering a fine silver tea pot from a craftsman and stonily refusing to take on the added expense of such frippery as a matching stand. Time proves the soundness of the silversmith's advice as a badly marred tea table

A So-Called Bachellor Tea Set
Made by William Kingdon, London, 1821, it was probably executed to special order

Huguenot Silversmiths: The Courtaulds

By Edward Wenham
Author of "Domestic Silver of Great Britain and Ireland"

NAMES may be merely a group of letters and as such have but little meaning. If for the sake of entertainment we turned the pages of any large directory we might discover that certain names left some of us cold while touching in others a warm glow. Patriots, for example, would be touched by names recalling men associated with the history of a country, while we collectors would be touched by names recalling the artists and fine old craftsmen whose work we seek so eagerly today.

Among silver collectors, a particular glow occurs at mention of the names of early goldsmiths (or silversmiths as we now refer to them). Fortunately we have more or less complete records of their names and history. In some cases the modern form may vary considerably from the original but there is usually no difficulty in recognizing them. For instance, although the names of many of the Huguenot craftsmen have been anglicized the change in most cases is only phonetic. Thus in Geslin, we might look for the original Ghiselin, the Huguenot silversmith who came to Philadelphia from England and worked for William Penn. Again, the modern Longmoor may well be the anglicized form of Longuemare, a South Carolina Huguenot. Others, such as Grignon, Legare and Quintard have remained unchanged.

Today the names of many of these Huguenot refugees from religious oppression are prominent in the world of finance and commerce, as for example that of Courtauld; the present members of this well-known firm being direct descendants of the celebrated goldsmith, Augustine Courtauld, who with later members of the family contributed so greatly to English 18th-century silverwork.

In addition to Augustine Courtauld, who is to be regarded as the founder of the family in England, there are four others of his name connected with silver craft who registered marks at Goldsmiths' Hall in the 18th century: Peter, half-brother to Augustine; Samuel, son of Augustine; Louisa Perina, widow of Samuel; and Samuel the younger, son of Samuel and Louisa.

It would seem probable that Augustine, Sr., was born at St. Pierre in the Ile d'Oléron about 1686 and was brought to England when his father fled from France in 1688. In *Silver Wrought by the Courtauld Family*, Samuel Courtauld says of the infant Augustine's arrival that it is traditionally thought he was "concealed in a basket of vegetables." His half-brother, Peter, was born in the parish of St. Anne, Soho, London, some few years later.

In time, both boys were apprenticed to the goldsmith, Simon Pantin, which fact might give us to think that their father also was a goldsmith. Any such supposition, however, is not supported by the two indentures. In the apprenticeship of young Augustine, dated 1701, the father is described as a wine cooper, which would infer he was a maker of wine casks, while Pantin's name is spelled in its French form, Pontaine. In the record of Peter's apprenticeship the father is described as a vintner (wine merchant) and Pantin's name appears in its anglicized form.

Having served the usual term of seven years under Pantin,

—*Thomas Lumley, Ltd.*
2. Superb example of Augustine Courtauld's achievement of fine form by beautiful proportions and bold, clear outline. A tray dating 1721-24. Width, 21½ in. Weight, 125 ounces. Sold in 1945 for $6,800.

—*Thomas Lumley, Ltd.*
Photo © Fortt, Fortescue & Gibbs
1. Pear-shaped caster with handsomely pierced cover by Augustine Courtauld. Date 1726-27.

—*Bracher & Sydenham*
3. Simplicity of form and outline, accented by subdued, delicate decoration (as in these tea caddies) characterize the silverwork of Augustine Courtauld. The pair, left and right, dated 1726-27; center casket, 1731-32. All three engraved with the arms and crest of the Still family.

ENGLISH SILVER

—Thomas Lumley, Ltd. Photo © Fortt, Fortescue & Gibbs
4. *Another example of the way Augustine Courtauld gained distinguished simplicity by leaving much of his silver surface plain. Vigorously shaped salver dating from 1730-31. Engraved with the arms of Blackett.*

young Augustine Courtauld started out on his own and entered his first mark at Goldsmiths' Hall in 1708. This, the first of four marks, was the first two letters of his surname—CO with a fleur-de-lis above. It might be well to mention that an appreciable number of early 18th century marks are the letters CO or Co, silversmiths at that time having to use the first two letters of the surname. But as each of the punches is accompanied by some device and the shapes of the punches themselves vary, they are easily distinguishable. In the same year, 1708, Augustine Courtauld entered another mark, his initials in small gothic letters, ac. It is this punch which is found on the miniature pieces, known as toy silver, of which he produced an appreciable amount.

His third mark, entered in 1720, was his initials AC with a fleur-de-lis above. An historical piece bearing this mark is the state salt-cellar of the City of London Corporation. This salt may be described as an example of Courtauld's rare venture into the field of fantasy. It has a large bowl ornamented with embossed and applied strapwork on four somewhat massive supports in the form of dolphins, the heads of which rest on shell-shaped feet. Around the rim of the bowl are four scroll brackets with female-head terminals, the brackets being intended to support a napkin or other cover when the salt was not in use. Hall-marked 1730-1, this important if not too beautiful example of his work is 10 inches high and 5 inches diameter at the rim of the bowl. Augustine Courtauld's last mark, AC in script capitals with a fleur-de-lis below, was registered in 1739.

Because the forementioned state salt displays a decided leaning toward the fantastic it is not representative of Augustine Courtauld's work at any period of his career. In general, his work indicates that he preferred to produce the more modified designs and ornamentation of the rococo style as illustrated in fig. 1, a caster of which the only decoration—apart from the engraved arms—is a small band of rococo motifs on the shoulder.

This simplicity of outline and avoidance of unnecessary ornamentation is characteristic of all the silverwork bearing his mark. Where decoration is used it is restricted to finely chased forms, delicate engraving, applied strapwork and flutings. An excellent example of his engraved work is shown in the three caddies in fig. 3. The smaller two of these bear the hall-marks for 1726-7, the other having been made by Augustine five years later, its hall-marks being 1731-2. In addition to the finely engraved bands round the panels and the lids, each of these caddies is engraved with the arms of Still of County Dorset, England.

One very notable example of Augustine Courtauld's reliance upon outline for beauty is shown in the large tray in fig. 2 which is devoid of any decoration other than the finely executed arms of Thomas Malin who married Mary Carbonell at St. Botolphs, Bishopgate, London, in 1722. In view of the fact that this tray bears the hall-marks for 1721-2, we may assume it was specially made as a wedding gift. It is some 22 inches wide, weighs no less than 125 ounces and was formerly in the collection of the late Thomas Hugh Cobb. When this collection was sold at Sotheby's in 1945 the tray met with remarkable competition from the buyers, eventually bringing $6,800. The salver in fig. 4, also by Augustine Courtauld, is another instance of a large surface being left plain except for the engraved arms, which are those of the Blackett family of Northumberland.

One often overlooked branch of the 18th century silversmith's craft is the making of silver toys. These attractive miniature pieces were produced in many shops as is evident from the number of men described as "goldsmith and toyman" in the lists compiled by Sir Ambrose Heal. And though Augustine Courtauld does not seem to have added "toyman" to his "goldsmith," he was nonetheless one of the foremost makers of these tiny pieces of which a number are illustrated here (fig. 5).

Among his toys it is not uncommon to find pieces copied from styles antedating his time, showing he used models of earlier periods. An example of this copying from the "antique" appears among those illustrated, namely, the curious tapering pot with a long tubular spout and conical lid—obviously a copy from the early lantern-shaped tea-pot, one of

—Ralph Hyman
5. *Miniature or toy silver pieces copied by Augustine Courtauld from full-sized models. He made numerous such miniatures. Note the old-style, lantern-shaped teapot (upper right) that harks back to the 17th century.*

A TREASURY OF OLD SILVER

6. Pyriform tea kettle and stand with subdued rococo decorations of flowers and scrolls. By Samuel Courtauld, Sr. Dating 1755-56.

which, made in 1670, is now in the Victoria and Albert Museum. He also made miniature tankards of the type fashionable in the time of Charles II; tiny pillar candlesticks with octagonal bases copied from the columnar sticks of the later 17th century; and this writer has seen a miniature silver fireplace that he made.

Several lads were apprenticed to him and at least two appear later in the records of London goldsmiths. One, Isaac Ribouleau, the son of Huguenot parents, began his apprenticeship in 1716, eight years later entering his mark and opening a shop in London in Lombard Street, at that time one of the centers of the craft. Another, Louis Ouvry, apprenticed to Courtauld in 1730, entered his mark at the Hall nine years later. Sir Ambrose Heal lists the name "Ouvry (or Ourry) Lewis, plate worker, Golden Crown, New Street, Covent Garden, 1740-42," which we may assume refers to Courtauld's apprentice. Also there is a record of a mark LO in script with a crown above; it was found on a plain mug, hallmarked 1740-1.

Very little is known of the half-brother, Peter Courtauld. After finishing his time with Simon Pantin in 1712 he apparently became a freeman of the Goldsmiths' Company but does not seem to have entered a mark until 1721. In that year he entered two marks: one, the first two letters of his surname, CO with a crown above; and the other, his initials, PC with a crown above. At this time he opened a shop in Litchfield Street, Soho,

London, but died eight years later and no work bearing his mark has been recorded so far.

Augustine Courtauld's son, Samuel, was apprenticed to his father in 1734, at the age of 14. On completing his apprenticeship he presumably continued to work in his father's shop in Chandos Street until his father's death in 1751, when he moved to 21 Cornhill. Silver-

—Parke-Bernet Galleries
7. Repoussé silver hot water urn in the neo-classical style. Bearing the marks of Louisa Courtauld and George Cowles, 1776.

work made by this Samuel (the elder) is mostly marked with his initials SC with a pellet between and a rising sun above, but he did use another mark—his initials and the pellet but without the rising sun; the latter, however, is rare. He issued two trade cards, the first of which describes him as "Goldsmith and Jeweller at the Rising Sun Shandos Street, St. Martin's Lane, London" and a more elaborate card after he moved to Cornhill, giving his address as "At the Crown in Cornhill Facing the Royal Exchange, London." Much of his work shows the influence derived from his father in the simplicity of its design and in the splendid workmanship but while the latter is characteristic of all the pieces bearing the mark of Samuel the elder, he later developed a tendency toward more exuberant rococo forms of ornamentation.

This later tendency became increasingly apparent as his years advanced. The pyriform kettle and stand of 1755-6 (fig. 6) shows subdued rococo forms in the finely chased flowers and scrolls on the shoulder of the kettle and in other motifs but another two-handled cup of five years later already displays all the exuberance the rococo style developed in England, an exuberance which became so popular that it was adopted by most of the London craftsmen with the result that many a fine design was lost beneath a mass of scrolls, shells, floral swags and other ornamental forms.

In 1749 Samuel Courtauld married the beautiful Louisa Perina Onger whose portrait was painted by Zoffany. She became the connecting link with the third generation of Courtald goldsmiths as represented by the son, Samuel the younger. This lad was only 12 years old when his father died in 1765 and Louisa undertook to carry on the shop in Cornhill alone, entering her own mark at Goldsmiths' Hall, her mark being LC in a lozenge-shaped punch. But while a number of examples bearing her mark are known in various collections it is rare, indeed, that one makes its appearance on the market.

After carrying on the business for slightly more than three years, Louisa

8. Adam style two-handled cup by Louisa Courtauld and her son, Samuel, Jr., 1778-79.

apparently decided that running a fashionable silver shop alone was too great a responsibility. In 1769 she took in as a partner an experienced craftsman named George Cowles. It was during the Courtauld-Cowles period that the rococo style finally gave way to the so-called neo-classic style introduced by Robert Adam. Consequently, examples bearing the mark of the partnership, LC GC, reflect the change observable in both form and ornament of all design after about 1765—a change well illustrated in the fine urn illustrated in fig. 7, which bears the London hall-marks for 1776-7.

In the following year, 1777, the partnership was dissolved, doubtless because Louisa's son, Samuel the younger, had joined his mother in running the shop. There would seem to be some doubt as to whether Samuel the younger served an apprenticeship or for that matter whether he was ever apprenticed. And though the combined mark of Louisa and her son Samuel was entered, the indications are that at no time did he show any great inclination to follow the goldsmith's craft.

In view of the short time that Louisa and her son were in business together it is not to be expected that examples bearing their combined mark could be plentiful. Yet such as are known suggest clearly that some important silver work was produced in their shop, and for a fashionable clientele. This is evident from the elaborate two-handled cup (fig. 8) which is typical of the formal style of the late Georgian period —the classic influence showing itself in the festoons of laurel, the guilloche band, flutings, acanthus leaves and other forms that Robert Adam had borrowed from ancient architecture and adapted to his own designs of architecture, interiors and furnishings.

Actually, Samuel the younger remained in business with his mother for a bare three years only. He then emigrated to the United States where he is believed to have become a merchant. The records show that he died at Wilmington, Delaware, in 1821, aged 69. After he left England, Louisa Courtauld sold the business in Cornhill to John Henderson. Thus after nearly a century the name of the Courtaulds disappeared from the list of active goldsmiths. Their fame, however, has never disappeared. It is still increasing.

MINIATURE GEORGE II TEA SET
The hall mark stamped on this tea set show that it was later sold and ceased to be used as a traveler's sample. *J.E. Caldwell & Co.*

Old English Silver-in-the-Little

By Harold Donaldson Eberlein

and

Cortlandt Van Dyke Hubbard

—*J. E. Caldwell & Co.*

An Early Georgian Tea Service
The shapes are unusual in miniature pieces of this type of silver.

"SILVER-IN-THE-LITTLE" has a peculiar fascination for all manner of people. It is the same with other articles of common utility deftly fashioned in miniature whether it be furniture, glassware, china, dolls' clothing, the smallest book printed from movable tyes, or what not. The minuteness of the achievement first excites wonderment, then admiration at the patience of the craftsman, and finally respect for his finished virtuosity. Collector and non-collector are alike affected. The only difference is that the collector desires to possess; the non-collector is content to admire. It needs only some such event as the exhibition of the Queen's Dolls' House, in England, to bring this latent hankering for things in miniature out into the open and create warm and active appreciation on the part of the general public.

Whatever other causes there may have been for the making of such Lilliputian silver services, tables, chairs, cabinets, books, dolls' frocks and caps, farm implements and other conceits, two purposes can be vouched for, at least as regards silver. First, they were made as samples of wares to be furnished at full size. Second, they were made by apprentices as proofs of their proficiency.

Some of the silver tea-sets, trays, coffee-sets, candlesticks and candelabra, goblets, mugs and the like, were made for the use of travelling salesmen in 18th Century England and were intended to be shown to prospective customers in the country who had no mind to go to the city to make their purchasers. Even after stage-coaches began to run with more or less frequency and tolerable regularity, a journey up to London from some village or hamlet in the deep country was an undertaking not to be entered into lightly or unadvisedly. Quite apart from the matter of expense, a pilgrimage of 50 or 60 miles under the prevailing travel conditions, was a subject for prayerful deliberation.

All the same, regardless of the hazards and discomforts of the road, the mistress of the house in Loamshire was keen to have her silver tea-tackle or set of table-

—*J. E. Caldwell & Co.*

English, But Probably Later
It, too, bears complete hall-marks.

ware complete with assorted sizes of spoons and two or three-tined forks, fashioned by the smiths who had their shops in London Town and would be sure to produce something very much in the approved mode. So down to the country journeyed the goldsmith's travelling agent, with a miniature tea-set in his bag to exhibit in hall or manor house, or the parlor of some prosperous merchant in Loamshire's county-town. It could be packed into a bag in little space and, should the bag happen to fall a prey to the highwaymen or be lost through some mischance of travel, the amount of precious metal risked was not too much to hazard for the prospect of a sale.

Besides the common report of this commercial use for silver-in-the-little, two circumstances strongly point to a confirmation. The majority of pieces found seem to be in patterns of the first half of the 18th Century while travel conditions were still extremely unsatisfactory and full of risk. In the late 18th Century when travel was much easier, not so many appear to have been made. Further, not a few of the pieces are without a hall-mark. If they had been intended for sale as fittings for a doll's house, for children's toys, or other purpose, they would of necessity have been fully hall-marked. On the contrary it would have been legally possible the larger work in a satisfactory manner.

In America, we know that miniature silver pieces were made and Paul Revere, that versatile genius and general handy-man of Boston, is said to have fashioned silver-in-the-little. So far, it is impossible to say with certainty that miniature silver pieces were used here for salesman's samples. They probably were, as the American silversmiths closely followed the practices of their British cousins. We do know that miniature pieces of furniture were made by cabinetmakers and kept in their shops to show customers as patterns from which orders could be given. There are fully authenticated records to prove this, and many of these miniature cabinets and sideboards are still in existence. If the cabinetmakers did this, what more likely than that the silversmiths followed suit?

—J. E. Caldwell & Co.

Miniature Silver of Queen Anne Period

Duly inspected and approved by the lord of the manor and his lady, or by the thrifty merchant and his spouse, these pieces of "silver-in-the-little" were packed again and back to town bumped and jolted the agent with an order for his master. He had probably arranged his itinerary for numerous stops so that he could make a number of visits in one neighborhood; just as today London tailors and shoemakers regularly send "their Mr. Jones" once or twice a year on a tour of certain American cities to show samples and secure orders from their regular customers. By the same analogy, we can readily imagine the London goldsmith's salesman, in the fore part of the 18th Century, exhibiting his wares in a private sitting-room at "The Bull" or "The White Hart" and bidding likely purchasers come there for an inspection of his goods and, probably, a glass of port at the salesman's charge.

to omit the hall-mark and so save the legal fee on samples obviously not intended for sale.

The pieces sold and sent out of England, in compliance with law, have been hall-marked. They also bear the modern stamp "Sterling. Made in England," as may be seen by the illustration showing part of the bottom of a small oblong tray with rounded ends, used as a setting for several of the tea-services shown in other illustrations.

There is likewise a strong probability that while some of these sets and single pieces were used as samples, not a few of them were the work of apprentices as proof of proficiency and ability to fashion correctly full-size pieces. It was a custom among silversmiths to require apprentices first to execute such miniature pieces perfectly. If they were deft enough to make miniatures, perfect to the least detail, they could safely be trusted to execute

As to miniature silver articles made by silversmiths' apprentices to prove their facility in handicraft and their fitness to fashion full-size pieces of tableware, it is possible to speak with more certainty. For example, it has been recorded that the young apprentices of the two famous Vermont silversmiths, Roswell and Bradbury Bailey, fashioned doll-size spoons as evidence of their craftsmanship. These miniature teaspoons, identical in pattern with the larger spoons made for customers, the apprentices were allowed to make and sell to whom they would for twenty-five cents apiece. One set of these apprentices' little teaspoons is still intact.

Whether these miniature silverware pieces are found in America, in England, or on the Continent, and they seem to have been of pretty general occurrence, they deserve attention for more than their mere curiosity and rarity. For both the collector and the non-collector, no less as reproductions than as originals, they should stimulate a deeper regard for the craft of silversmithing and a more widespread appreciation for the subleties of contour displayed by the handiwork of past generations of silversmiths.

English Standing-Cups

By Edward Wenham
Author of "Domestic Silver of Great Britain and Ireland"

WITH whom you share a cup, with him share your friendship—that is in brief the tradition of the standing-cup. Raising a glass to honor a distinguished guest at dinner; the "Here's how!" or similar salutation when two or three foregather on holidays; the now almost forgotten custom of passing round a quart pot of ale in the taproom of a wayside inn: each symbolizes the ancient ceremony of the standing-cup which is still observed at banquets in the halls of London City Livery Companies and colleges.

Far back along the ages it was the custom to pass a large cup round the company, each in turn drinking to one or more of the others present. The man who drank stood up and held the cup with both hands. By so doing he exposed himself to a dagger thrust. To protect him from treachery the man next him also stood, to be his pledge or as we would say, be responsible for his safety, indicating his willingness to pledge the other by raising his sword to defend him while drinking. It is this custom that is observed in modified form at the passing of the ceremonial cup to the present time.

At important dinners held in the halls of Livery Companies, after the dinner and grace is said, the master and the wardens of the Company drink to their guests; then the cup is passed round the table, each guest drinking from the cup, wiping the rim with his napkin and passing it to his neighbor. This form of observing the old custom, however, has not the romance of the more formal practice where the man holding the cup stands and bows to his neighbor while the pledger, also standing, removes the cover from the cup with his right hand and remains holding it as the other drinks. This may be regarded as repeating the ancient custom of keeping the right or dagger hand occupied and so preventing treachery toward the man drinking.

Various quaint customs connected with the standing-cup are to be found in old records. One describes the ceremony observed at Corporation dinners in Lichfield, England, where the two toasts—"The King" and "Weale and Worship"—are drunk from a massive silver cup holding upward of four quarts, which was given the Corporation in 1666 by Elias Ashmole, founder of the Ashmolean Museum at Oxford. According to this account, "The Mayor drinks first and, on his rising, the man on his right and the one on his left also rise. The Mayor then hands the cup to the one on his right when the one next to him rises, the man on the left of the Mayor still standing. Then the cup is passed across the table to him when his left hand neighbor rises; so that there are always three standing at the same time." Another early reference speaks of the ceremony as it was observed at parish meetings and churchwardens dinners at St. Margaret's, Westminster, London. Above the head of the person drinking at these events the cover of the cup was held by his neighbors on his right and left. Here too, three men stood at the same time.

Whether it be the Anglo-Saxon drinking horns, the simple, mediaeval mazer bowls or the massive standing-cups of Tudor and Stuart times, each typifies the age-old importance of drinking vessels—and age-old it is, for the first Book of Kings records that "all Solomon's drinking vessels were of gold and all the vessels of the house of Lebanon were of pure gold; none were of silver."

In great houses, standing-cups were displayed on the cup borde; the more numerous and more magnificent the cups, the higher the social status of the master of the house. Incidentally, cup borde means literally a board or plank on which drinking cups are placed; actually it was a series of open shelves constructed in steps and from the name we have our word "cupboard." The cupboard as we know it, however, is more closely connected with the early box-like chest which, stood on end and fitted with shelves enclosed by a door, was known as an ambry.

Few drinking horns have survived but enough have come down to us to show, in the splendid mounts with which they are ornamented, the skill of the 14th-century goldsmiths. One of the finest is the so-called wassail-horn, 25 inches long, at Queen's College, Oxford, said to have been given by Robert Englesfield, founder of the College, who died in 1349. It is a buffalo horn with massive silver-gilt mounts and there is a similar horn at Corpus Christi College, Cambridge, though the cover of the latter is missing.

Among early drinking vessels sought by collectors the simple mazer bowls are perhaps the rarest.

—New College, Oxford
1. *Coconut cup with 15th century English silver-gilt mounts.*

—Victoria and Albert Museum
2. *The Howard Grace Cup, a Tudor example made in London 1525-26.*

—© W. Dennis Moss, Cirencester
3. *Anne Boleyn Cup (London 1535-36) in Cirencester Parish Church.*

ENGLISH SILVER

These were the common cups from the 13th century to the days of the Tudors, those of poorer folk being a plain turned bowl while those of the more wealthy were ornamented with silver or silver-gilt mounts and enamel work (fig. 7), the finest sometimes being raised on a stem with an elaborate foot and fitted with a cover. The name "mazer" has an unusual origin. The suggestion has been made that it is associated with the old word "maze," to stupify or bemuse, the assumption being that indulgence in the contents induced mazing. Actually, the word refers to the wood of which the bowls are made rather than to the bowls themselves, for it derives from the Old German *masar*, meaning "a spot," from which we also have the word "measles." The wood for these bowls was generally maple selected from that part of the bole where a number of branches grew closely together, the part less likely to warp and which when turned gave the spotted effect often referred to as "bird's eye" maple.

It is unfortunate but true that our high appreciation of early works of art finds expression in terms of money; but our keeness to acquire such works being so much greater than the opportunities to possess them, this form of appreciation seems unavoidable. It is a natural result that as searchers for early works increase in number available examples gradually go out of circulation and the curve of values rises ever more steeply. The sharpness of this rise becomes apparent when we select the prices paid for some of the mazers that have appeared in the present century. In 1902, one was sold for $850; in the following year, another for $700. By 1905, the widening interest in these bowls showed itself in a bid of $2,500; three years later, one known as the Tokerys mazer—with silver-gilt mounts of 1534—brought the sum of $11,500, a figure which was exceeded in 1929 when the Saffrom Walden or Pepys mazer realized no less than $14,500.

While a large number of standing-cups or hanaps as they are also called, are in the possession of various English corporations and colleges, many are owned by private collectors. Moreover, in quite recent years several important examples have found their way to the market. These often massive cups, when not in use, were at one time kept locked in a chest known as a *hanaperium*, a word later abbreviated to hanaper to denote a box in which valuable documents were kept. This box was often a wicker basket covered with leather and similar to those formerly used for holding clothes or samples when traveling — thus from "hanaper" we have the familiar word, "hamper."

It is probable that the earliest standing-cups referred to as hanaps had turned wood (mazer-like) bowls with covers. Later ones have bowls formed of silver or of a coconut or ostrich egg with silver mounts. Cups with coconut bowls (fig. 1) mounted in silver or silver-gilt and raised on a stem and foot seem to have been popular in the late 15th and early 16th centuries. They were revived for a short period nearly three centuries later, and examples of the late 18th and early 19th centuries are sometimes met with. They are listed in old wills and inventories as *note argento, blak nutte*, etc., the earliest such mention being a *cyphum de nuce Indye cum pede apparatu argente* in a will of 1259.

Ostrich-egg cups are often referred to in early documents as "griffin egg." The mounts are similar to those with the coconut bowls and, with authenticated English mounts, are equally rare. A particularly fine example appeared at the Swaythling sale, London, in 1924 and its rarity is reflected in the $27,500 paid for it (fig. 6). It is 18½ inches high and the mounts bear the London hall-marks for 1623-4.

Any lengthy study of early standing-cups brings the discovery that the types and forms are so numerous as to make it by no means easy to recall all the many shapes and ornamental variations. In addition to those already remarked, bowls were made of serpentine, crystal or ivory and there still exist examples with a nautilus-shell bowl surmounting handsome silverwork (fig. 9). The earliest

4. *Elizabethan gourd-shaped cup, London, 1598-99.*

5. *Silver-gilt steeple cup, London, 1619, that brought $16,500.*

6. *Silver-gilt mounted ostrich-egg cup, London, 1623-24. H. 18½ in.*

known surviving English standing-cup is the so-called King John Cup, dating from about 1350, belonging to the Corporation of King's Lynn. According to legend it was given to that town by King John but the style of the cup and the costumes of the figures engraved on the panels point to its belonging, instead, to the period of Edward III (1327-77) who did not appear on the scene until two centuries after John of Magna Carta fame had passed to his fathers.

We could continue at length on the subject of English standing-cups in public collections but the private collector is more concerned with those that have appeared and may well appear again on the market. And though we purpose to restrict our reference to some that have been offered in the last 25 years, it is of interest to mention two which were sold from the Dunn-Gardner collection in 1902—a sale which may be said to have established values for English silver at a level above any previously known. A James I standing-cup of 1604-5 brought $20,000, a figure which, some might suggest, was influenced by the fact that the cup, as the inscription has it, *was made of the Greate Seale of Irelande in Anno Domini 1604, after the Deathe of the Blessed Queene Elizabethe, the Most Blessed Prince that ever Reigned.* Yet no such influence could have been centrally involved in view of the high prices paid for other cups at that sale, such as $20,500 for a Tudor font-shaped cup.

Twenty-two years after the Dunn-Gardner sale, came the dispersal in 1924 of part of the Swaythling collection which included several great standing-cups. The prices then realized (doubtless considerably stimulated by commissions placed by Mr. William Randolph Hearst) exceeded both the expectations of the owners and those recorded at previous sales of English silver. Even so, the high prices paid at that time have since been surpassed. For example, let us refer to a set of three silver-gilt steeple-cups bearing London hallmarks for 1611-12. When these were offered at the Swaythling sale they realized $22,500, yet six years later, $16,500 was paid for a single steeple-cup hall-marked 1619-20, which is one of the many instances that might be quoted to illustrate the consistent rise in the values of fine standing-cups (fig. 5).

In the evolution of the shapes and ornamentation of these cups a marked change is noticeable in those of the early 16th century, by which time, in England, the former Gothic gave way to Renaissance forms. Traces of the mazer bowl remain in some of the bowls and something of the horn-shape in others but the dominant influence both in the shapes and in the elaborate decoration is derived from German and, to a lesser extent, Dutch goldsmith work.

These influences are more particularly noticeable in cups of the later Tudor period. One type of that time (fig. 2) shows an interesting adaptation in the style of the bowl: the main or middle part is cylindrical, with a slight taper in which it is possible to see a relic of the horn-shape, while in a bowl-like lip fixed to the upper part of

7. *Mazer bowls, such as this silver mounted one dating about 1450, once were ceremonial drinking vessels.*

8. *The 15th century Rodney Cup that fetched $38,000 at the Swaythling sale in 1924.*

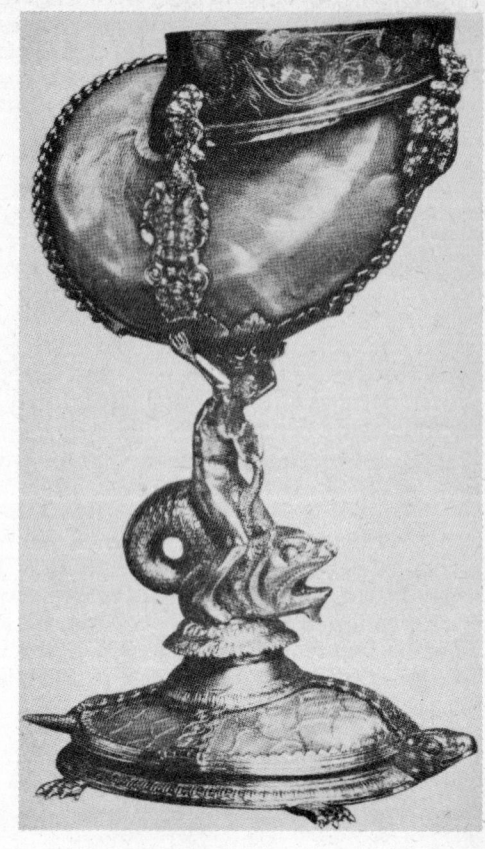
—Former Coll. Mr. W. R. Hearst
9. *Elizabethan nautilus cup with handsome silver-gilt mounts dating from about 1580.*

10. *Two-handled standing-cup of James I period (1603-25), a severely simple example with a cone-shaped finial on the cover.*

ENGLISH SILVER

the cylindrical section there is a distinct resemblance to the shallow mazer bowl. The cover is usually a low dome with a finial in the form of a figure holding a staff or spear in one hand and a shield in the other—a type of finial fairly common in later 16th-century cups.

One characteristic of this type of Tudor cup is a bold protruding member immediately below the cylindrical section; in some instances this is engraved, but as a general rule like the foot, stem and cover, it is boldly embossed with lion masks, fruit, foliage, flowers, strapwork and other ornament in a manner closely resembling that favored by the contemporary goldsmiths of Augsburg and Nuremberg.

Shapes of various large fruits were also adapted as bowls for cups, and a few in the form of a cantaloupe still survive. The majority, however, have bowls of the type known as gourd-shape and these were doubtless introduced from Germany. The gourd-shaped bowls bear a close resemblance to an inverted pear; but where the pear shape begins to taper it is constricted to a "waist," so forming a large globular section at the top joined to a smaller globular section below. Most of these cups have a stem formed as part of a twisted tree trunk on a high foot (fig. 4), and while occasionally the bowl is plain, it is not unusual to find it engraved or embossed in the prevailing style.

At the end of the Tudor period the so-called steeple-cups were introduced (fig. 5) and remained popular throughout the reign of James I (1603-25). These derive their name from a high steeple-like finial copied from the steeples found in architecture of the 16th and early 17th centuries. The bowl with the cover suggests the shape of an egg, another characteristic being a plain baluster stem with three applied brackets and a high spreading foot.

As might be expected in view of the then enforced austerity, silver articles made in the time of Cromwell (1649-60) are few and far between, and any that do survive are very simple in character. The typical standing-cup of that time has a slightly tapering cylindrical bowl—devoid of decoration except for a wide band of matting—on a plain baluster stem and molded foot, the upper surface of which is usually matted (the term "matted" implies a dull surface produced by a tool). The cover which is flat or has a slight dome continues upward in a high cone-shape not unlike, but larger than, one of the extinguishers which accompanied the tray candlesticks, formerly found on the hall table to light one to bed.

This cone generally has a plain baluster finial, although one Cromwellian cup that appeared in the market some 15 years ago has a finial in the form of the figure holding a staff and shield mentioned above. This particular example which bore the London hall-marks for 1650-51 brought $6,000.

As the 17th century advanced, standing cups were made without covers. It is probable that the earlier cups were fitted with covers as some protection against poison, and, as this method of disposing of an enemy became less "fahionable," covers were regarded as unnecessary. But even if society as a whole gained more sense of personal security, standing-cups when they lost their covers lost much of their imposing character—just as a mug or can lacks the dignity of a covered tankard.

Some few late Stuart standing-cups with covers do exist and they show very clearly the reaction against the enforced austerity of Cromwellian times. In place of the former simple outlines many cups dating after 1660 are extravagantly ornamented, indeed, often fantastic in design.

By the end of the 17th century, the great standing-cups were passing to give way to the less imposing yet attractive two-handled cups which became fashionable after the Restoration in 1660. Of these and the various beakers and other individual wine cups we may treat in a future issue, for it may be interesting to recall how the shapes of many of them have come down through the centuries and reappeared in our modern tableglass.

EARLY GEORGIAN MILK JUG

This unusual vessel was made by Thomas Langford, London, 1715. Coffee and teapots of this period were much more plentiful than was this diminutive milk jug.

Sheffield Plate; An Accident

Discovered in 1742 by Boulsover, It Soon Was an Important English Industry

By SEYMOUR B. WYLER

THE discovery of the process known as Sheffield plating was an accident. Yet it revolutionized the trade life of a city and later became a leading industry in England. It is perhaps the only one of the fine arts which can be termed 100 per cent English in origin.

In 1742, in the garret of a small building called Tudor House, a mechanic, one Thomas Boulsover, was repairing the blade of a broken knife. Entirely by accident he fused silver and copper and discovered that when these two metals were heated to a certain degree, they became inseparable. He realized that this strange occurrence might be turned to good purpose and on further experimentation found he could manufacture small things, such as buttons, boxes, and buckles of this silver-veneered copper. These are the earliest known specimens of Sheffield plate.

But although Boulsover indeed discovered the process he was not destined to father the industry. The man he employed to go on the road and merchandise his new product, cheated him so outrageously that he was left without resources to continue, beyond the few pieces he had already manufactured. However, during the first few months of his experimentation in Sheffield plating, he had taken as an apprentice a young man named Josiah Hancock. Having vision and acumen, the latter sensed that there was a fortune in the new process if properly handled. Here indeed was a cheap substitute for silver which had become very high in price because of Government taxation. There was a ready market in England and Europe and Josiah Hancock and other makers capitalized on it.

During the first 20 years of Sheffield plating, many beautiful articles were produced which often equalled the solid silver originals in design and workmanship. In fact, the first manufacturers, with a quick eye to the possibility of deception, impressed hall marks on the new products similar to those on silver pieces. Specimens showing the imitation hall marks are very rare. The small goblet illustrated, made by Fenton Matthew & Co. in 1760, is a fine example of such a piece.

Of course the silver manufacturers protested to the Guild, and the hall marking of Sheffield plate was forbidden. By 1784, however, the industry had grown to such proportions that they were granted permission to impress a maker's mark on any piece. In fact the rapid growth of Sheffield plating was evidenced in 1773 when the city of Sheffield was granted an Assay Office.

The history of Sheffield plate divides itself into two periods. During the years 1750 to 1780, there were many embossed objects, for the original manufacturers knew that a profusion of design and ornamentation nicely concealed those defects which so often appeared on the first pieces of plate. The corresponding pieces produced in solid silver were in much simpler style.

From 1780 until 1820, the finest Sheffield plate was produced, and produced in quantity. By this time, the majority of leading cutlers in Sheffield had begun to manufacture plated ware and the industry was at its height. With the advent of the Brothers Adam, the demand for extreme simplicity had its effect on design in all crafts and Sheffield plate was no exception. Tea services, cruets, candelabra, trays, and other household appointments were manufactured in quantity for the first time in this ware.

As the years passed, the style designs of the master silversmiths in England influenced those of Sheffield plate more and more. In this latter period, too, we find white metal or German silver first used.

Then came the discovery in 1838, by Elkington of electro-plating, and the curtain was rung down on the old process of Sheffield plating. Its life had been relatively brief but many fine pieces had been produced in that time. Consequently, from the collector's standpoint, Sheffield plate presents an admirable field of endeavor, especially as the prices have not yet mounted to the dizzy heights eventual scarcity will one day drive them. The demand, however, is already considerable and the supply obviously limited.

In every branch of art there are always outstanding names. So it is with the story of Sheffield plating. These arranged chronologically are:

Josiah Hancock	1755
Thomas Law	1758
Fenton Matthew & Co.	1760
Holy Wilkinson & Co.	1784
Matthew Bolton	1785
Robert Gainsford	1808
Creswick	1811
J. Watson	1830
Wilkinson & Co.	1836

LONDON MADE TUREEN OF 1803

—S. Wyler, Inc.

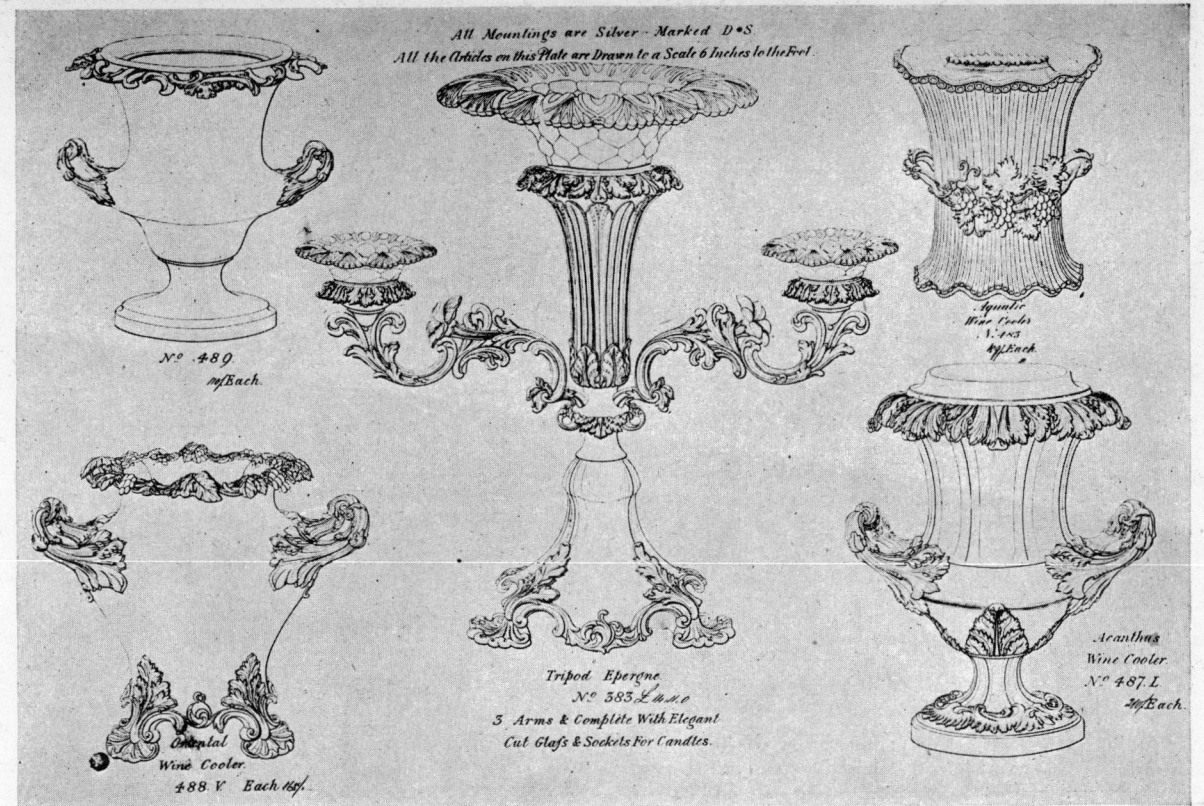

—Author's Collection

Four Wine Coolers and an Epergne of 1810 as Engraved by James Dixon & Sons

Lettering on it states that "All mountings are Silver . . . Marked D*S." Description of each piece includes the price. That of the three-arm espergne complete "elegant cut glass and sockets for candles" was £14:11:0. The wine coolers ranged from 110 to 210 shillings each. All prices were inserted in hand writing.

Making Sheffield Plate Was Big Business
By Carl W. Drepperd

IN the first Boston directory, 1789, seventeen goldsmiths—most of whom were silversmiths—are listed. Paul Revere is one of them. Samuel Minot is another. But Minot is listed as more than a goldsmith; he is also an "importer of plated ware." The plated ware that Minot imported is the ware that, for almost two centuries has rejoiced in the name "Sheffield Plate." Collectors at home and abroad have an avid interest in this ware. Dealers in antique silver display it with some pride and sell it quite readily. Yet all of us, collectors included, when standing so far away in time from the highwatermark of a business, are apt to overlook the business

—Robert Ensko, Inc.

Monteith Punch Bowl, 1800 or Earlier

From the catalogue of Love, Silverside, Darby & Co., who registered their Sheffield plate mark, June 2, 1785. The engraving carries no description other than "No. 179."

—Robert Ensko, Inc.

Teapot and Locked Caddy

These two pieces of Sheffield plate in classic Adam design, dating 1800 or earlier, are also from the illustrated trade catalogue of Love, Silverside, Darby & Co.

A TREASURY OF OLD SILVER

—*Author's Collection*

Label on Dixon Sheffield Catalogue

Their earliest registered mark was Dixon & Co., with star, of Birmingham, entered, September 8, 1784. The last, J. Dixon, preceded by the rose of York, was entered July 20, 1835, by James Dixon & Son of Sheffield.

that produced the goods we are enjoying as antiques. To most collectors, Sheffield Plate is the near-silver of our ancestors; plate almost as rich as the real thing—solid silver—and certainly made in as many delightful styles and patterns, and in many more things than were ever fashioned of the solid white metal of the Easterlings. Being one of those hateful people, a digger-after-facts, it is quite in character that I began collecting facts, documentary facts — about Sheffield Plate, rather than collecting the plate itself. By this simple process

—*Robert Ensko, Inc.*

Two Candlesticks and Maker's Trade Card

The oval card, dated 1800, reads "Love, Silverside, Darby & Co. Silver and Plated Manufacturers Sheffield. An assortment of their Manufacture at their warehouse No. 25 Gussiter Street, London."

I discovered that making Sheffield Plate was big business at Sheffield, and elsewhere, in England; that it was sold all over

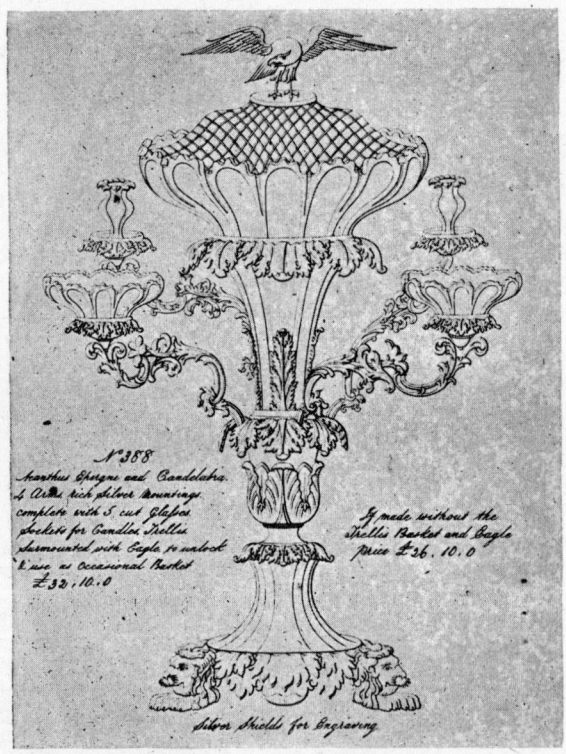

—*Author's Collection*

A Chippendale Epergne

This design reflects some of the most elaborate in his Director. Plate from the Dixon catalogue, about 1810-20. Price complete £32:10:0 or without trellis basket and eagle, £26:10:0.

—*Author's Collection*

Sheffield Communion Plate

Engraved plate from Dixon catalogue. Illustrated are chalice, flagon and patten with pocket service at upper right. The silver inserts for engraving are outlined on the chalice and flagon. Prices ranged from 30 shillings for the three-quarter pint chalice to 90 shillings for a two quart flagon.

ENGLISH SILVER

the world; that commercial agents were on the spot in every so-called civilized country; and best of all, that the Sheffield Plate industry issued catalogues so generous in size, so comprehensive in scope of illustration that, if one persisted (and had a purse big enough), one could reconstruct the entire "line" of Sheffield Plate offered between the years 1760 and 1830.

Thomas Boulsover (1704-1788) is credited with the discovery of fusing silver sheets on a copper base in 1743. He may, however, have read in certain ancient and current tomes the fact that silversmiths from the 14th to the 17th Century were cautioned against putting tin under their silver. Frederick

—*Author's Collection*

Epergne or Candelabrum at Pleasure

Lithograph plate about 1828-32 from catalogue bearing no maker's name. It was designed for "six branch and centre for seven lights or large rich cut centre basin and six smaller to match. Price £45.

Bradbury, in his *History of Sheffield Plate* mentions the fact that plating was not unknown before Boulsover made his discovery that copper could be the base upon which plates of sliver were fused. In Bradbury, too, one can find all about the early makers of this ware, read about its growth from a snuff-box and button business into a wide-world trade in all kinds of table wares, lamps, epergnes, et cetera. Bradbury even reproduces some Sheffield catalogue pages and, one may gather, the catalogues are far rarer than the wares they advertise. Which is quite true. The Metropolitan Museum of New York owns two complete catalogues of Sheffield. One of these, issued by Shemeld, Parkin & Co., (about 1781) has been identified by comparing the illustrations with examples of marked ware in the Victoria and Albert Museum, London. Another, issued by Theops-Richards & Co. (1813-1814), has the makers identity established by a pasted-on card. This catalogue is numbered and, shades of Samuel Minot, its number is 46752! If but one firm issued 46,752 catalogues, what must have been the total distribution of all makers who issued

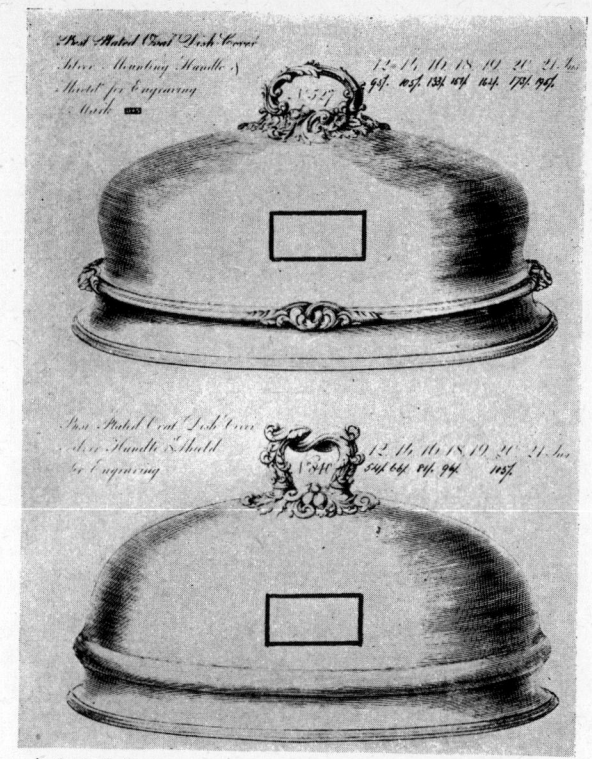

—*Author's Collection*

Two Oval Dish Covers

Plate engraved for Dixon catalogue about 1810-20. Both covers have silver handle and insert for engraving. Prices ranged, according to size, from 54 to 195 shillings.

catalogues? It is perhaps only because, in the years following the end of true Sheffield Plate production (after 1840), the catalogues were destroyed as rapidly as they had once been issued, that we cannot find them as readily as we can find old American almanacs.

When I found two of these Sheffield catalogues within ten days, at points two hundred miles apart, and both were not only rich in pictures, but doubly valuable because both were fully "priced" in respect of each item, in pounds, shillings and pence, I called upon Stephen C. G. Ensko to display (you know how collectors are) my treasures. Mr. Ensko, intrigued

—*Author's Collection*

An Elaborate Sheffield Tray

Lithographed plate about 1828-32, from catalogue without maker's name. This piece was made with silver handles, feet and engraving insert. Prices ranged from 60 to 336 shillings according to size and details of workmanship.

by the uniqueness of my priced copies said "I have a few of these but, unfortunately, they are not priced. Whereupon he hauled out a magnificent catalogue, issued by Love, Silverside, Darby & Co., dated 1800. This one illustrates one hundred ten items. Some of the plates bear evidence of issue before 1800 and this is further suggested by the fact that only up to 14 are the first pages numbered consecutively; thereafter some plates bear numbers as high as 187. This catalogue is particularly rich in candlesticks and lighting fixtures, salt cellars, mugs and castors. Some teapots and tea sets are of the 1785-1798 period; all of which leads to the interesting conclusion: Sheffield catalogues were made up to cover the needs, habits, and pocketbooks of the populations certain agents were tapping in terms of sales. It may well be that Love, Silverside, Darby & Co's Complete Catalogue would run to over 250 pages!

One of my finds is the fully identified catalogue of James Dixon & Sons (makers of Sheffield Plate marked D * S) and its date is approximately 1825. This catalogue pictures 116 items, some of which bear numbers as high as 510. The display is again rich in candlesticks, lighting fixtures, epergnes and castors, although there is a large folding page of ecclesiastical plate. My second catalogue is a mixture of plates by two makers, embellished with a label of about 1842 bearing the legend "Patterns of best Sheffield Plated Ware, priced for First Quality Sheffield Plate, with strong silver edges and ornaments, or First Class Electro Plate." A few of the plates are lithographed by Victor Chagot, Sheffield; others are by T. Underwood, Birmingham. One of the plates by Underwood displays an "Epergne or Candelabrum at Pleasure," at forty-five pounds sterling. Maclure and Macdonald of Glasgow lithographed several plates in this same catalogue which, in addition to the lithograph plates, contains forty-six engraved plates. With the exception of the lithographed plates above noted, all found bound in one catalogue, all the catalogue pages noted are engraved, and are plate printed. Mr. Bradbury mentions one commentator who has said that the Sheffield plate makers spent as high as from ten to twenty pounds per page for catalogue engraving, and as much as fifteen shillings per hundred pages for printing.

Your modern analyst, given these facts, would say, in the vernacular, "Brother, there was money in that business." And he would be right. Sheffield Plate, selling for less than silver, but looking as good as, if not better than most custom made silver, was a money making business. For proof of that let the reproductions of some of the pages speak for themselves. Pounds, shillings and pence don't lie, when written as prices in the days when Sheffield Plate was selling everywhere in America, at comparable prices in dollars and cents. Big business, this Sheffield Plate Business, international in scope, straight line production in big factories, and sales agents and retailer dealers everywhere.

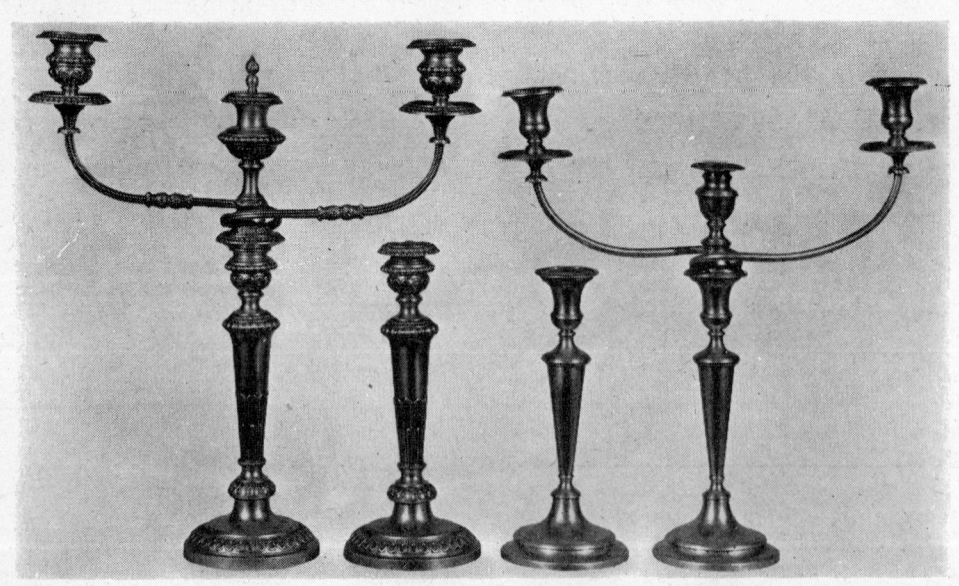

—*S. Wyler, Inc.*

CANDLESTICKS OF BOTH SILVER AND SHEFFIELD
Made by John Green & Co. in 1803, the bases are solid and the branches Sheffield plate

—*S. Wyler, Inc.*

SHEFFIELD GOBLET OF 1760
Made by Matthew Fenton & Co. It Bears Counterfeit Silver Hall Marks.

Silver Plate of Georgian England

By Alice Hoyt Coutant

FOR the average collector of old English silver the period of greatest interest lies between the years 1714 and 1830. During this Georgian period, so called because of the successive reigns of George I, II, III, and IV, the art of the silversmith achieved real greatness both as regards beauty of design and excellence of execution. Consequently it is not only well worth collecting but there are still plenty of fine specimens to be had today at reasonable prices.

In order to see this period in its proper perspective as regards silver history, one must look back for a moment to the political and social trends of the Stuart and Queen Anne years that immediately preceded it. The last half of the 17th Century saw the end of the Civil Wars and the Restoration of the Monarchy. The former had proved disastrous to art in general and to that of the silversmith in particular. Further, the demands of Charles I for money for his war chest had resulted in the melting down of vast quantities of silver.

With the accession of Charles II and subsequent peace and prosperity, there came a tremendous reaction. A large quantity of ceremonial and decorative plate was made for the coronation by Sir Robert Vyner, goldsmith-banker and mayor of London; the livery companies of the City of London ordered loving cups and other plate to show their wealth; the Church ordered communion plate and ornaments for the altar; and the noble and wealthy families equipped their homes with such lavishness that their inventories show the possession of plate running into several tons weight of silver. The diaries of both John Evelyn and Samuel Pepys make frequent reference to the display and ostentation of the court and to the extravagant quantities of silver furnished the numerous mistresses of the Merry Monarch. There was a bed made of massive silver for the apartments of Nell Gwyn.

And so, for the palaces of the King, for the royal chapels and for the great houses of England, such as Knole Park, Ham House and elsewhere, there was an amazing amount of silver made during the last quarter of the 17th Century. The pieces for decoration and display far exceeded anything made before or since. There was much silver furniture; such as beds, cradles, large tables, stands, toilet tables and high mirrors. Sconces, candelabra and candlesticks of silver held the candles which shed their light over the rich interiors of these homes. Even fire dogs and fire screens were of silver and on the chimney shelf stood huge vases of the metal, elaborately wrought.

For the table there were epergnes, fruit baskets, bread baskets and meat dishes. For the service of wine and beer there were posset bowls, beakers, tankards and standing cups. Sir Robert Vyner made a wine cistsern for the coronation of Charles II which may be seen at the Tower of London and has been used at the coronation of the Kings and Queens of Great Britain ever since down to that of King George VI last May.

In the Morgan collection there is the famous tankard given by Queen Mary to one Simon Jansen for having safely conveyed King William to the Hague in 1691. The sides of the tankard are plain; engraved on the front are the arms of William and Mary, surmounted by the royal crown. It has the figure of a seated lion as a thumb piece and on the cover is an inscription which, translated, reads:

When Simon fills this cup with wine
Her Majesty's brilliancy in it doth shine
And as he the cup to his lips doth lift
He remembers full well the Royal gift.

These limping lines are more than offset by the genius of the craftsman who made the tankard.

In addition to the wine cisterns or fountains, we have standing cups such as Samuel Pepys presented to the Cloth-workers Company in 1667 and the unique one in the form of the Royal Oak, surmounted by a crown which Charles II presented to the Barbour Surgeon's Company in 1676, in commemoration of his memorable escape. Another interesting piece in use at the time is the monteith for cooling glasses—a bowl fitted with a movable rim which is notched or scalloped, its name is supposedly derived from a Scotchman named Monteith who wore a cloak with a scalloped border.

Because of this extravagant use and display of plate, the last quarter of the 17th Century was known as the "silver age." After the Restoration large pieces became less common and with increased comfort and elegance in the homes, a number of new utensils were introduced. Tea, coffee, and chocolate now became known. Coffee achieved an immediate success and coffee houses sprung up all over England. Men foregathered in them to drink the new beverage, to gossip and discuss politics. So great was their reputation as centers of political agitation that Charles II tried to suppress them. Chocolate was used more in the late 17th and 18th Centuries and tea, introduced as a medicine and for a time selling at a price between £2 and £5 per pound, did not become a popular drink until the middle of the 18th Century. After 1650, therefore, we find coffee, tea and chocolate pots; tea and coffee spoons; and, for a time, silver tea cups made after the style of the Chinese tea bowl.

During the late Stuart period silver design showed marked Dutch influence, tulips, anemones, acanthus leaves, fruit, animals and amorini were embossed in bold relief. With the coming of the Huguenot silversmith after the Revocation of the

—Metropolitan Museum of Art

A Late 17th Century Cup with Cover
The hallmarks show it was London-made in 1682. The maker's touch is E N

37

Edict of Nantes, 1685- a great change appeared in the art of the silversmith. Heavy in weight, beautiful in outline and proportion, the silver pieces of the Queen Anne and early Georgian periods needed no other ornamentation than the exquisitely designed armorial bearings and mantlings found on most of the pieces and which in excellence of taste and execution have been rarely exceeded either earlier or later.

The Early Georgian period lasted from 1696 until 1725; the Rococo lasted from about 1725 until 1770. Up to about 1740 a considerable proportion of the work seemed to combine the forms of the new period with something of the simplicity of the old but with a marked tendency towards richer effects. The engraving which heretofore had been used only for heraldic motifs now began to play a more important role and during the years of George II's reign the craftsmanship of the engravers was extremely high. The Rococo style, which came from the Continent and achieved its greatest beauty in the Louis XIV style in France, was characterized by the use of unsymmetrical forms, broken lines and the lavish use of the scroll ornament.

Among the first to use this style was the Huguenot silversmith, Paul Lamerie, probably the greatest silver craftsman of all time. The epergne which he made in 1734 is an example of the early Rococo style and easily ranks as the finest ever made. A copy of it is now in the Victoria and Albert Museum. In that same year he made two beautiful chandeliers, which were hung in the Kremlin and were considered the most notable in existence. In fact so many of his pieces executed in the Rococo style have become famous that "Lamerie style" has become almost synonymous with Rococo. We must realize, however, that he worked in all the styles that succeeded each other during his long career from 1712 until 1751 and that the height of the Rococo fashion did not arrive until several years after his death.

The largest piece made at this time was a wine cistern, 5½ feet long, 3½ feet deep and 3½ feet wide, weighing 8,000 ounces and with a capacity of 60 gallons. It was made by Charles Kandler of St. Martin's Lane who, after three years labor, finished it in 1734. It was sold by lottery, won by a Sussex gentleman and soon after acquired by the Empress of Russia who put it in the Winter Palace at St. Petersburg. One can only hope that it is still in existence.

Because the liquid for which they were designed was a decided luxury, early teapots were, of course, small. With the coming of the Rococo period tea had become more common and the price more reasonable. The size of pot naturally increased and now came that most beautiful design of all, the inverted pear shape. This when ornamented with the fine engraving of the day was indeed a thing of beauty. Nor did the tea caddy lag behind. It had developed from a simple box with lock and key to a vase-shaped canister elaborately embossed.

The end of the Rococo period came rather suddenly in 1770. Again an influence swept over the Continent and later into England which completely changed existing forms of domestic art. Excavations at Pompeii and at Herculaneum had awakened an interest in classical form throughout Europe. Artists and architects travelled to Italy to study, rich travellers bought all sorts of objects found in the ruins and shipped them to England to adorn their homes. Illustrated books on Greek and Roman art began to appear. Designers in England became acquainted with classical forms and adapted them to modern needs. Of course, the great exponents of this style were the Adam brothers and Robert Adam designed plate for some of his clients whose houses he had built. The silversmiths Rundell and Bridge executed these designs, as well as the designs of that versatile sculptor, John Flaxman, several examples of whose work are to be seen in the royal collection at Windsor Castle. Flaxman, it will be remembered, also designed for Josiah Wedgwood.

The classical period was characterized by the use of the classical urn decorated with floral swags, draped linen suspended between oval shields, rams' and lions' heads and acanthus leaves. Engraving ceased to be applied as profusely as during the Rococo period but a new type, called "bright cut," was developed by the Birmingham silversmiths and reached heights of great beauty between the years 1770 and 1800.

All through the history of the English silversmiths we find the names of women. In many cases it is not known whether they were the actual craftsmen or whether they simply carried on a business left to them by husband or father. But in the case of Hester Bateman who registered her mark in 1774 in London, there is no doubt but that she was a craftsman. Her work is considered the supreme example of the classical period in the art of the silversmith and is notable for its beauty of outline, delicate proportions and for the matchless excellence of engraving.

The so-called "Adam period" ended with the 18th Century. The first 30 years of the 19th were marked by two types of decoration, that derived from the classical and that derived from the later and more massive periods of Roman art. The most notable craftsman of these years was Paul Storr.

—Metropolitan Museum of Art

Ornate Silver-Gilt Cup

Made in London, 1755, by the famous Huguenot silversmith, Paul Lamerie, it is an ultra example of the ornate Rococo style.

—Clapp & Graham, Inc.

Typical Pieces of Georgian Table Silver

These pieces are—top to bottom, left to right—Tray by Edward Jay, London 1791; four candlesticks, William Cafe, London, 1762; tankard, James Bell, London, 1716; pair of covered gray boats, Henry Cowper, London, 1788; coffee-pot, Gabriel Sleath, London, 1737; ewer, Jacob Marshe, London, 1773; teapot, William Bayley, London, 1798; patten, John Eckfourd, London, 1702; gravy boat, John Lupp, London, 1746; and pair sauceboats, James Stahl, London, 1777.

The London Companies and Their Plate

By Waldo Hopkins

SURVIVALS from the Middle Ages and the old guild system are the seventy-six "livery companies" that still exist in London. Once they were genuine corporations composed of members of a particular trade and possessed of distinct power in such guild matters as apprenticeship, quality of production, and the like. The term "livery" is also a survival of a time when clothes, indeed, made the man, and one glance at his dress told whether he were a gentleman or an artisan. Further, members of the various guilds or trades wore distinctive uniforms and so could be neatly pigeonholed in an economic scheme where individuals were supposed to stay put.

Some companies had their own buildings where guild matters were disposed of and large banquets were held. The others met in Guild Hall, which was another name for town hall. Gradually power passed into the hands of wealthy members and so shifted away from the trade altogether. For instance, Samuel Pepys became Master of the Clothworkers' Company, in 1677, and subsequently gave the organization a very fine piece of plate. Pepys had many interests besides that of keeping a diary, but there is no record that he was ever a clothworker.

In direct proportion to the wealth and importance of the various companies were the gold and silver plate, the paintings, and other artistic possessions that accumulated from the 15th Century on. Today, some of the finest examples of old English plate are owned by certain of the livery companies.

The elaborate sideboard dish, with the Goldsmiths' Company arms in the center supported on either side by a pair of unicorns and with a most ornate border of small figures and scrolls, is an example. It and its companion piece, a helmet ewer, are part of an exhibit of nearly one hundred pieces of silver-gilt plate on display in the British Pavilion at the New York World's Fair. This collection, which was loaned by various London companies, is expected to remain in this country for at least another year. Meanwhile, the plate left in London has been removed to places of safety where it is likely to remain until peace is once more assured.

The sideboard dish is also symbolic of an era when neither those above nor below the salt had cause to worry about which fork to use for fish, meat, salad, etc., since these refinements in table equipment did not come into general use in England until after the Restoration. Previous to that the well-worn adage, "Fingers were made before forks," was in full force. Consequently, a basin and ewer, preferably of silver, were a necessary part of a table service.

By 1741, when Paul Lamerie made this superb basin and ewer for the Worshipful Company of Goldsmiths, forks had long been present on well-appointed dining tables, and the once essential ewer and basin had become just sideboard ornaments. By the third quarter of the 18th Century they had ceased to be made.

Although Huguenot-born, but English-trained Lamerie worked in various silver styles during his long career, which covered the first half of the 18th Century, his name is as closely associated with the rococo in silver as is that of Scotch Duncan Phyfe with the pedestal base and acanthus-carving motif in furniture. However, he was among the first to use this style so characterized by irregular forms, broken lines, and scroll ornament. This sideboard dish is probably the most spectacular example of this great artist's work in this ornate style which became so popular in England during the latter years of his life. In fact, the height of the rococo fashion came several years after his death, but his work in this manner, beginning in the late 1730's, and continuing to the end of his career, was of such high artistic merit that it has never been surpassed. It is doubtful if it has ever been equaled.

The history of these livery companies and their collections of fine examples of the silversmith's art is that prominent men in London often gave them pieces beginning with the 15th Century.

—*The Worshipful Company of Goldsmiths*

Lamerie in His Most Elaborate Manner

This basin, for display on a sideboard, done in silver gilt, has in the center, in high relief, the arms of the Goldsmiths' Company and an elaborate border of fine details. It was made with a helmet-shaped urn to match, in 1741. Both bear Paul Lamerie's mark.

How to Read English Hall Marks

By Alice H. Coutant

A Typical Set of Hall Marks

Enlarged from a piece by Paul Storr, London, 1793-94, these, left to right, are: P S, maker's mark; Leopard head crowned and Lion passant, the assay city; Sovereign's head, duty stamped; and S, the date letter.

AFTER the Romans left Britain, coinage was in chaos for several centuries. Coins were of all shapes and sizes. Quality and weight of silver varied greatly and the practice of clipping coins, although punishable by death, was common. Towards the middle of the 13th Century, a number of North German merchants came to England and formed a guild in London. They made their own coins which soon became notable for honesty of weight and fine quality.

Called "Easterlings," probably because of the geographical position of the country where they originated, the term soon applied to their coins as well. Then, by the end of the century it had been shortened to *Sterling* and this, derived from the name given to the honest product of honest men, became the accepted term for the alloy which has been of such a high standard in England for over 600 years.

Sterling silver is an alloy of 925 parts pure silver in 1,000. This standard, decreed by King Edward I in the year 1300, has been adhered to ever since, except for a few years when an even higher standard prevailed. No other country holds such a record. England is unique in the careful control and accurate marking of silver plate produced by her craftsmen.

Study of these marks over such a span of time is naturally complicated and difficult. Therefore, a general outline of the system that has been in force so long may well serve as a guide.

When a craftsman finishes a piece of silver it is punched with the maker's own mark. For well over a century the silversmith used the same emblem as that over his shop, a bird, a fish, an animal, a flower, or a star. Sir Thomas Gresham (1519-1579), a silversmith-banker, founder of Gresham College and The Royal Exchange, used a grasshopper as the sign over his shop and on the silver plate made there. Consequently a gilded grasshopper may be seen today on the weather vane of the Royal Exchange building in the City of London which occupies the site of Sir Thomas's shop.

After the maker has marked his wares, he sends them to the nearest assay office of The Worshipful Company of Goldsmiths and Silversmiths to be assayed. There each piece receives three and sometimes four marks in addition to that of the maker. First it is assayed and, if found of sterling standard, punched with the sterling mark, a lion passant if assayed in England, a thistle if in Scotland, and a harp if in Ireland.

Next, a letter is stamped on the piece signifying the year the assay was made. About 20 letters of the alphabet are used, A to U omitting J. The style of the letter is changed for each cycle, as is also the shape of the shield in which it is punched. Lombardic, Gothic, Roman, and Script are used.

After the date letter has been punched, the special mark of the assay town where the test was made is affixed. This is a leopard's head for London, an anchor for Birmingham, three sheaves with a sword between for Chester, and a crown for Sheffield. Scottish silver is marked with a castle for Edinburgh and with the coat of arms of the city, called the tree, fish and bell, for Glasgow. Irish silver bears the figure of Hibernia for Dublin. These seven are the only assay towns of Great Britain at the present time. During the past, various towns have had an assay office for short periods. The most notable ones are York, Exeter, Newcastle, and Cork.

King George III, as Americans have good reason to know, was prolific in his ideas for raising funds by taxation and, in 1784, issued a Royal Decree which levied a tax on all silver. Thus still another mark to show that the tax had been paid became necessary. It was collected at the assay office and the fifth mark, a Sovereign's head, was added to the four already described. Therefore, we have the head of George III, George IV, William IV, and Queen Victoria on silver objects produced between the years 1784 and 1890 when both tax and mark were discontinued.

Only four marks appear between 1890 and 1935 but from

May 29 to December 31, 1935, a special mark, the profiles of George V and Queen Mary stamped in an oval shield, was used to commemorate the Silver Jubilee of the reign of Their Majesties. Silver bearing this mark is of special interest to collectors and has already appreciated in value.

During the last quarter of the 17th Century when the extravagant display of wealth at the court of the Stuart Kings and in the homes of the nobility reached a height which caused historians to call it the "silver age," demand for plate became so great that silversmiths, faced with a shortage of bar silver, melted down coins to get material for making their wares. Naturally, by the end of the century there was a distinct scarcity of coins and of silver for the mint. Accordingly, in 1696 it was decreed that all silver objects, other than coins, should be made of a higher standard than "sterlins," namely 958 parts pure silver in 1,000. This became known as the "Britannia standard" because it was marked with the figure of Britannia in place of the lion passant. It was enforced from 1696 until 1720. After the latter date, it was allowed if a craftsman wished to develop a piece in the finer metal. Whenever this happens the piece is always marked with the figure of Britannia. Much of the "Jubilee" silver was made in this standard.

London is and always has been the most important assay town in Great Britain. From the year 1478 until the end of the reign of George III in 1821, the mark was that of a leopard's head crowned. Since then the leopard's head uncrowned and looking more like the face of the famous Cheshire Cat has been in use.

The following gives in very brief form the names and marks of the assay towns of most interest to collectors.

London
1300 to 1478. 3 stamps. Maker's mark, lion passant and leopards' head crowned.
1478 to 1696. 4 stamps. Maker's mark, lion passant, leopard's head crowned, date letter.
1696 to 1720. 4 stamps. First two letters of maker's name, figure of Britannia, leopard's head crowned, date letter.
1720 to 1784. 4 stamps. Maker's mark, lion passant, leopard's head crowned, date letter.
1784 to 1821. 5 stamps. Maker's mark, lion passant, leopard's head crowned, date letter, Sovereign's head.
1821 to 1890. 5 stamps. Maker's mark, lion passant, leopard's head uncrowned, date letter, Sovereign's head.
May 29th to December 31st, 1935. 5 stamps. Maker's mark, lion passant, leopard's head, date letter, Sovereign's head.
January 1st, 1935 to date. 4 stamps. Maker's mark, lion passant, leopard's head, date letter.

Sheffield
1773 to 1784. 4 stamps. Maker's mark, lion passant, crown (town mark), date letter.
1784 to 1890. 5 stamps. Maker's mark, lion passant, crown, date letter, Sovereign's head.
1890 to date. 4 stamps. Maker's mark, lion passant, crown, date letter.

Birmingham
1773 to 1784. 4 stamps. Maker's mark, lion passant, anchor (town mark) date letter.
1784 to 1890. 5 stamps. Maker's mark, lion passant, anchor, date letter, Sovereign's head.
1890 to date. 4 stamps. Maker's mark, lion passant, anchor, date letter.

Chester
1668 to 1700. Various, but 3 stamps, maker's mark, 3 sheaves and sword (town mark), date letter most commonly used.

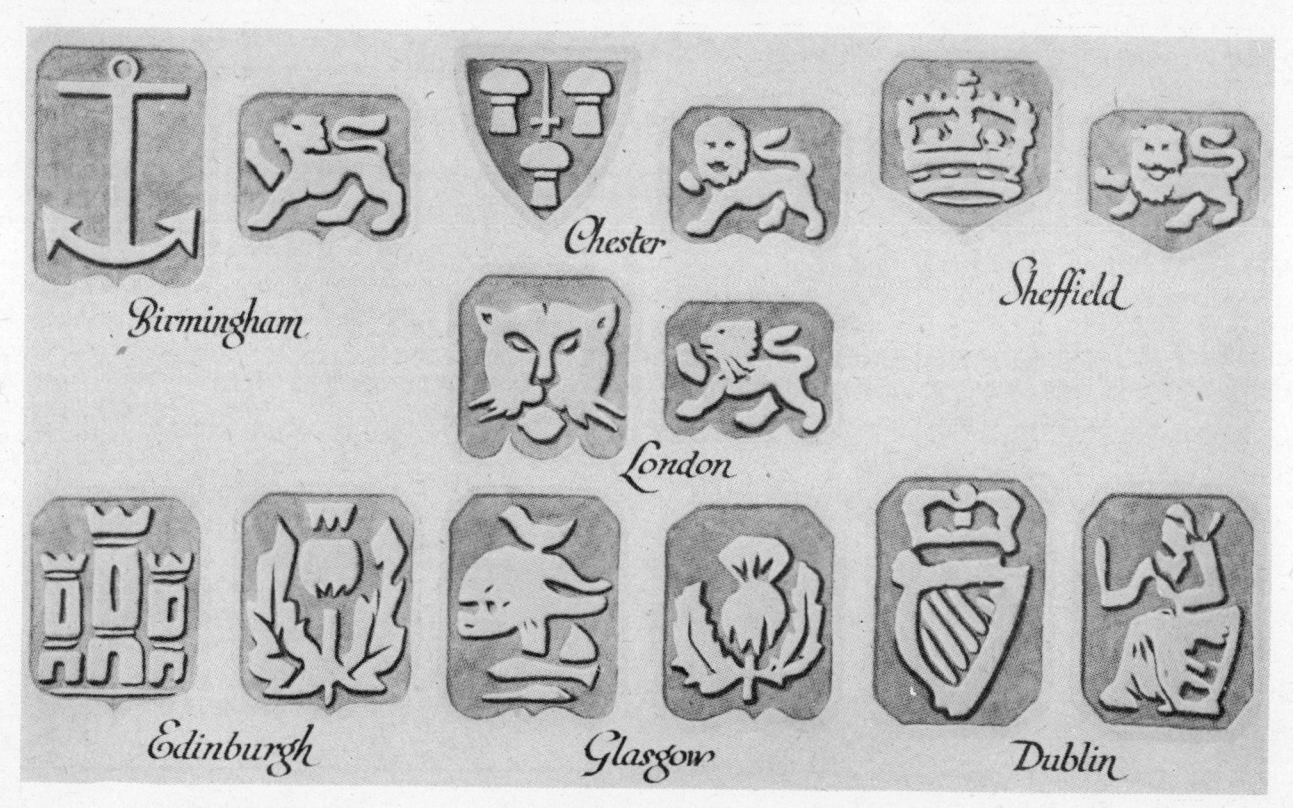

Marks of the Principal English, Scotch, and Irish Assay Cities
Left to right these are: Birmingham since 1773; Chester since 1668; Sheffield since 1773; London from 1300; Edinburgh since 1552; Glasgow since 1681; and Dublin since 1638.

The Scottish Silversmiths

by SEYMOUR B. WYLER

Scotch Silver Sauce Boat. Robert Lowe, Edinburgh, 1753-54.
Metropolitan Museum of Art

THE characteristic traits of a people are often reflected in the quality of their art. The austerity and simple tastes of the Scotsman is brought to the fore by the work of the earliest silversmiths. The majority of silver articles made were definitely for practical use, rather than for purposes of decoration. This is shown by the fact that most of the early Scotch silver was used either in churches or else embraced those pieces used in the art of drinking.

Perhaps the most definitely Scotch of all silver articles was the quaich. This originally was a small two-handled bowl made of wood with silver stripings and used for drinking spirituous liquors. However, a few of the more affluent Scotchmen had these quaiches especially made to order in solid silver. Very few of these pieces were made, therefore they have come to be recognized as the most valuable pieces of Scotch silversmithing to be found. Among other articles, definitely attributed to the Scotch silversmiths, were mulls which were made of large or small horns mounted in silver and used as snuff boxes. Tankards, candle cups, flagons, lugs and mazer cups are all found among the earliest examples of Scotch silver. A Scotch silversmith from Edinburgh named Monteith was the originator of the Monteith bowl, which was named for him.

The earliest Scotch silver which was made in a recognizable quantity, dates from the early 18th century and was very simple in design. However, towards the end of the 18th century, the influence of the English and Irish silversmiths, with their flair for decoration, was impressed on the Scotch silversmiths. Consequently, many pieces of the later 18th century and the early 19th century are ornate, but of definitely fine quality.

The legislation to govern the fineness of silver made in Scotland dates back to as early as 1457, when the first statutes were enacted. The penalties for misrepresentation were so severe that deception was often punishable by death. During the reign of James II, a deacon was appointed to inspect the silver of each maker, and if the test for fineness was correct, the deacons' mark was impressed on the piece together with the maker's mark. However, in 1759, the thistle was introduced and used instead of the deacons' mark, and is still used today. In 1784, the head of the sovereign was also impressed to denote payment of duty. This was not removed until 1890 when the duty on silver was abolished.

The two most important assay offices in Scotland are located in Edinburgh and Glasgow. The Edinburgh hallmark is a three-towered castle, while the Glasgow mark consists of a tree, bird and bill. Both places used date letters. However, silver was also assayed at Aberdeen, Stirling and several other smaller provincial towns, as each individual city originally had the right to assay its own silver. This differs widely from the English legislation on the early plate, which compelled all pieces to be sent to London. Today, however, more than ninety per cent of all Scotch assaying is done in Edinburgh.

The cities in Scotland where silver was produced were Edinburgh, Glasgow, Aberdeen, Dundee, Inverness Perth, Stirling, St. Andrews and Leith.

Unfortunately, there is very little early Scottish silver available for today's collector, because even the wealthy lairds and chieftains did not indulge in lavish home appointments. Since the early Scottish silversmiths could not find sufficient work in any one town, they led a nomadic existence, making small pieces to order, here and there. Also, because of the fact that much of the silver was melted during the 17th century for political reasons, but little remains to be found today.

The careful attitude towards spending money, so often characteristic of the Scotch as a people, had its effect on silversmithing. For this reason complete tea services are practically non-existent, as the families would add one piece at a time to their sets every few years. Consequently, to find a Scotch silver tea service of identical date letter and maker, is virtually an impossibility.

From the standpoint of the dealer or collector, the original marks used by deacons in Scotland have been invaluable in determining the approximate dates of the earliest Scottish pieces. Date letters were not inaugurated for many years to come. Frequently, in the provincial towns, just the name of the city was impressed. Therefore, the dating of many old pieces must be approximate.

It is interesting to note that in the earliest days of silversmithing and goldsmithing in Scotland, it was the general custom for the client to bring his own silver or gold to the craftsmen to be wrought to his order. It appears that dishonest craftsmen adulterated the metal and outrageously cheated the customer. Because of this, the amount of alloy permitted to be used was regulated by law. Perhaps in no country was stricter adherence to this legislation demanded and for that reason nearly all of the Scotch silver found today is up to legal standards. The same standards as set up by the laws of 1483, regulating the quality of the metal, are still used today.

Scotch silver presents to the collector a field of great endeavor. The pieces to be found today are rare and high in price. There are, however, so many willing and ready to purchase these fine specimens that very few remain in the open market for any length of time.

Pair of Scotch Silver Beakers, Maker Unknown. Edinburgh, 1776.

Irish Plate Was Widely Made

By Seymour B. Wyler

ALTHOUGH plate was produced in Ireland as early as the 10th Century, very few examples antedating 1600 are still extant. As is usually the case, this dearth of medieval silver was due to patriotic causes. A turbulent island from the start, constant political upheavals took heavy toll of family silver as the enthusiastic champions of the various causes cheerfully surrendered their plate for the common good.

But there is little doubt as to the ability of the earliest Celtic silversmiths. The discovery of the famous Ardagh Chalice, made in the 12th Century, conclusively proves the true merit of their craftsmanship. The similarities of basic forms as compared with English silver are always to be noted, but the decorative scheme was for the most part original, rather than copied from the arts of continental Europe.

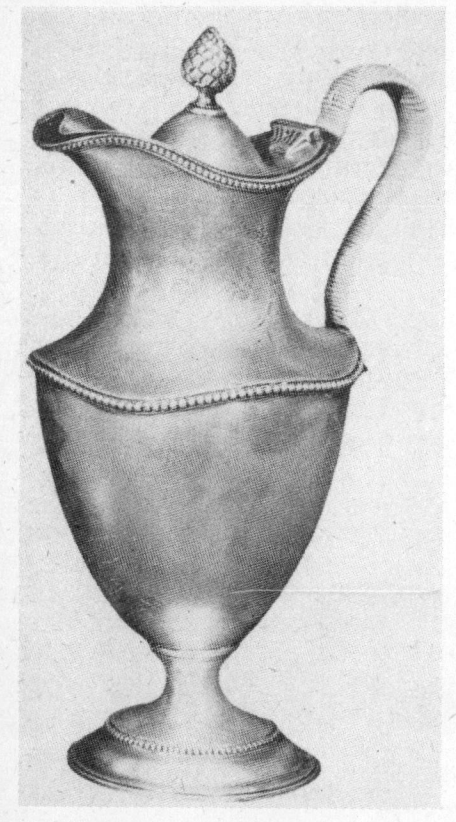

The silversmiths in Ireland were greatly influenced by everyday farm life and its environs, for the originality of design found on so many pieces. Particularly noticeable are the pastoral scenes and figure subjects, so dear to the hearts of the countrymen of Ireland. The chasing on pieces of Irish plate is always to be recognized. This may be accounted for by the fact, that after being subjected to the process of chasing, the silversmiths had not apparently cared to risk the delicate though necessary process of flat hammering the article again. Pieces chased in this particular style are to be found nowhere but in Ireland.

By the middle of the 18th Century, the prevailing rococo styles waned as the Classic influence, introduced by the Brothers Adam, grew in favor. For many years, however, the delicate embossing, enclosing escutcheons for crests and coats of arms, on pieces of plain silver was distinctly reminiscent of the earlier elaborate designs.

In 1607, Charles I granted the charter to the Dublin Goldsmiths Co. which gave them the exclusive control of the craft. At this time two hall marks were inscribed: the crowned harp, being the King's mark, and the maker's mark. In 1638, date letters were first brought into use. It is interesting to note that on Irish silver, successive date letters were often missing. This can only be accounted for by the fact that, due to historical events, Irish corporations were annulled for a time and little gold or silversmithing was carried on.

In 1730, the Irish Parliament imposed a duty of six pence per ounce on all plate, and the figure of Hibernia was stamped on as a duty mark, to denote payment of tax. In 1807 the duty was raised to one shilling per ounce and the King's head impressed as a duty mark. However, no notice was taken of the Hibernia, and both marks were used together until 1890.

But the craft of the early Irish silversmith was not confined to Dublin. The city of Cork, with its natural silver mines, became a large center for silversmithing, and pieces were produced there as early as the 17th Century. The actual dates of the Cork products can only be approximated, however, as no date letters were used, except on pieces sent to Dublin to be assayed. In 1710, the word *sterling* was often inscribed, not as a town mark, but to indicate that the plate was equal in quality to that of the English silversmiths.

There was also a small quantity of silver made at Youghal, Limerick, Galway, and other small towns. However, specimens of Irish provincial silver are indeed very rare. Church plate in particular was practically always the product of either Dublin or London. On many provincial pieces was impressed

—S. Wyler Inc.

A DUBLIN BOWL
Made about 1730 by D. P. whose full name is yet to be discovered.

—S. Wyler Inc.

A DUBLIN WATER JUG
Made by R. Woodhouse, 1736

A PAIR OF GEORGE I. IRISH BEAKERS

They were made in Dublin about 1715 but bear no maker's touch mark.

the word *dollar*, thus bearing witness to the custom, prevalent not only in Ireland but in America, of melting Spanish dollars for use in the silver craft.

The various silversmithing towns in the provinces also adopted and used identifying marks. Cork, for example, had a ship and castle; that of Youghal, a figure of a yawl, (Heraldic Lymphad); that of Galway was an anchor; Limerick-made pieces bore the word *Sterling* or *Starling;* and Belfast pieces carried the impression of an upright hand.

The story of silver making in the provinces may be said to end with the year 1848. Very little was made from then on and today, practically all Irish plate is Dublin-made.

Perhaps the most distinctive piece of Irish silver was the dish ring, often erroneously termed potato ring. These were introduced in Ireland about 1750 and were one of the principal articles of table plate produced. They were used as stands for crystal dessert bowls, soup bowls, or wooden potato bowls and enhanced to the fullest degree, the fine piercing and delicate rococo for which Irish silver is particularly noted.

Other Irish products were drinking mugs of every conceivable size, which must have been made in quantity to judge from the number to be found today. Also, many of the silversmiths specialized in making important pieces, such as epergnes, elaborate candlelabra,

IRISH SILVER MARKS

From left to right, top: Crown harp, Hibernia, King's head, Queen's head, ship and (lower row) castle, the mark of Cork; the yawl of Youghal, the hand of Belfast, the anchor of Galway and the word Sterling of Limerick.

and complete dinner services, all in competition to the English trade.

Who were the men that produced these pieces of Irish silver, so eagerly sought after by the collectors of today? Out of the scores that once worked in Dublin and the provinces, a few names emerge. Some are well known; some are but names; while for many more only a baffling initial gives any clue to the identity of the man who wrought the piece so marked.

In Dublin, the earliest well known silversmith was William Cook who was working about 1640. He was followed by Joseph Stoaker whose working years were from 1650 to 1670. From then until the Georgian period, there seem to have been no outstanding craftsmen. Then came Henry Daniell and John Hamilton, 1710-1730; Robert Holmes and John Moore, 1730-1745; Matthew West, Richard Sawyer, William Law, and Michael Keating, who were at work from approximately 1760 to 1820.

In the other cities, there were such men as Robert Goble, 1680-1712; William Bennett, 1730-1760; John Nicholson and Richard Stevens, 1780-1800—all of Cork. In Galway, there was Richard Joyes, 1695-1725; in Belfast, Matthew Bellew, 1790-1810; in Limerick, Joseph Johns, 1730-1760, and George Moore, 1760-1785; and in Youghal, in County Cork, were John Sharp, 1620-1640, and Austin Beere, 1720-1740.

These are but a few names among the many craftsmen who once produced the plate for which Ireland is justly famous. If data regarding the silversmiths of this unique people is meager, correspondingly rare are examples of their work. Perhaps in no country where so much plate was produced, has so little remained intact through the years. Most of the fine pieces of old Irish plate are today in museums or private collections. Therefore, when a good example of the Celtic craft comes on the market, it is immediately sought after by all who appreciate interesting design and excellent workmanship.

SAUCE BOATS AND TAZZA OR PATTEN

The boats were made in Dublin, 1734, by John Wilme and were once owned by Admiral Lord Vernon, while the patten is the work of Thomas Parr, London, 1703, who had probably migrated from Ireland.

American Silver Styles and their English Background

By Joan Prentice

Associate Curator of Decorative Arts,
Philadelphia Museum of Art

(*All photographs courtesy the Philadelphia Museum*)

AN UNUSUAL opportunity for tracing the development of styles in silver was offered at the Philadelphia Museum of Art in a recent exhibition. It included works by leading silversmiths of France, England and America from 1660 to modern times. The exhibition was arranged in a communicating series of twenty period rooms representing successive phases of artistic devlopment in each of the three countries. In no other American Museum could such a comprehensive group of interiors be found to serve as background for the treasures of a single craft. An analysis of the silver styles on display, the influences affecting their development, and the contributions of craftsmen responsible for new styles, was presented by Fiske Kimball in the Museum Bulletin for March.

Included in the exhibition were 700 or more pieces of silver, English predominating. Many effective comparisons were possible, a few of which are here illustrated. Their dates cannot, however, be taken as indications of precedence in every case as a style often prevailed even in Paris or London, the principal centers of production, for twenty years or more. In fig. 1, for example, the French candlestick (a) happens to be of later date than the English one (c), yet the type was originated on the Continent then adopted by England and subsequently brought over to America. Reaching the provinces after a considerable lapse of time, styles were longer continued there than in the capitals. In Scotland and Ireland, for instance, belated examples persisted long after they had been superseded by new fashions at the capital, while in far-off America, tankards and other popular forms of silver continued to be made a hundred years after the first models had appeared abroad. Further similarities between provincial and American pieces are the general use of a makers mark only, and the arrangement of initials of the owners in a triangle, one letter for the surname of the family being placed above two for the christian names of husband and wife.[1]

The close relation of early New York silver to that of Holland, due to the immigration of numbers of Dutch craftsmen to that city, is well known. Also well known is the fact that all the characteristic American forms of beaker, tankard, caudle cup and mug, salver, tea and coffee pot, cream jug and sugar bowl, to mention but a few, have their forerunners in Europe, principally in England.[2] There still remains to be undertaken a comprehensive study of American silver based on style, an account which would take into consideration the persistence of types long after their initial introduction, and coordinate successive developments as the main American centers of production shifted from Boston and New York prior to 1750, thence to Philadelphia in the last decades of the 18th century and thence to Baltimore where our finest silver of the 19th century was made. Such a study would be all the more valuable as little American silver is dated. Outside the period of the Baltimore experiment, which remained in effect from 1814 to 1830—an experiment based on the English system of hall marks—the exact date of individual pieces of American silver is known only in a few rare instances where the date is actually inscribed or the occasion for which the piece was made is recorded.

Fig. 2. *Casters, from left to right: (a) English, by Charles Adam, London, 1719, lent by the Philadelphia Museum of Art. (b) American, by Simeon Soumaine, New York, after 1719, lent by Mrs. Maurice Brix. (c) English, unidentified silversmith, 1698, lent by Mr. Forsyth Wickes. (d) American, by I. B., New York, c. 1700, lent by Mrs. F. S. Crofts.*

The exhibition and Bulletin, on which the present article is based, suggested not only a more precise chronological arrangement of American silver than has hitherto been attempted, but offered at first hand such a large-scale comparison of our silver with that of other countries as to permit the relationships to be rather fully comprehended. The conclusions drawn have been that the close dependence of the American colonies on Europe, and chiefly on England, has remained almost unchanged since the 17th century as far as styles in the decorative arts are concerned. In fact, excepting the Revolutionary years from 1775 to 1790, when trade with England ceased and a few essentially American contributions began to occur in furniture and silver designs, European styles have prevailed among us.

The American silver here illustrated falls within the major categories of late baroque, rococo, neo-classicism, and romanticism. Most of the pieces are, as the phrase goes, "finds," their existence being scarcely known to the public till now. Another such find was an urn (illustrated elsewhere),[3] by Paul Revere, made in Boston for Hannah Rowe in 1791 as ledgers show.

Fig. 1. *Early Candlesticks (each one of a pair) from left to right: (a) French, by Pierre Masse, Paris, 1689, lent by the Walters Art Gallery. (b) American, by H. B., New York, 1700-1710, lent by Mr. and Mrs. Walter M. Jeffords. (c) English, by I. B., London, 1676, lent by the Museum of Fine Arts, Boston.*

Fig. 3. *Left to right. Chocolate pot, by Lamerie, London, 1744, lent by Dr. A. Hamilton Rice. Coffee pot, by Joseph Richardson I, Philadelphia, 1754, lent by the Historical Society of Pennsylvania.*

Fig. 4. *Left to right. Teapot, by John David, Philadelphia, c. 1790, lent by the Baltimore Museum of Art. Coffee pot, by John Lynch, Baltimore, c. 1804, lent by Mrs. Morris Duane.*

The practical aspects of identification on the basis of style can best be demonstrated by a brief review of the development of 17th century candlesticks as shown in fig. 1. Evolving from the pricket type of earlier times, socket candlesticks appeared in Europe in the 16th century. English table candlesticks of this sort are known which date from 1637, though few survive. The double-tiered base is a characteristic feature which reached the height of its popularity in England from about 1660-1695 and in France a little earlier. This style was brought to America in the last years of the 17th century. It is reflected in 1686 in a simple pair, still with square bases, by Joseph Dummer[4] and continued to be made after 1700 (fig. 1b). The later examples show the later developments of octagonal bases and deep gadrooning.

The muffineer or caster, the finest examples of which were made in France, came into fashion in England in the 17th century reign of Charles II. They remained cylindrical in form until the end of the century. Usually made in sets of three for sugar, salt and pepper, or, as some say, for sale and two kinds of pepper, they were, in the 18th century, fitted into frames with accompanying glass bottles for oil and vinegar. The covers of these utilitarian vessels show the evolution of pierced work from the geometrical perforations of the 17th century to the exquisitely executed intricacies of the 18th centry, a development which found its most elaborate expression in England in the openwork cake-baskets and *épergnes* of the third quarter of the 18th century. The early forms are illustrated in the right hand group of fig. 2, c and d. Soon the bodies took more complicated shape and the cover piercings became more advanced, as in fig. 2, a and b. The close relation of American types to the English is quite apparent.

Few silver pieces wholly characteristic of the late baroque style—with its lavish display of extravagant ornamentation as exemplified in large wine coolers, massive centerpieces and other magnificent appurtenances of English banquet halls—were made in America. The six American baroque sugar boxes known to exist, four by Winslow[5] and two by Coney, are very similar and are undoubtedly derived from European originals. The dating and placing of period porringers by the design of the handles, and the changes which took place in the development of tankard tops and bodies are well understood.

The rococo aspects of American silver, however, have been relatively neglected. True, not many pieces of American silver, wholly rococo in character, were made, but there were probably more than have so far been identified. A newly discovered group of such silver recently was acquired by the Historical Society of Pennsylvania. The group consists of five pieces, four by Joseph Richardson I (who also made the superb tea kettle in the Mabel Brady Garvan Collection, Yale University[6]), and one by Phillip Syng. Of particular interest in this group, because of the unusually early date, is a set of three pieces—a coffee pot with its accompanying sugar bowl, by Richardson, and tray by Syng—known to have been made for the wedding of Sarah Shoemaker and Edward Penington in 1754. The coffee pot is compared in fig. 3 with a chocolate pot by Paul de Lamerie whose technical skill as a silversmith was unmatched by any of his contemporaries. The first intimations of the exuberant rococo style which stimulated craftsmen to

Fig. 5. *Left to right. Candle Cup, by I. W., London, 1671, lent by the Philadelphia Museum of Art. Covered Cup, by A. E. Warner, Baltimore, c. 1835, lent by Miss Annie B. Hays.*

Fig. 6. *Left to right. Teapot, by J. E. Terry & Co., London, 1827-28, lent by the Philadelphia Museum of Art. Terrapin dish, by Samuel Kirk & Son, Baltimore, 1846-1861, lent by Mrs. M. Stevenson Easby.*

full expression of their powers, appeared in Paris just before 1700. Flashing through the various stages of its development from flat chasing to elaborate asymmetrical *repoussé* work, it began to wane in France towards the middle of the century. Active in England from about 1735 to 1765, it found an echo in America from about 1750-1780. Among other examples are a fine bowl of 1753, by Richard van Dyke[7] and a *repoussé* teapot, by Gabriel Lewyn, dating about 1765.[8]

The neo-classic style which followed the rococo was prompted by the excavations at Herculaneum and Pompeii. It was introduced in England by Robert Adam, probably on his return from Italy in 1758. It reached France somewhat later, beginning to be felt at the time of Louis XVI though not reaching its full effect until the early 19th century. Coming to America directly from England, the neo-classical style was reflected here in two tendencies, one dependent on English precedents, the other slightly independent. The vase-shaped urns which replaced tea kettles; the cream pitchers decorated with bands of beading and shallow flutings; the round or oval teapots with straight spouts; the silver soup tureens, rare in America: all follow English models exactly; but tea and coffee pots with galleries and galleried sugar urns seem to be of American origin. No parallel for them, so far as we know, exists abroad. This decoration, particularly associated with Philadelphia during the great period of its history (fig. 4a), found favor elsewhere in America, especially in Baltimore (fig. 4b), many of whose silversmiths were Philadelphia trained. It also was used occasionally in Boston as is borne out in the attribution to William Homes, of Boston, of a fluted and engraved sugar bowl owned by Miss Annie B. Hays, a piece originally belonging to the owner's great-great-grandmother, Mary Throop Jenckes (1775-1850) of Providence. A particularly interesting feature of this sugar bowl, once part of a tea set, is the small straight-topped gallery which is attached to the cover of the bowl rather than to the body.

Coming on to the 19th century, that orphan age ignored and even scorned by many critics, we find that dependence on English fashion was again the rule. The center of American silvermaking had moved to Baltimore which grew rapidly into a large city after 1800 and tripled its population by 1830. Unfortunately little that was new or original was produced in the Victorian era. Craftsmen harked back to earlier periods, reappropriating and reusing old styles, for the most part ignorantly and tastelessly. However, in fig. 5b, we see an example of 19th century American silver with an air of individuality. To be sure it was derived from a much earlier English piece (fig. 5a), yet it nevertheless manages, by virtue of severity and the formal band of ornamentation around the rim, to convey a certain Empire impression, and by its triangular feet to show some individuality of its own. Fig. 6 exemplifies the naturalistic tendencies of the age, which were popular then, and we venture to prophesy will be so again. In any event its forms are eminently successful.

A study of the decorative arts, as well as that of the fine arts, requires an understanding of the principal styles or tendencies which arise in different sections of the world at different times and succeed one another in ever changing sequence. All manifestations of the artistic creative mind thus become part of a general cultural pattern. If the attempt just made at the Philadelphia Museum to show not only a sequence of changes in silver designs but to gather together the major aspects of interior decoration from three countries during the better part of three centuries, should awaken an increased interest in the evolution of style, it will have served its purpose.

FOOTNOTES

1. E. Wenham: "English Provincial Silver—Its Relation to American Colonial," *Connoisseur* 96:20, Oct. '35.
2. F. H. Bigelow: *Historic Silver of the Colonies and its Makers* (1917). C. L. Avery: *American Silver of the XVII and XVIII Centuries*. The Metropolitan Museum (1920).
3. Philadelphia Museum Bulletin, Vol. XLI, March 1946, p. 77. *Antiques* 49:296, May 1946.
4. *Masterpieces of New England Silver* (ill. exhib. cat.) Gallery of Fine Arts, Yale University (1939), Fig. 8.
5. One ill. *Antiques* 32:309, Dec. 1937.
6. Philadelphia Museum Bulletin, Vol. XLI, p. 74, March 1946. *Antiques* 49:296, May 1946.
7. Exhib. Cat. *American Silver*, Museum of Fine Arts Boston (1906) Pl. XI, No. 321.
8. J. H. Pleasants & H. Sill: *Maryland Silversmiths 1715-1830* (1930) Pl. XXXII.
9. Similar to an earlier piece by the same maker. J. H. Pleasants & H. Sill: *Maryland Silversmiths (1715-1830)*, (1930), Pl. XLIV, No. 6.

RARE SILVER CAUDLE CUP

The work of the early Boston silversmith, William Cross, this two-handled cup of early American design was once the property of the Mather family of Massachusetts. In 1945 it was sold at auction to a museum for $2400.
Parke-Bernet Galleries

17th Century New York Silver Was Both Dutch and English

By Harold Donaldson Eberlein
and
Cortlandt Van Dyke Hubbard

—Metropolitan Museum of Art

Garrett Onclebagh Tankard with Ship Decoration

NEW YORK silver of the 17th Century differs perceptibly from the silver made at the same period in the other American colonies. It was the product of two altogether distinct traditions, two separate sources of inspiration. The first was Dutch, the second was English. The amalgamation that inevitably came about resulted in a distinctive character that marked the silverware of New York origin till the middle of the 18th Century, or even later.

Practically all New York silver that has come down to us was produced after the city passed under British rule in 1664. The Dutch residents, little affected in their cultural outlook by the political change, were essentially conservative and tenacious of their usages and wonted mode of life. They continued to require their bowls, beakers, and other silver plenishings to be in the Dutch manner. And then smiths, for a long time, continued to fashion their handiwork according to Dutch precedent, with a few modifications. On the other hand, such English smiths as settled in New York followed English ways, and their work reflected contemporary design in England. Hu-

—Clapp & Graham

Typical Sturdy Craftsmanship

At the left a Tankard by Simeon Soumaine; the right one by Bartholomew Schaats.

AMERICAN SILVER

guenot craftsmen adapted their cunning to the tone of their new environment and did not bring in any appreciably French influence.

By the end of the 17th Century, the Dutch and English in the province were about evenly balanced in numbers. Social fusion of the two elements began very soon after New Amsterdam became New York, but the process was slow. Equally deliberate was the fusion of Dutch and English influences in silversmithing, but the outcome of this gradual blending was a recognized type. The stages in its creation may be traced by successive comparisons.

shipping became lawful prey for colonial privateers. Slow communication between England and the colonies often left the latter in doubt about the exact relations at the moment between the mother country and the hostile powers. Then the colonists' inclinations and cupidity decided their course of action.

Actually, the border line between privateering and piracy was shadowy. Under the respectable aegis of letters of marque, piratical seizures were by no means unknown. Furthermore, an openly connived-at traffic went on with notorious pirates at Madagascar. They even came to trade

—*Metropolitan Museum of Art*

Ornate Work Was Also Done
A Snuffer and Stand by Cornelius Kierstede.

—*Gallery of Fine Arts, Yale University*

A Teapot by Nicholas Roosevelt

It may seem a far cry from colonial silver to piracy, but the connection was very real. As mercantile venture expanded, and New York ship-owners and merchants prospered, they gladly heeded the urge to fit out privateers and augment profits by prizes captured at sea from the enemy. The risks were not much graver than those incident to ordinary marine commerce. The rewards could be vastly greater. England was at war, off and on, with France and Spain and at such times French and Spanish

outside the very port of New York. Nominally disapproving irregularities of commerce, some provincial governors forebore to inquire too closely into the doings of influential merchants. During Col. Fletcher's rule, these illicit and magnificiently profitable practices seem to have gone altogether unchecked. His successor, Lord Bellomont, dragged the scandal into the light of day and bombarded the Lords of Trade in London with denunciations of "the continued groth of Piracy." In 1698 he wrote: "This city hath

been a nest of pirates, and I already find that several of their ships have their owners and were fitted from this port, and have Commissions to act as privateers, from the late Governour here."

Captain Kidd set out from New York to suppress piracy, then turned pirate himself. Apropos trafficking with freebooters, the Earl of Bellomont notes " 'Tis the most beneficial trade, that to Madagascar with the pirates, that was ever heard of, and I believe there's more to be got that way than by turning pirates and robbing." His lordship's efforts to suppress these practices roused bitter resentment and opposition.

We can readily surmise what a golden stream must have poured into the coffers of New York's "merchant adventurers" during Gov. Fletcher's régime. Affluence derived from trade, legitimate and otherwise, enabled the citizens to indulge in luxury. Silver coin a-plenty gave the smiths ample metal to fashion silverware. An eloquent memorial of the direct connection between silverware and piracy, or near-piracy, is the tankard Garrett Onclebagh made, now in the Metropolitan Museum. In defiance of Lord

named ... John Windover and the Huguenot, Bartholomew Le Roux, the latter energetically espousing the people's cause at the time of the Leisler Rebellion in 1689.

Although they did not work in the 17th Century, and some of them were not born till the opening years of the 18th, such men as Peter Van Dyck ... often termed the greatest of New York's silversmiths ... Adrian Bancker, Simeon Soumaine, the Ten Eycks and others ought to be mentioned in connection with 17th Century silver. They worthily carried on its tradition with only such changes as might be expected from conservative craftsmen in the course of orderly evolution. They also perpetuated the tradition of their predecessors in the discharge of public duties.

Most of the 17th Century New York silver that has survived belongs to the last quarter of the century. One of its outstanding characteristics is massive substantiality. It is just as pronounced in generous solidity and weight of metal as was the proverbial Dutch burgher in his bodily sturdiness. Again, it is marked by rugged simplicity of contour. The shapes are not at all lacking in grace, but they are forthright in line, like the mental habit of their makers, and they do not show the delicate subleties of form that occasionally distinguish pieces of other origin. While many pieces made in New England and elsewhere are fashioned of thinner metal, with edges tapered off, and more curves, more slender shapes, more refinements of line, early New York pieces are usually of somewhat ampler size, made of thick silver, and the edges are abruptly cut off. They show the careful workmanship of good craftsmen, but they lack that finish which marks the more sophisticated artist. There were, too, certain types of design and ornament that characterized early New York silver. The chief articles made at this period include tankards, beakers, baptismal basins, porringers, bowls, cups, mugs, wine tumblers and teapots with, of course, the usual complement of spoons, candlesticks and the like.

The previously mentioned fusion of Dutch and England tradition traceable in early New York silver cannot be better exemplified than by the ubiquitous tankard. The fact that tankards were made at all indicates a distinct stage of fusion. So far as we know, they were not made nor used in Holland. They *were* made and used in England, and the type New York smiths fashioned was more like the broad, flat-topped, plain Restoration tankard of England than like Continental or other colonial tankards, but was usually larger, heavier and of more massive aspect. The capacious size of New York drinking-vessels perhaps indicates local hospitality and aptitude for consuming liquid refreshment.

The New York tankard had a flat lid of two stages and the top often became a vehicle for engraved enrichment, frequently of elaborate character. Other colonies came early to use domed lids, with or without finial; the New York lid continued flat. The whorled thumb-piece, or so-called corkscrew shape, was a feature of rarest occurrence in the rest of the colonies, but was known in England at the date. Above the moulded base was often a stamped or moulded foliate border, seldom used elsewhere in America and probably derived from Continental precedent. In the mantlings of armorial bearings engraved on tankards, and on other pieces also, swags and drops of fruit and flowers, and likewise other decorative motifs apart from heraldry, showed Dutch or German inspiration. On the backs of the handles a common ornament consisted of stamped or moulded masques or

Wine Tumbler by Van der Spiegel

It also bears mark of Benjamin Wyncoop.

An Unmarked Funeral Spoon

The Handle is engraved "Maria V Renselaer Obit 24 Jann 1688/9"

—Metropolitan Museum

—Metropolitan Museum of Art

Tankard by Benjamin Wyncoop

Bellomont, a number of merchants financed the *Nassau*, under Captain Giles Shelley, for the Madagascar trade. On its return, they are said to have presented this testimonial to Shelley. His arms were engraved on the drum and a likeness of the ship on top of the lid to commemorate the incident.

Prosperous in their craft, 17th Century New York silversmiths were men of consequence, like their fellows in New England. Of Jeuriaen Blanck, "goutsmidt," whose name appears in 1643, we know little. The term "goldsmith," by the way, originally designated a worker in the precious metals; the name silversmith did not come into common use till the 18th Century.

Of those who wrought a little later we know much more. Ahasuerus Hendrickse, trained in Holland, took his oath of allegiance to the King in 1675; thence onward he was a prominent figure. He made "jewellery, rings, funeral spoons, and beakers and, as well, fashioned the silver spears, pikes and sword-hilts affected by the militant burghers."

Carol van Brugh was likewise a person of note. He it was who made "the gold cup presented to Gov. Fletcher in 1693, the bullion for which was purchased for £106 and turned over to Vanderburgh (van Brugh) to fashion," the Council providing "that the revenue from the ferry be used for no other purpose until the bill for this was paid." This testimonial was presumably for Fletcher's attitude in favoring trade.

Garrett Onclebagh, who made Shelley's *Nassau* tankard, belonged to a prominent family, was a respected member of the Dutch Reformed Church, and served several aldermanic terms, though he seems to have fallen under a cloud in later life. Jacob Boelen, who had learned his craft in Holland, also figures conspicuously in civic affairs. Jacobus Van der Spiegel was an ensign in Captain Walter's company, sent to Albany in 1689 to protect the northern frontier against the impending French invasion; later a captain; assessor for the West ward in 1694-95; and, in 1698, "elected to the highly honorable position of constable." Cornelius Kierstede, a man of local note and of influential family connections, one of New York's most original and skillful silversmiths, fashioned some of the finest pieces of early Manhattan's plate. He later removed to New Haven owing to interest in a copper mining project. And so it goes. Benjamin Wynkoop, Bartholomew Schaats and nearly all the early silversmiths bestirred themselves in civic matters. Of the silversmiths who were not Dutch, two especially must be

—Clapp & Graham

Elaborate, Early New York Work

The Tankard at the left bears the touches of Cornelius Kierstede and Philip Goelet; that at right the mark of Jacob Boelen.

—Clapp & Graham

A Cream Pitcher by John Le Roux

cherub heads with pendants of fruit, foliage and flowers. These characteristics were distinctly typical of 17th Century New York tankards. Mugs were really small tankards without lids and often had a re-inforcing moulded band about the body between base and rim.

Typical of New York design of the period were also tall, flaring beakers of heavy silver with substantial moulded base, the sides engraved with interlacing strapwork patterns and sprays of flowers, leaves and fruit. When intended for church use, symbolic figures of Faith, Hope and Charity were often embodied in the design. Beakers made elsewhere were lighter, smaller, and generally lacked all surface ornament save arms, initials or monograms. Again, characteristic of the period in New York were the bowls, with or without handles, their sides often divided into panels and embellished with repoussé or embossed motifs. Repoussé and embossed ornamentation, for other articles also was typical of New York. The motifs generally betrayed Dutch or Continental derivation. How elaborate such ornament could be may be seen from a snuffer-stand by Cornelius Kierstede.

Marks used by the 17th Century New York silversmiths varied. Jacob Boelen used I B (with a rose below, in shield); I B (with crown above, in cartouche); and I B (in shaped rectangle). Jacobus Van der Spiegel used I V S (in trefoil), I V S (in rectangle) and other variants. Benjamin Wynkoop used WBK (in a heart) and B W (in long oval). Bartholomew Schaats used B S (with fleur-de-lis below, in heart-shaped shield) and B S (in a square). Cornelius Kierstede used C K (in rectangle) and C K (a diamond or lozenge and two pellets below, in a shield). It is always likely that variations of these may turn up and also that more marks, of makers hitherto credited with only one mark, such as Garrett Onclebagh or Ahasuerus Hendrickse, may come to light. Then, too, there are some marks that have never been identified; they always carry the stimulus of possible solution. Unmarked pieces are tantalizing. We can only conjecture and suggest strong possibilities of their authorship.

17th Century New York silver is highly satisfying for its intrinsic good qualities of form and workmanship, its strong and pleasant individuality, and because it faithfully reflects both the personality of its makers and the social life that called it into being.

By Keonraet Ten Eyck of Albany One of a Pair of Salvers

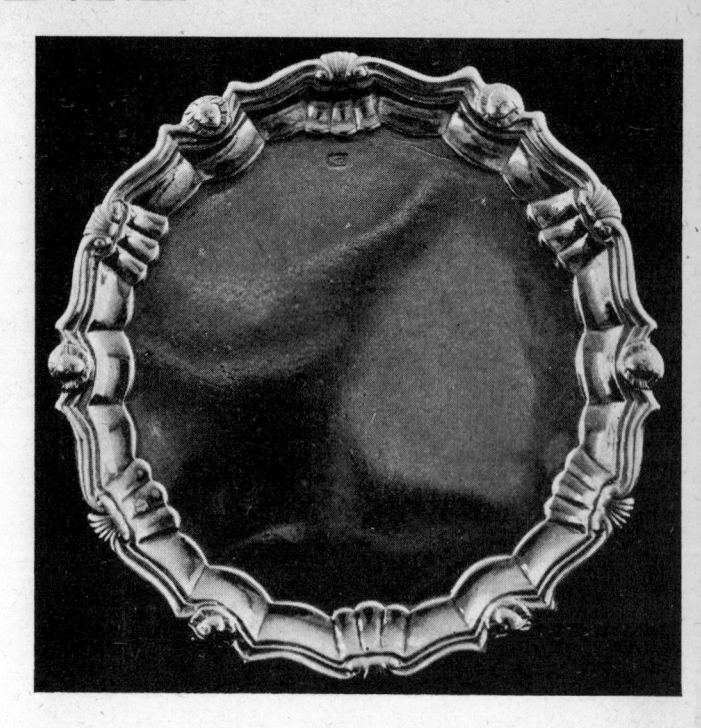

—*Clapp & Graham*

Museum of the City of New York

EARLY NEW YORK SPOON

This spoon was made by the New York silversmith Henricus Boelen who died in 1755.

The Drowne Silversmiths of Portsmouth

By Stephen Decatur

UNDOUBTEDLY the name of Samuel Drowne is as well known as that of any of the early silversmiths of Portsmouth, N. H., but locally, at least, it is more generally remembered because of the prominent part its owner played in the affairs of his community during the period of the American Revolution and in the years immediately thereafter. Like many other American silversmiths of the time, he was an ardent supporter of the patriot cause and, in fact, he was concerned in an affair which, since it antedates the fights at Lexington and Concord, is considered by many historians as marking the true beginning of the Revolution.

Early in December, 1774, a rumor became current in Boston that the British intended to send troops to occupy Fort William and Mary at the mouth of Portsmouth Harbor. On the thirteenth of the month, Paul Revere galloped to Portsmouth with letters to the Committee of Correspondence there reporting this expected move. The following evening a party of several hundred men from Portsmouth and neighboring towns went down the river in boats and, in spite of the fire of the small garrison, landed, stormed, and captured the fort. As it turned out there were no casualties on either side, a happy chance which may explain why this exploit has not achieved greater prominence. The originator and one of the leaders of it was Captain Thomas Pickering, Drowne's brother-in-law, and the silversmith was a member of his company.

The principal object of the patriots in this affair was to secure the powder stored in the fort before the British troops could get it and upwards of four hundred barrels of the precious material were taken and secretly removed upriver to places of safety. This part of the program was engineered by Drowne and he arranged it so successfully that the authorities were unable to recover a single barrel. Later, some of this powder was used at the Battle of Bunker Hill where, it would seem, there was, unfortunately, not enough.

Samuel Drowne was a member of an interesting family to which Shem Drowne of Boston, a prominent coppersmith, also belonged. Leonard Drowne, the first of the name in this country, settled near Portsmouth about 1670, but ultimately the family removed to Rhode Island. The silversmith's father, also named Samuel, was a grandson of the original settler. He was first a minister of the Calvin Baptist denomination, but later became an Independent Congregationalist preacher and in that capacity was called to Portsmouth in 1758. Although devout Christians, the members of his flock, being seceders from the established churches, were not highly regarded; commonly they were contemptuously referred to as "New Lights." In fact, Governor John Wentworth of New Hampshire issued a special edict permitting all ministers in the Colony to perform the marriage ceremony "except one Drowne."

Samuel, the silversmith, a son of this preacher, was born in Providence, Rhode Island, in 1749, and died in Portsmouth in 1815. He married Mary, a daughter of Captain Thomas Pickering, one of the largest landowners of Portsmouth, a prominent citizen and a military officer who was killed in battle with the Indians at Casco to the eastward. The Captain Thomas Pickering of the Fort William and Mary exploit was, of course, a brother of the silversmith's wife. He was a captain of privateers and was killed in 1779 during the capture of a British letter of marque, a vessel much more powerful than the 20-gun ship *Hampden*, which he commanded.

A few months after the capture of the fort, Samuel Drowne was placed in charge of the leading Tories in his neighborhood to see that they conducted themselves discreetly. In 1778 he was a member of Colonel John Langdon's Company of Light Horse, an organization especially formed from

—*Charles H. Batchelder and Others*

Spoons and Sugar Tongs by Samuel Drowne

He was the first of his family to follow the silversmiths' craft in Portsmouth. His dates were 1749-1815. The spoon identified as Number 5 is the earliest. It was made for Captain Lear, father of Colonel Tobias Lear, secretary to General George Washington, and bears the Lear crest. Numbers 2 and 3 are excellent examples of Drowne's "feather-edge" work. They, and Number 1, were made for the Treadwell family of Portsmouth. Number 9 has been reversed to show one of his known marks, "S. Drowne" in rectangle.

—*Metropolitan Museum of Art*

Beaker by Samuel Drowne

Other pieces of silver than spoons and kindred flatware for table use are comparatively rare, although this beaker is evidence that he did make pieces of hollow ware.

among the gentlemen of Portsmouth, to assist in the operations in Rhode Island, and was with it during the attempted capture of Newport. In 1789 Drowne was one of the Committee of Twelve appointed to arrange for the reception of President Washington on his visit to Portsmouth and he further served as a selectman of his town in 1799 and 1804. He was arrested and carried to Exeter for trial in 1795 for alleged participation in riots arising from dissatisfaction with Jay's Treaty. He had then been a deacon for many years, and the spectacle of this dignified gentleman in the dock inspired a great deal of amusement. However, his detention was easily shown to have been a mistake; he had merely been passing by at the moment of the disturbances.

The silversmith lived on the southern side of what is now State Street, not far from the waterfront, and, as was the usual practice at the time, he had his shop in the same building. His spoons and flatware are not too difficult to find, but pieces of hollow ware by him are exceedingly scarce. His best known mark is "S. Drowne" in a rectangle with shaped ends. He also used "S.D.," capitals in elongated oval.

While the best-known silversmith of the family, Samuel Drowne, was not the only member of it to follow this profession. His brother Benjamin, 1759-1793, of Portsmouth also, was a silversmith. Since he died at a comparatively early age, examples of his work are quite rare and, practically speaking, are confined to spoons. Like his brother, he made a good marriage, his wife being Frances, a sister of the Major William Gardner, whose name is so familiar to visitors to Portsmouth through its connection with the beautiful Wentworth-Gardner mansion, one of the finest Georgian houses in the country. Benjamin was also a vigorous supporter of the patriot side during the Revolution and in 1780 was on the staff of Colonel Thomas Bartlet's regiment of New Hampshire militia. His name is omitted from many lists of silversmiths, but he used the mark "B. Drowne," capitals in rectangle, and possibly also "B. D.," capitals in rectangle. His house and shop were diagonally across the street from those of his brother.

Samuel, the silversmith, had two sons who followed in their father's footsteps. This younger generation dropped the final "E" from their surname. The eldest was Thomas Pickering Drown, 1782-1849, whose mark, "T. P. Drown," capitals in rectangle, is generally familiar. He was prominent in local affairs and in 1817 abandoned his silversmithing to become town clerk, an office which he held until 1826. Then for ten years he was connected with the Portsmouth branch of the United States Bank; but, with the abolishment of this institution during Jackson's administration, he seems to have returned to his original trade and then possibly worked in Newburyport for a few years, although this has not been verified. His early work closely resembles that of his father, but, apparently, is not as highly regarded.

Daniel P. Drown, 1784-1863, the other son of Samuel, is listed as a silversmith as late as the Portsmouth directory for 1860-1861, but it is doubtful if he ever worked independently, since no pieces of silver with a mark which could be his have been recorded up to the present time, although, of course, it is possible some exist. Undoubtedly, however, he worked with his father in his early years. During the War of 1812 he was a lieutenant of New Hampshire troops; then he was deputy sheriff until he succeeded his brother as town clerk in 1826, an office he retained until 1832. Two years later, when serving as a selectman of the town, he was appointed Collector of Customs for the Portsmouth district, retaining that office until 1841, when he became connected with the railroad. He was afterwards a justice of the peace, and the Commissioner for the State of Maine in New Hampshire. Thus, he could have had but little opportunity for following his trade, but it may be that for a few years prior to his death he did so.

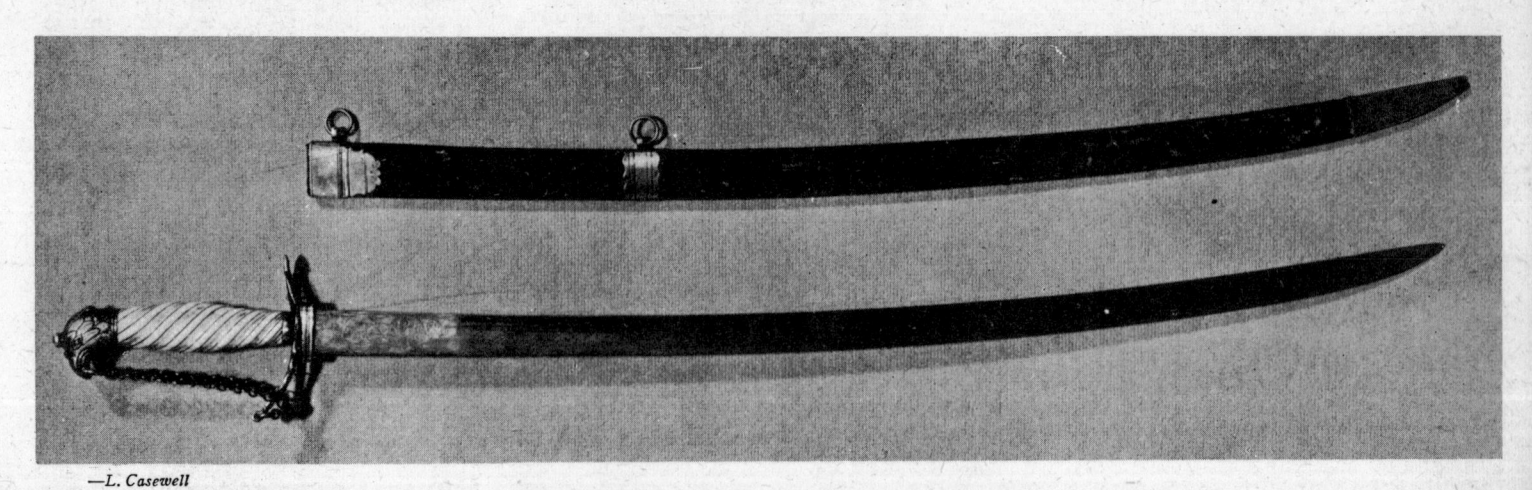

—Charles H. Balchelder and Others

1   2   3   4

Spoons by Thomas Pickering Drown

He was the elder son of Samuel Drowne and along with his younger brother, Daniel P., also a silversmith, dropped the final vowel from the family name. Spoon Number 1 is too early in style for this craftsman's period. His dates were 1782-1849. This spoon is one of a half dozen that he made to match a set of spoons made by his father (see Numbers 2 and 3 in illustration of Samuel Drowne spoons). Number 2 has been reversed to show his mark, "T. P. Drown" in rectangle. The coffin-shaped handles of Numbers 2 and 3 may be considered the earliest work of this silversmith, while the bright-cut spoon, Number 4, is a decorative treatment also used at times by his father, from whom he presumably learned engraving as well as silversmithing.

—L. Casewell

Sword with Scabbard by Samuel Drowne

The silver hilt, that ends in a bird's head, and the mounting bear his mark. It was made circa 1775. The scabbard, as was general at this time, is of finely tanned leather. The blade was probably a European import.

Philadelphia Silver by Ghiselin and Syng

By Harold Donaldson Eberlein

and

Cortlandt Van Dyke Hubbard

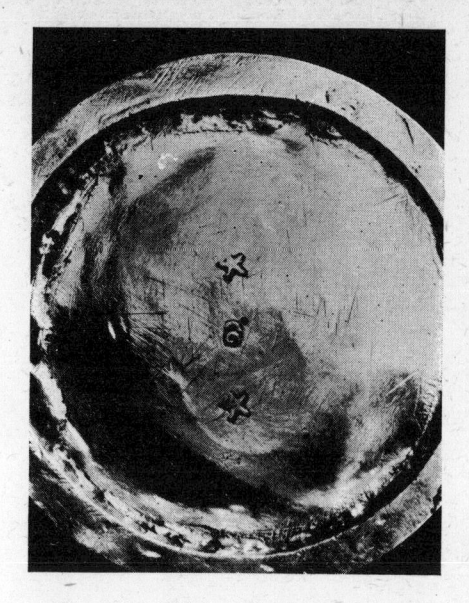

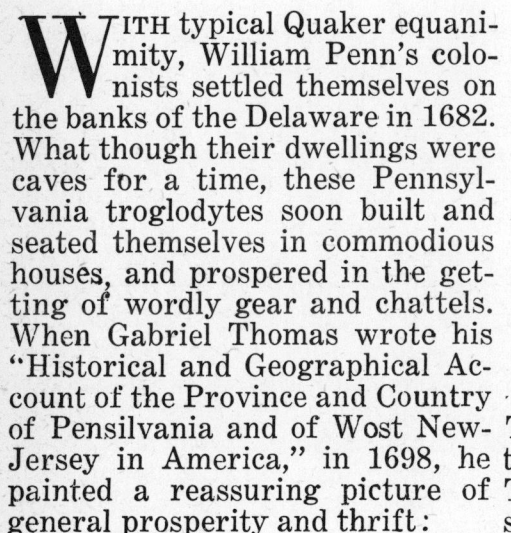

Cesar Ghiselin's Touch

The base of the Christ Church beaker. It bears the letters C G with five-jointed stars before and after.

WITH typical Quaker equanimity, William Penn's colonists settled themselves on the banks of the Delaware in 1682. What though their dwellings were caves for a time, these Pennsylvania troglodytes soon built and seated themselves in commodious houses, and prospered in the getting of wordly gear and chattels. When Gabriel Thomas wrote his "Historical and Geographical Account of the Province and Country of Pensilvania and of West New-Jersey in America," in 1698, he painted a reassuring picture of general prosperity and thrift:

"the Industrious (nay Indefatigable) Inhabitants have built a *Noble* and *Beautiful* City ... which contains above two thousand houses, all Inhabited; and most of them Stately, and of Brick, generally three Stories high, after the Mode in London. ... And for Silver-Smiths, they have between Half a Crown and Three Shillings an Ounce for working their Silver, and for Gold equivalent."

Though he looks at the infant city through rose-colored glasses, Thomas is matter-of-fact in his statements. His mention of prices current for silversmithing is pretty good evidence that at least one silversmith was working in Philadelphia at the time. Penn, we know, from the outset of his colonizing scheme encouraged craftsmen of various sorts to establish themselves in his "greene country Towne." In his "Further Account of the Province of Pennsylvania," published in 1685, the Proprietor states that French

Syng Flagon and Alms Basin and Beaker by César Ghiselin

The flagon is engraved "Gift of Col. Robert Quarry" and bears the touch P S in rectangle. The alms basin and beaker are marked C G with five-pointed stars on either side.

—Christ Church, Philadelphia

55

Cream Jug by William Ghiselin Working 1750-62

It is marked twice on the bottom. This touch is crude capitals W and G with pellet between.

—*Pennsylvania Museum of Art*

(Huguenots) and Dutch had already arrived as settlers.

Whether there were or not any silversmiths in this group, the first recorded manipulation of the white metal for Philadelphia was an illicit proceeding that caused a tempest in the judicial teapot in the very first year of the Colony's founding. Charles Pickering, one of the "first purchasers," a personage of substance and consideration in England and of conspicuous importance in the Province, "maltster, ship-owner, merchant, lawyer, miner, planter, yeoman, copper and iron worker, forest ranger" and a few more things besides "goldsmith," as he styles himself in his will, through his effervescent versatility and dynamic enterprise generally managed to be in the center of the stage, often in a scrape.

On August 24, 1683, before the Privy Council, "Wm Penn, Prop^er and Govr," the

"Govr Informed ye board that it was Convenient Warrant should be sent from this board to apprehend some persons upon suspition of putting away of bad money."

Charles Pickering, Samuel Buckley, and Robert Fenton were the persons "aprehended" to be tried for "Quining of Spanish Bitts and Boston money, to ye Great Damage and abuse of ye Subjects thereof."

In view of the scarcity of circulating coin, and with John Hull's "Pine-Tree Shillings" in mind, Pickering apparently had the happy thought of relieving the situation. Where he got his "24 pounds of Bard Silver" we do not know; it was too soon for anything to have come from the small lead and silver mine in Chester County. When asked at the trial the names of those to whom he had paid out his false coinage, he refused to tell, "saying the Money that any p^rson rec^d of him he would change it and that noe man should Loose any thing by him." William Penn, as governor and judge, charged the jury; when the jury brought in the verdict, he sentenced Pickering to make

"full Satisfaction in good and Currant pay to Every Person that shall within ye Space of one Month bring in any of this false Base and Counterfitt Coyne" (to be called in by proclamation), and that it "shall be melted into gross before returned to thee and that thou shalt pay a fine of *fourty pounds into this Court, toward ye Building of a Court house in this Towne*, and Stand comitted till payd and afterwards fined Security for they good abearance."

Cream Pitcher by Philip Syng, the Younger

Made circa 1750, it bears the touch twice of P S in a rectangle.

—*Pennsylvania Museum of Art*

A Syng Braiser Made About 1780

It is twice marked on the bottom with the touch P S in shaped cartouch separated with two leaves, the mark of Philip Syng, the younger.

—Pennsylvania Museum of Art

Buckley was fined £10, and Fenton, a servant, was set an hour in the stocks.

Although the Grand Jury had found a true bill against him for a "Heynous and Grevious Crime," for which he got the foregoing sentence, Pickering seems to have lost no standing in the community. He redeemed the "Spanish Bitts and Boston money" he and his associates had coined and, in less than a month after his indictment, appeared in Friends' Meeting, of which he was a member,

"offering to submit himself to the will and pleasure of the meeting, and to do anything that the meeting should order, which might Remove any Scandal that the truth was likely to Suffer through him being concerned in paying and passing moneys not Current."

On March 14, 1685, the Privy Council of the Province adopted a resolution that

"It is ye sence of this board that the Petion^r [Pickering] in reference to privileges and ffreedom, Stands in an Equal Capacity with other Persons of his Station in the Province."

In May, 1690, he became a member of the Provincial Assembly.

Aside from Pickering's "quining" escapade, Philadelphia had several silversmiths working before the end of the 17th Century. The names of César Ghiselin, William Paschall, and Johannis Nys all occur at an early date. Exactly when Paschall and Nys began to ply their craft we do not know. In his will, dated December 6, 1695, Paschall calls himself "silversmith"; and Nys, who had worked first in New York, is named in William Penn's cashbook in 1700 and in the Dickinson Ledger under date of September 5, 1700.

We do know, however, that César Ghiselin is the first gold and silversmith *recorded* to have been working in the Province. He was on the tax-list of 1693, and in the will of Peter Dubac, gentleman, dated October 14, 1693, we find:

"I give and bequeath unto my loving friend Cesar Guislin of ye s^d town of Philadelphia, Goldsmith, the sum of twenty four pounds current Silver money of this Province, which he oweth unto me, & also a barr of Gold, weighing an ounce and eight penny weight which he hath now in his custodie, the said Cesar delivering up to my executor eight ounces he hath of mine in broken gold and powder."

William Penn's cash-book, under date of December 4, 1701, has the entry:

"By Exps, p^d ye Goldsmith's note (Pticulars were given before but are lost) Caesar Ghiselin £1-14-0."

In Pentacost Teague's Ledger, October 24, 1708, Ghiselin is charged £14-2-0 for 35¼ oz. of silver; three days later, he is credited with silver and gold "rec^d by my boy Peter" and for a "firle on my cane." The ledger of Thomas Coates shows "Cash paid Cesar Ghiselin £5 on 12th mo., 15, 1711." Sundry other records indicate Ghiselin's activities at his craft.

He seems to have been of Huguenot stock and to have come from London to Philadelphia. Although the names of his parents and the date of his birth have not been definitely determined, it is likely that his father was Nicholas Ghiselin of Rouen, naturalised in London in 1681-2, according to the records of the Huguenot Society of London. To have been on the Philadelphia tax-list of 1693, César must have been born about 1672. His denization was issued in London, September 28, 1698 (while he was living in Philadelphia); his papers were afterwards recorded in Annapolis. His wife, Catherine, appears to have been the daughter of Pierre Reverdy, a Huguenot refugee from Poitou who fled to London, migrating thence to New York and afterwards to New Castle, Del. The records of Christ Church, Philadelphia, show that César and Catherine Ghiselin had nine children, Nicholas, William, Mary to have paid five shillings a year in 1723 and 1724. Catherine Ghiselin died in April, 1726, and there is record that Ghiselin paid pew rent in St. Ann's in 1727.

It was about this time, however, that he returned to Philadelphia, for in his will, dated January 27, 1728-9 (William Paschall, gold-

Inkstand by Philip Syng, The Younger

Made 1752 at a cost of 27 pounds, 16 shillings, for the colonial state house, this was used by signers of the Declaration of Independence.

—Independence Hall

Katherine, Hanah, Septima, and four daughters who died in infancy.

Some time between 1716 and July, 1718, Ghiselin removed to Annapolis and took up land there. In April, 1720, he was chosen a Warden of St. Ann's Church and seems to have served on the Vestry till 1725, or possibly longer. Vestry minutes of June, 1725, mention reservations in pews for "housekeepers of this Vestry to sit in" and, in the second pew, seats were appointed for "Mr. César Ghiseling and his wife Catherine and his daughter Hanah," an accommodation for which César is recorded smith, already mentioned, was one of the witnesses) he describes himself as of Philadelphia. He died in February, 1733, and was buried in Christ Church Yard. His son William, who continued to live in Annapolis, was executor. The inventory of César Ghiselin's belongings shows that he had on hand a considerable quantity of gold and silver, besides jewelry materials, and that his shop was well appointed with all the requisite tools and implements. William Ghiselin, the Philadelphia silversmith who worked in the middle of the 18th Century, was his eldest grandson, the son of Nicholas.

None of César Ghiselin's account books have come to light, so we cannot tell just what he did or for whom he worked. Unfortunately, too, very few examples of his work have come down to us, though one cannot help feeling that a good deal more of it must be somewhere in existence. The few authentic pieces known are two spoons, in private ownership, and the alms plate and beaker belonging to Christ Church, Philadelphia, both of them inscribed "the gift of Margaret Tresse spinstor to Christ church in Philadelphia." The alms plate is 9¾" in diameter and the beaker is 4¾" high; both are marked on the bottom with C G stamped in a crude rectangle between two five-pointed stars. Two tankards bequeathed by his son-in-law were, in all likelihood, Ghiselin's work, but their whereabouts are unknown. In 1721, while this vestryman-silversmith was working in Annapolis, the Corporation of the City of Annapolis commissioned him to make twelve silver spoons to be given as prizes at the local horse races, a sporting touch. None of these have been found though several of them, like as not, may be tucked away and turn up some day. In the *Maryland Gazette*, November 16, 1752, is an advertisement:

"Found a Gold Ring, the Maker's stamp C G having a posey on it. The Owner may have it by applying to the finder."

This ring was almost certainly a piece of Ghiselin's work, fashioned during his Annapolis period; the "posey" was not recognized as a star. By one unfamiliar with marks, the mistake might readily have been made. The few known pieces of Ghiselin's work show a high order of craftsmanship. Though severely plain, their purity of line imparts distinction and a virile, yet reticent, individuality.

The other vestryman-silversmith was Philip Syng, the Younger. Ghiselin left a grandson of his name to carry on the craft. Syng had a silversmith father, two brothers, a silversmith son and nephew. Philip the Younger, the middle member of the Syng dynasty, was one of the finest silversmiths of his day; he was also a conspicuous and useful member of the community throughout his life.

Philip Syng the Elder, "goldsmith and gentleman," sprung of an old Shropshire family, followed his craft in Cork. In 1714, with his wife and three sons, Philip, John and Daniel, he sailed from Bristol and landed July 14, in Philadelphia. There seems to have been some connection of family or ancient friendship between Philip Syng senior and the Honourable John Hart, Esq., who had come from England that same year as governor of the Province of Maryland. Almost immediately after landing at Philadelphia the elder Syng went to Annapolis. He was apparently back in Philadelphia by September 29, since on that the lad's eleventh birthday, he placed young Philip apprentice to a silversmith there. Who that silversmith was we do not know; we can only surmise. It may have been César Ghiselin. If that was the case, and if the elder Syng had some influential connection in Maryland, as Dr. Jordan suggests in his genealogy of the Syng family, it might have had something to do with Ghiselin's removal to Annapolis a few years later. We know only that both men belonged to the small Church of England party, were connected with Christ Church, and that the Church of England people at that time were perforce just as clannish as were the overwhelmingly numerous Quakers. All the rest is pure conjecture.

Whether the elder Syng soon afterwards went back to Annapolis for a time, or stayed on in Philadelphia, is not clear. We do know, however, that he was working in Philadelphia for a number of years during which he fashioned some important pieces of silver, such as the flagon at Christ Church; that his shop, "over against the Market House, next Door but one to the Crown," is mentioned in an advertisement in 1720; and that, in 1722 or 1723, he left Philadelphia for Annapolis where he remained till his death at the age of sixty-six, May 18, 1739.

Philip the Younger stayed in Philadelphia and continued the business. He was a young man of parts who soon gained a well-deserved reputation for silverware of the highest quality in design and workmanship. He likewise identified himself so fully with the life of the city that he was constantly in evidence in one capacity or another. His diversified contacts doubtless helped his business but his varied interests were so spontaneous and genuine that it would be unjust to attribute ulterior motives to his ubiquity, notwithstanding his close association with that astute young opportunist, Benjamin Franklin.

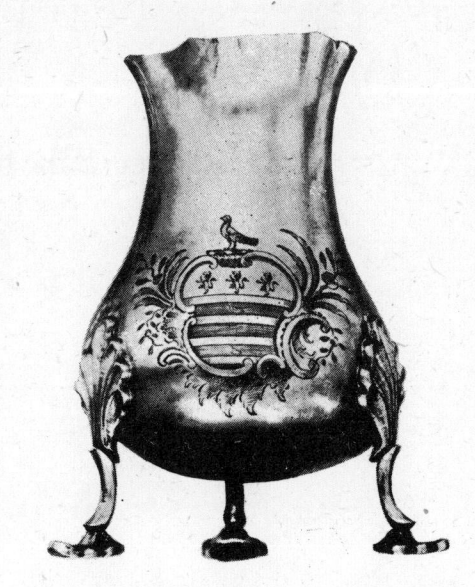

—*Pennsylvania Museum of Art*

Armorial Engraving on Jug

This finely executed engraved coat of arms is on the front of the William Ghiselin cream jug.

He was an early and active member of the American Philosophical Society and was treasurer of that venerable body from 1769 to 1771. In 1747 he was elected to the Vestry of Christ Church and served as vestryman for several years. In 1748, when there were alarms of French ships coming up the Delaware to attack Philadelphia, he vigorously furthered the building and manning of the "Association Battery" for the city's defense, a measure that met strong opposition from the powerful Quaker element. In 1750, he was one of the founders of the Academy, the school that ultimately became the University of Pennsylvania. The Academy or college served as a kind of political headquarters for the Church party, just as the Pennsylvania Hospital did for Quaker leadership. In 1752, when mutual subscribers formed the Philadelphia Contributionship for Insuring Houses against Loss by Fire, the first fire insurance company in America and one of the oldest in the English-speaking world, Syng was one of the twelve original directors.

With his already assured reputation as a silversmith of the first rank, and constantly in the public eye as he was, it was natural that the Pennsylvania Assembly, in 1752, should commission Syng to make the silver inkstand for the State House in Philadelphia, now Independence Hall, that same inkstand that was afterwards used at the signing of the Declaration of Independence, and also in signing the Constitution in 1787.

When the Quakers had generally withdrawn from all active part in government affairs just after the middle of the century, Syng's integrity and capacity for public service resulted in his choice as City Treasurer in 1759, an office he held for ten years. In 1765 he was a member of the Provincial Commission of Appeals, and was also a signer of the Non-Importation Agreement, in the same year. In addition to his house and shop in the city, he had a country place near Ardmore called Prince of Wales Farm. He died in 1789 at the age of 86, and was buried in Christ Church Yard.

Such, in brief, is the outline of the life of Philip Syng the Younger. Between his arrival in Philadelphia in 1714, as a lad of eleven, and his death in 1789, he had seen the city grow from raw infancy to imposing maturity as the metropolis of the country.

His work is characterized by elegance of contour as well as substance of body and delicacy of finish. The jewelry he wrought is generally distinguished by the same qualities. His mark was P S

A TREASURY OF OLD SILVER

in a rectangle, usually repeated several times, flanked by leaves impressed. There are variations in the number of times the rectangle with P S occurs and in the disposition of the impressed leaf or leaves.

Philip Syng the Younger lived in a period more favorable for silversmithing than did César Ghiselin. Until 1722, when the Assembly sanctioned a restricted and conservative issue of paper currency, there was a dearth of silver coin in circulation. There was no easy surplus, as there was in New England or New York, that could be melted and fashioned into plate. The colonists were often forced to adopt a system of barter. It was to relieve this pressing embarrassment that Charles Pickering had coined his "Spanish Bitts and Boston money" in 1683, an enterprise for which he cannot be altogether blamed. More than 20 years later James Logan writes William Penn,

"We have now 'tis true nor money nor credit, yet we live quiet and easy and want nothing."

The trouble was that "the province was drained of money to pay for importations which the developing country" had to have.

—*Pennsylvania Museum of Art*

Trencher Salt by Philip Syng, Sr.
Three times on the base it bears the touch P S in a heart.

SILVER TEAPOT BY JACOB HURD

The inscription on this teapot reads "The Gift of Theo: Burrill, Esq. to the Revd. Mr. Nath. Henchman Pastor of ye first Church in Lynn July 5th, 1737."
Museum of Fine Arts, Boston

William Gilbert, Silversmith of New York

By Stephen Decatur

WHEN Gerrit Cosine, or Cozyn as the name was spelled on the old Dutch records, died in 1769, he bequeathed to his daughter Catherine "his Mahogany Dining Table, his Mahogany Card Table, his Looking Glass," and a carefully itemized list of articles which included "a silver tankard, marked G C, and a silver teapot, silver sugar box and cover of silver, 6 silver table spoons, 6 tea spoons, silver tea tongs, silver mugg, and silver Punch ladle." In a way this legacy was in the nature of a load of coals for Newcastle, for Catherine's husband was William Gilbert who, at the time, was a rising young silversmith of the City of New York. In Cosine's will his son-in-law was referred to as W. W. Gilbert, and this was the appellation by which this craftsman was generally known, although he was baptized in the Dutch Church in 1746 as plain William, the son of William and Aalte (Verdon) Gilbert. Undoubtedly, he adopted the extra initial as a convenient means for distinguishing himself from the many other gentlemen of the same name then resident in New York. For instance, at that period there was a William Gilbert, baker, who had a son William, Jr., a few years older than the silversmith.

No record has as yet appeared of Gilbert's apprenticeship. Very possibly he served under the same master as did another prominent silversmith of the time, Ephraim Brasher, as the latter married William's sister, Ann Gilbert. But evidently young Gilbert finished his term at a rather earlier age than was customary, since he and Catherine Cosine were married in 1767 when he was barely past his twenty-first birthday. At that time the spirit of resistance to arbitrary acts of the British Government was growing rapidly in America and, from the first, Gilbert identified himself whole-heartedly with the patriots. In spite of his comparative youth, early in 1775 he was made one of the sixty members of the "Committee of Observation" and on May first of that year was elected to the "Committee of One Hundred" which superseded the former body and took over the management of local affairs

—*Museum of the City of New York*

William Gilbert, Silversmith

A pastel portrait by James Sharples. This was probably painted in New York during the last decade of the 18th Century.

—*Museum of the City of New York*

Another Gilbert Sugar Bowl

Here, the base is circular. Bands of beading are combined with simpler "bright-cut" engraving for the decorative design. Loaned from the collection of Herbert L. Pratt.

—*Museum of the City of New York*

Sugar Bowl by Gilbert

The urn shape was a favorite form with this silversmith. This piece, with "bright-cut" engraved decoration, bears the monogram T H L in the oval beneath the balancing leafage sprays on the side.

—*Museum of the City of New York*

A Footed Silver Salver by Gilbert

This piece bears the Bayard crest, engraved in the center. Originally, it belonged to Nicholas Bayard (1736-1798), who had married Catherine Livingston.

in the city. When the British forces occupied New York, the Gilberts, along with almost every other supporter of the cause of liberty, prudently left town to preserve their safety and it was seven years before they could return home. Where they lived during that time has not been discovered, but it was presumably either in eastern Connecticut or northern Westchester County, since William Gilbert enrolled in Colonel John Lasher's regiment of New York militia. His brother-in-law, Ephraim Brasher, also served in this organization and probably both these silversmiths were present with it at the Battle of Long Island. Gilbert rose to the rank of captain, while Brasher became a lieutenant.

The Gilberts seem to have returned to New York as the British went out. Under date of November 26, 1783, which was the day after the redcoats evacuated the city, General Washington was presented with a document entitled: "The Address of the Citizens of New York, who have return'd from exile, in behalf of themselves and their suffering Brethren," in which the Commander-in-Chief was thanked for his services in ridding the city of the English troops and so enabling those patriots who had been forced to flee to return to their homes. Among the signers of this paper were the silversmith, who in this instance signed as William Gilbert, Jr., his father, and Ephraim Brasher.

A news item which appeared in the *New-York Gazette* or *Weekly Post-Boy* on August 27, 1770, gives the approximate location of Gilbert's shop prior to the Revolution. "Tuesday Night last some Villains broke into the shop of Mr. Gilbert, Silver-Smith in the Broad Way, and robb'd the same of near two Hundred Pounds in Plate, &c. Diligent Search has been made after the Thieves, but we Have not heard of any discovery being made." Undoubtedly the site was well down Broadway, south of Wall Street, and since Gilbert is listed in the New York City Directory of 1786 as being then on Broadway, it is probable he returned to his old stand after the Revolution for some years at least. Probably, too, as was customary, he resided at the same address. But later he moved his shop to 26 Dey Street and about the same time he acquired a splendid estate on Greenwich Lane in Greenwich Village, then on the outskirts of town. His land began about a block north of Washington Square and ex-

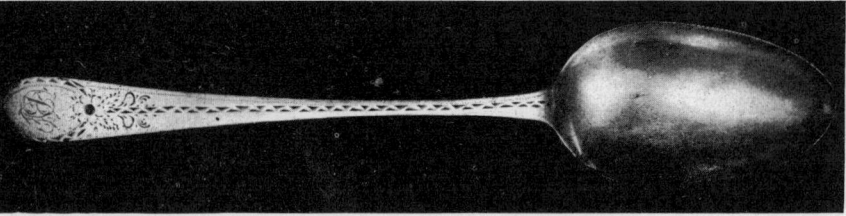

—Stanley B. Ineson

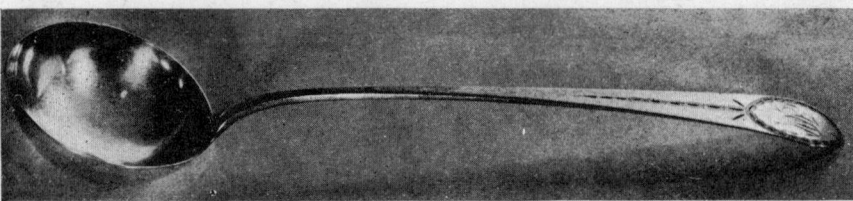

—Museum of the City of New York

Two Pieces of Flatware by Gilbert

Above, a dessert spoon; below, a ladle. Both are decorated with "bright-cut" engraving. On the spoon it extends the entire length of the handle. The ladle is from the collection of Mrs. Robert B. Noyes.

—Metropolitan Museum of Art

A Gilbert Cream Pitcher

The shaping of the base, in concaved octagonal form, is unusual. The touch-mark, Gilbert, in script, can be seen on the side of the base.

—Museum of the City of New York

Silver Mug by Gilbert

This piece originally belonged to Nicholas Bayard and bears his family crest on the side. The shaping of the handle is unusually bold.

Gilbert's Touch-Mark

This one, his surname in script letters, is the one most frequently used. He had three others, but pieces bearing them are rarely found.

tended nearly to 11th St., while across town it ran from near 5th Ave. almost to 6th Ave.

By 1800, Gilbert had become a prominent and influential citizen. One may picture him being driven to his shop each morning by his coachman behind a handsome span of horses. He had been an Alderman, representing the West Ward, at the formation of the first city government after the evacuation of the British and he continued to be re-elected to that office each year until 1788 when he was chosen as one of the city's representatives in the State Assembly. He was also a member of the Assembly in 1789, 1790, 1791, 1792, 1793, and from 1803 to 1808. He was Commissioner of Excise for several years, was in charge of the renewal of tavern licenses in 1786, in 1794 became an Associate Justice for New York City. In 1801 he was Assistant Alderman for the Seventh Ward and Alderman for the Eighth Ward in 1804, while in 1803 he was Prison Inspector. In 1809 he was elected to the State Senate, an office he held for four years and in his final year as a member of that body was also a member of the Council of Appointment. Thus when he retired at the end of 1812, Gilbert's public service had extended over a period of thirty years, or nearly forty years, if his pre-Revolutionary and Revolutionary activities are included. He was also interested in the affairs of his community in other directions besides politics. Thus, for example, in 1791, he became Treasurer of the Museum of the St. Tammany Society, otherwise known as the American Museum, apparently soon after its organization by John Pintard. Of course, too, he was a member of the Gold and Silversmiths' Society.

When, on December 2, 1784, General Washington arrived in New York for a short visit, he was received with tremendous enthusiasm by the inhabitants and the City Council voted him the freedom of the city to be presented to him in a gold box. The making of the box was entrusted to Gilbert and it is, of course, the most important piece of work he turned out. The payment warrant was approved by the Council on January 18, 1785, for the sum of 46 pounds 16 shillings to W. W. Gilbert for "A Golden Box to enclose the Freedom presented to his Excellency, General Washington."

Most of the examples of Gilbert's work which have been examined seem to date in the period between the close of the Revolution and 1800. During these years the vogue for neoclassical designs, under the influence of the Adam brothers, was most potent. The silversmith made much use of the Grecian urn motif for his hollow ware and in the handling of this graceful form he achieved a notable success.

Mabel Brady Garvan Collection, Yale University.

EARLY AMERICAN SUGAR BOX

This very fine and extremely rare sugar box was the work of Edward Winslow of Boston, circa 1700.

William Cario, Father and Son, Silversmiths

By Stephen Decatur

ALTHOUGH the work of the early American silversmith William Cairo had been well and favorably known to collectors for over half a century, nothing was known of the gentleman himself until comparatively recently. Even his place of residence was a matter of uncertainty, and perhaps a greater conflict of authorities existed concerning it than about that of any other fellow craftsman of the period. Now, however, much has been learned regarding his life and, in fact, evidence has come to light which seems to make it certain that actually there were two silversmiths of the name—doubtless father and son.

Prior to these discoveries, Cario was variously assigned to Philadelphia, Boston, Portsmouth, or New York. The latter city was the most favored for his home and it was the only place connected with Cario with any appearance of definiteness, it being said that the silversmith was born there in 1721 with sometimes the additional statement that he was made a freeman there in 1742. But three years ago several indisputable facts concerning him were found, among them proof that he had worked in Portsmouth, and in Newmarket, New Hampshire, during much of his life at least. This information was quickly supplemented by the researches of Mrs. Helen Burr Smith, through whose efforts the complete story of the latter part of the silversmith's life was made available. However, amid the data assembled there were certain facts which could not easily be reconciled with each other; particularly conflicting were the indications regarding Cario's age. Consequently, a further investigation has been conducted, with the result that something can be said of William Cario, Senior, a hitherto unknown silversmith, although the information is still far from complete.

Cario is an uncommon name and, since one Michael Cario, an Englishman who had served his apprenticeship in London, was a silversmith first in New York and later in Philadelphia in the approximate period 1728-1745, it is easy to understand why it was thought that a William Cario, also a silversmith, belonged to one or the other of those places. It is possible, too, that a child of this name was born in New York in 1721, although a reasonably careful search has failed to reveal any record of it or, for that matter, any confirmation of the story that a man of this name was made a freeman there in 1742. However, these points are unimportant, since in any event such a person could not have been either one of the silversmiths. But it would seem probable that a relationship existed between Michael and the two Williams, father and son.

The first clue to the true identification of William Cario—the silversmith whose work was known—came when attention was drawn to an old tombstone in the ancient Point of Graves burying ground in Portsmouth, New Hampshire. The inscription on it states that it marks the resting place of "Mrs. Abigail Cario, wife to Mr. William Cario, died Sept. 17, 1767." This occurrence of a name identical with that of the silversmith prompted an investigation of local records and evidence was quickly forthcoming to show that they were one and the same. At the same time, several examples of his work were seen which were traced to original ownership in Portsmouth or its vicinity.

The proof that the gentleman of Portsmouth was the silversmith may be found in a deed of 1765 covering the disposal of the estate of William Pevey, or Peavy, of Portsmouth. (N. H. Deeds, Vol. 91, fol. 417.) It shows that Pevey's daughter, Abigail, was the wife of William Cario who is referred to as a "goldsmith." The marriage of the couple took place in Boston and the record of their marriage intentions may be found in the Boston records under date of July 5, 1759. While no documentary evidence has appeared to show the date at which Cario reached Portsmouth, silver articles made by him for residents of that town have been seen which confidently may be dated prior to 1760, and his marriage to a Portsmouth girl in 1759 is a further indication that he was there sometime before that date. In any event, the history of his life after 1760 is clear.

Within a year after the death of Abigail, a William Cairo married Lydia Coxcroft. The nuptials took place in the South Church in Portsmouth, whose records further reveal the baptisms of four children born to the couple between 1769 and 1774. During these years the silversmith seems to have taken an active interest in the affairs of his community; his name appears on several petitions to the Governor and Council of New Hampshire and he was also a signer of that curious and interesting document of 1772 entitled "Protest against Theatrical Performances" which is now in the care of the New Hampshire Historical Society. About 1774 or 1775 Cario removed to Newmarket, a small but then flourishing town fifteen miles inland from Portsmouth. In 1776 he signed the "Association Test" there, proving his adherence to the patriot cause, and his name appears on several petitions of its inhabitants drawn up during the ensuing fifteen years. In 1790 he bought land in Newfields, a part of Newmarket, from Ste-

—New Hampshire Historical Society

Communion Cup, by Cario

Made by William Cario II, it was a bequest to the church in Newmarket, New Hampshire, where this silversmith worked after leaving Portsmouth. The inscription reads: "The Gift of Deacon Joseph Judkins, to the Church in Newmarkett, by his Last Will 1770."

—New Hampshire Historical Society

The Atkinson Silver Waiter

Shown here is the underside of this piece of English hallmarked silver with the engraving by William Cario. Recorded on it are the names, dates of death and ages of forty-eight Portsmouth residents from 1740 to 1771 at whose funerals Theodore Atkinson, as a pallbearer, received mourning rings. Evidently he sold these, bought this waiter and had the names of the people whose rings he had received engraved on the back. This engraving also includes the lettering "W·Cario—Sculp."

phen Hardy, the father of another silversmith then working in Portsmouth. The silversmith's house on this property is still standing and, undoubtedly, he had his workshop in its ell. There he died in 1809 and the inventory of this estate discloses not only a long list of silversmith's tools and materials, but a supply of pewter as well, so that apparently he worked in this metal as well as in silver. It was said of him that "in 1809 he was among the last of our townsmen to wear the gentlemen's short clothes and kneebuckles."

So far, nothing has been mentioned which is inconsistent with his having been born in 1721. However, the following obituary was printed in the Portsmouth *Gazette* of August 1, 1809: "Died—At Newmarket on the 20th of July very suddenly. Mr. William Cario, formerly of Portsmouth, aged 75, leaving a wife and one child to mourn the loss.

"To highly paint the character of a deceased friend appears superflous; suffice it to say Mr. Cario has been the kind husband, indulgent parent and affectionate friend to his numerous acquaintances, which, with many other pleasing traits in his character, rendered him worthy of imitation." As ages in such notices were generally given in round numbers, this would indicate that Cario was born about 1735, unless an error was made. However, two advertisements appeared in Boston newspapers which are given in *The Arts and Crafts in New England*, by George Frances Dow. Quoting from that work, the earliest reads: "William Cario—By applying to Mr. Cario, Jeweller, may be seen a Silver Spoon that was taken up in the Street about three weeks ago and has not been advertised. —Boston, Mar. 7/14, 1737." The second says: "Notice is hereby given, that William Cario is removed from his late Dwelling near the Rev. Dr. Colman's Meeting House, to the South End of the Town over against the White Swan, where all sorts of Jeweller's work is made & sold after the best and newest Manner, likewise fine Sword Blades, and Canes Sold and mounted there.—Boston, Oct. 23/30, 1738."

These advertisements make it clear that a William Cario, a jeweler and silversmith, had a shop of his own in Boston as early as the first month of 1738. He could hardly have been less than twenty-five years of age at that time and so born not later than 1712. Thus, if this silversmith be the same as the one of Newmarket, the latter must have been close to one hundred years of age at the time of his death rather than aged seventy-five as stated in the obituary. It would seem that such an advanced age would have been mentioned in the death notice; furthermore, at such an age, the silversmith could not have been actively engaged at his trade as his inventory implies.

Thus, the existence of two William Carios is indicated and this is confirmed, with every appearance of certainty, through two newly found bits of information. The first is an entry in the *"Vital Records of Newbury, Massachusetts"* recording the marriage on September 5, 1735, of William Cario and Mary Ann Pollard, "both of Boston." Undoubtedly, this refers to the jeweler of Boston and, on the face of it, implies a runaway marriage. The date, 1735, is too close to the year of birth of William Cario of Portsmouth and Newmarket, as stated in his obituary, to be a mere coincidence; in all probability he was the son of this couple and so was aged about seventy-three at his death, rather than seventy-five, a small discrepancy almost to be expected. Second, a silver mounted sword has been seen, which dates circa 1740-1745, and which originally was owned by a gentleman of Portsmouth. It bears a hitherto unrecorded silversmith's mark, W·C, in rectangle with clipped corners. Considering the date of this sword, its place of ownership, Cario's advertisement in the Boston newspaper, and the fact that the initial mark of William Cario of Portsmouth and Newmarket is known, together with the improbability of the new mark belonging to another New England silversmith with the same initials—since all their marks are believed to be known—it may be confidently assumed that this new mark can belong only to William Cario, Senior.

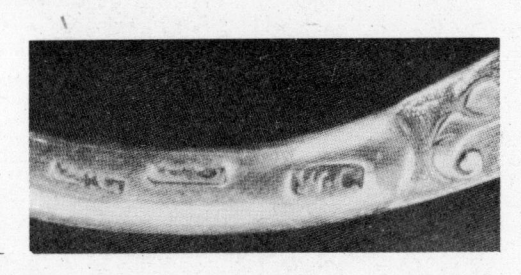

It will be observed that the marriage intention record of William Cairo and Abigail Pevey in 1759 makes no mention of "Junior." Although by no means conclusive, this might mean that the older man was then dead, unless, indeed, this was a second marriage of William, Senior, rather than the first marriage of his son, an hypothesis which in some respects seems the more reasonable. In any event, the elder was dead by 1769 when the younger man began to sign petitions without any "Junior" to his signature. But nothing has as yet been found to indicate where the older man lived before he appeared in Boston in 1735; it is entirely possible that he was born in New York. The sword suggests that he later moved to Portsmouth and there is another pointer in the same direction.

In the possession of the New Hampshire Historical Society is a massive silver waiter which was originally owned by Theodore Atkinson, 1697-1779, a resident of Portsmouth and for many years a member of the Governor's Council of New Hampshire. The tray is English, made in 1750, and on it are engraved the names of forty-eight individuals with the dates of their deaths, ranging from 1740 to 1771. The engraving is signed "W. Cario— Sculp." It is not probable that Atkinson would have established such a memorial on an old tray, hence it would seem that the list was begun when it was new—that is, about 1751, at a time when William, Junior, was too young to have done the

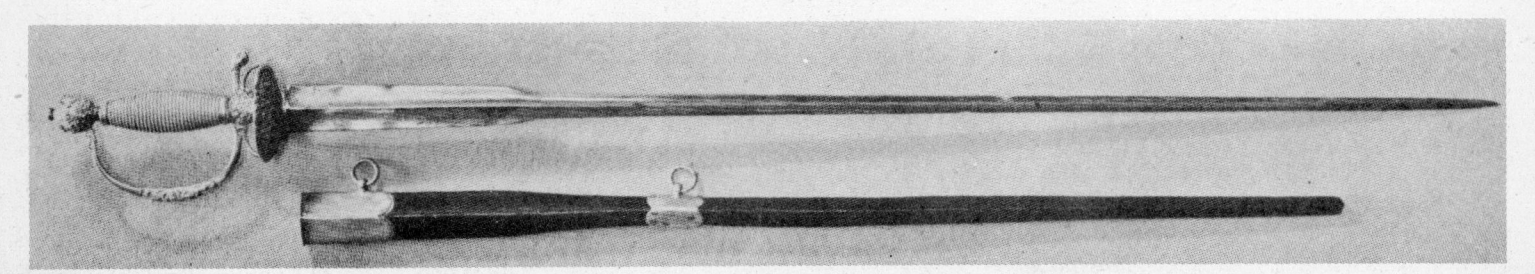

—Society for the Preservation of New England Antiquities

Tablespoons, by Cario

Three of these spoons bear the touch-mark of W·Cario and the other that of Benjamin Burt. Obviously, the latter was a replacement made at a later date. Although these spoons are engraved with various initials, they are part of a set originally made by Cario.

Mark of William Cario

These are the initials W·C in clipped rectangle. This mark is from the Peirce sword. Two imperfect impressions of the same mark can be seen at the left.

—J. Winslow Peirce

Sword, with Silver Hilt and Scabbard Mountings by William Cario I

Made between 1740-1745 for a member of the Peirce family of Portsmouth, this is the only specimen that has been found so far bearing the touch-mark of the elder Cario.

work. If this be the case, then the engraving was begun, at least, by William, Senior, and since the article would not have been carried back and forth between Portsmouth and Boston, it follows that the silversmith was living in the former place. Incidentally Atkinson's choice of names for inclusion on his waiter has been the subject of speculation for at least a century. In the second volume of Brewster's *Rambles about Portsmouth*, published in 1869, there is an extended account of this tray, and the author then remarked: "It will be seen that neither the death of his (i. e. Atkinson's) son nor of his wife has been noticed. He alludes to the death of one of Governor Benning Wentworth's sons, and omits those of the other two. He also omits the death of Governor Benning's first wife. Those acquainted with the history of Portsmouth will notice that he omits husbands and notices wives, and vice versa. Indeed, the most interesting point in this matter is to get at the standard of qualification for record upon the waiter."

As a possible explanation of this puzzle it is suggested that the names represent persons at whose funerals Atkinson, a man of great personal popularity, received gold funeral rings. It is, of course, general knowledge that such articles were presented with a thorough understanding that the recipients, who were, in general, the pallbearers and a few other intimates, would eventually dispose of them. The list has twenty names up to and including 1750, the year in which the waiter was made, and if these represented rings, it is quite probable that their combined value would have purchased the tray and paid for the first engraving. From time to time thereafter, Atkinson could have had more engraving done as partial payment for other rings. The waiter would thus be a permanent, consolidated memento. This theory, of course, easily explains the omission of names from the list which otherwise might be expected to appear, since Atkinson might well have been out of town when a funeral occurred. Besides, he probably would not have been asked to be a pallbearer for every member of the various families represented.

Therefore, the two craftsmen, from present knowledge, may be summarized as follows:

William Cario, Senior, born circa 1712; died before 1769. Worked in Boston 1735-1738 and later in Portsmouth. His touch-mark was probably W·C, capital initials with pellet between in rectangle with clipped corners. This is illustrated from the hilt of the Peirce sword.

The other Cario touch-marks, all of which are undoubtedly those of William Cario, Junior, born circa 1736; died 1809, who worked in Portsmouth 1758-1775 and in Newmarket 1775-1809, are: (A) Initial W·C in rectangle with pellet between. (B) Initial and surname in capital letters with pellet between in serrate rectangle. (C) Initial and surname with pellet between, large and small capitals, in rectangle with enlarged front end.

Note: this last mark has not been seen by the writer on silver articles of a later date than circa 1770, although such may exist. Thus there is a possibility that this mark may belong to William, Senior.

TWO-HANDLED COVERED CUP

Made by Peter Feurt of New York and Boston, a silversmith of the early 18th century, bears the inscription "Mrs. G. Apthorp to her Great Grand Daughter Sarah Apthorp Morton." Another inscription under the coat of arms states that the cup at an earlier date was a gift of Henricus Hope.

Mabel Brady Garvan Collection, Yale University

Paul Revere, His Craftsmanship and Time

By William Germain Dooley

A SPECIAL exhibition, "The Work and Environment of Paul Revere," has just opened at the Museum of Fine Arts, Boston. AMERICAN COLLECTOR readers will notice the coincidence with the appearance of Esther Forbes' best selling book, *Paul Revere & The World He Lived In*—a graphic story of Boston during the Revolution and the early Republic. Like the book, the museum's exhibition is far more than a showing of Revere's work. It brings together, much of it for the first time, a collection of rare early silver, 18th and 19th century American antique furniture, prints, needlework—one piece of which has been traced to Revere's ownership by a descendant—and last but not least, an unparalleled group of Copley and Stuart portraits that not only give us impressions from the life of Revere and his wife, but also vivid character studies of the leading group of patriots in Miss Forbes' carefully documented but lively study. These men would include Samuel Adams, John Hancock, James Otis, Joseph Warren, General Knox and others active in those stirring times, not unlike the present in their urgency.

It was Warren who started Revere off on his famous ride; later it was Revere's grim duty to identify his friend's body, months after he had fallen at Bunker Hill, by two artificial teeth which he had made for him. Portraits by Stuart include those of Revere and his wife in their latter years, the rotund Henry Knox, famed for his almost superhuman feat of bringing the heavy cannons captured from the British at Ticonderoga to Dorchester—artillery that forced the evacuation of Boston; and Dr. Samuel Danforth, handsome and fearless Tory who remained in America and lived to see old enmities so far forgotten that he was the physician called to Revere's deathbed in 1818.

—*Museum of Fine Arts, Boston*

St. Memin Portrait of Revere
This crayon drawing depicts him in his later years. This French artist did not come to the United States until 1795 and returned home in 1814.

—*Museum of Fine Arts, Boston*

Revere Silver in Rococo Style
The sugar bowl and tray bear the Chandler coat-of-arms and the coffee pot that of the Sargent family.

Then, too, the museum has gathered a considerable group of some of the finest New England furniture of the period, some of it made by Revere's neighbor, John Seymour, from whose shop in Creek Lane came forth the cabinetwork that has given him the title of master of American tambour front furniture. There are also block front pieces of the Boston rather than the Newport style, some good Salem casework, and a group of 18th century chairs in that sturdy simplicity that was a hallmark of America's best. A bow front chest of drawers, dating from about 1775, is also said to have been owned by the patriot, and has come to the Museum as a bequest of Mrs. Pauline Revere Thayer, a direct descendant, along with the needlework above mentioned—a pole screen with the panel showing a rustic park scene, with two lovers, a milkmaid in the background, and a church in the distance.

It is impossible to give in an exhibition of this sort, any adequate glimpse of Revere's versatility, beyond silversmithing, rolling copper and working brass and engraving copperplate, making false teeth, setting up a powder mill, printing currency, casting bells and cannon, commanding a regiment, and overall engaging in continued and intense political activity. Nevertheless it is a showing of more than ordinary vividness, and of especial interest to antiquarians.

For instance, the museum has delved into its Revere silver collection—by all odds the most important and comprehensive known—and even here been able to show only a portion of it, roughly divided into the church silver and the domestic plate. Most of these are well known, but it would not be amiss to point out such rare items as the large two-handled urn, one of his major works. It bears the inscription:

TO PERPETUATE
the Gallant defense
Made by
Capt GAMALIEL BRADFORD
in the Ship Industry on the 8th july 1800
when Attacked by four French Privateers
in the Straights of Gibraltar.
This URN is Presented to him
by
SAMUEL PARKMAN

A Revere Tea Set in Adam Style
These pieces were presented to Edmund Hartt, constructor of the frigate Boston. *The sugar bowl bears the presentation inscription and the others his monogram.*

Revere's Print of Harvard
Engraved after Joshua Chadwick, this print bears the title beneath the view, "A Westerly View of the College in Cambridge." The buildings depicted are Holden Chapel, Hollis, Harvard, Stoughton, and Massachusetts halls.

This historic piece has been lent by the Massachusetts Historical Society. Then there is the famous tea set in the Adam style made for Edmund Hartt, builder of the frigate *Boston*, and also the *Constitution* or "Old Ironsides," for which ship Revere furnished the copper. Here also is a fluted covered sugar bowl from Revere's own Charter Street house, and willed by him to his unmarried daughter, Harriett. A teapot made for Moses Brown of Providence is shown, with the receipted bill on which credit for turning in a salver is noted in the cost, evidence again of the melting down of earlier plate for new fashioned pieces.

This Moses Brown piece is also entered in one of the Revere daybooks, precious lists of documentary evidence that have caught more than one swindle in counterfeit Revere silver. These journals are still owned by the family and are carefully guarded. On one open page, among other things, can be seen a bill in 1765 to "Mr. John S. Copley. To a Gold Setting for a Picture, to the Making, to the Glass." Here is one more testimony of Revere's versatility.

It is fitting, too, that Copley should have painted Revere as a vigorous young man, in his shirtsleeves at his bench, a teapot in hand, engraving tools nearby, the silver resting on a leather pad to protect it while working. Considered by many to be the finest of the Revere portraits, its reproduction, unfortunately, has not been permitted for this showing. Under the picture the Museum has placed a very similar teapot, with identical inverted oviform shape and spout, but with repoussé work of a type that the silversmith might have added. This is also a family bequest.

Exhibited also are the Harvard print by Revere, and several others from the famous Boston collection of Valentine Hollingsworth. Most interesting perhaps is the Boston Massacre print by Revere, shown here in two versions, and between what is thought to be the original Henry Pelham print from which Revere copied his plate.

Underneath is given the text to a remarkable letter from Pelham to Revere. It reads:

"Sir:

When I heard you was cutting a plate of the late Murder, I thought it was impossible, as I knew you was not capable of doing it unless you copied it from mine, and as I thought I had entrusted it in the hands of a person who had more regard to the dictates of Honour and Justice than to take undue advantage of the Confidence & Trust I reposed in you. But I find I was mistaken . . . as truly as if you had plundered me on the Highway. If you are insensible of the Dishonour you have wrought on yourself by this Act, the World will not be so. However I leave you to reflect upon and consider of one of the most dishonourable Actions you could ever be guilty of.

H. Pelham"

It is known that more than five hundred of Pelham's version were printed, but none have been positively identified. Revere having captured the Boston market, it is quite possible that they were shipped to sympathizers in England and used in 1770 in W. Bingley's *Short Narrative of the Horrid Massacre in Boston*. In defense of Revere it must be said that pirating of print designs was common at the time. Also, by 1774 the two had again become fast friends.

In the midst of all these objects, Esther Forbes worked for a number of years, fortunate in the fact that John Singleton Copley was a precise, unflattering portrayer of character. Here in the magnificent gallery where the Revere portrait takes the leading role, the other actors, truly men of action, are seen as in the eyes of their contemporaries. It is this fact, along with the shrewd and careful arrangement of the entire show by the Museum curators, Edwin J. Hipkiss, W. G. Constable, H. P. Rossiter, and Miss Gertrude Townsend, that make it an important event.

Pre-Revolutionary Revere Silver
Cream Pot made for Lucretia Chandler. Her husband, John Murray, a loyalist, fled to Nova Scotia. Their ship was overtaken by an American privateer and this cream pot was brought to Boston where it was sold at a prize court auction.

A Tea Set Made in 1786 by Ephraim Brasher

—Gallery of Fine Arts, Yale University

Ephraim Brasher, Silversmith of New York

By Stephen Decatur

MANY Early American silversmiths, it is well known, took prominent parts in the public affairs of their times and served their country or their communities ably and well. In this connection, of course, the name of Col. Paul Revere of Boston comes first to mind, to be followed, perhaps, by that of Samuel Cranston, who became governor of the Colony of Rhode Island and Providence Plantations. Although New York cannot boast of having produced a silversmith of corresponding fame, nevertheless in the person of Ephraim Brasher it possessed a member of the craft who was able, at a critical time, to render services to his fellow citizens which, if not spectacular, were of almost inestimable value.

With the close of the Revolutionary War and the recognition of the independence of the United States, business in the new nation was at a standstill. As it attempted to revive, and the shipping trade, especially, gave evidences of surprising vitality, an acute shortage of hard money developed which seriously hampered the efforts of the merchants. Gold and silver coin had almost disappeared from circulation, much of it drained from the colonies during the years of fighting, the balance hoarded away as a precaution against the uncertainties of the times. The weak government of the Continental Congress had no mint, no bullion, and no credit; its paper money had fallen greatly in value and was steadily continuing to depreciate. As a medium of exchange for business transactions this script was practically worthless, as no one would accept it except at a ruinous discount.

Under the circumstances, specie was a necessity and any coin, whatever its origin, was pressed into service. Consequently gold and silver coins became profitable to import. Every vessel making a successful

—Wayte Raymond, Inc.

A Brasher Doubloon

He minted these coins for the State of New York in 1787. On the obverse at left, the design shows the sun rising over a mountain with the word "Excelsior" beneath and "Nova Eboraca Columbia" as the outside legend. Brasher's name in minute letters appears immediately beneath the mountain. On the reverse, his touch E B in an oval is stamped on the shield of the spread eagle.

—Museum of the City of New York

Covered Sugar Bowl

It is 5-3/8 inches tall and the base is 2-7/8 inches in diameter. The script initials J C S on the side are surrounded by a floral decoration typical of Brasher's engraving.

—Museum of the City of New York

A Brasher Tankard

The tankard bears in script on the lid the initials E L for Edward W. Laight, the original owner, who was a New York merchant and officer in the militia. The tankard is 6-1/2 inches tall and the base is 5-5/8 inches in diameter.

69

voyage to a foreign port brought back foreign coinage and this money immediately passed into circulation. Coins of France, England, Spain and Portugal, and of their colonies in the western hemisphere appeared in everyday use. Since these pieces were of every conceivable design, denomination and degree of fineness, there was naturally much confusion. Nevertheless, in default of anything better, they were a great aid to business.

Such a heterogeneous currency, however, offered a great opportunity to counterfeiters and they were not slow to take advantage of it. By 1786 the country was flooded with bogus coins, in fact bad money became so common that it was unsafe to accept a coin until it had been examined and pronounced genuine. The situation was a severe handicap to business and everyone suffered much vexatious delay and loss.

At the time Ephraim Brasher was a leading silversmith and jeweler of New York. Fortunately he was also an expert on precious metals and this knowledge enabled him to decide on the genuineness of coins. Probably at first he merely acted in an expert capacity, but in all events he soon conceived the idea of stamping each good piece which passed through his hands with the punch he used for the silver of his manufacture. This mark was E. B. in a rectangle. Brasher's reputation for probity was unquestioned; it was immediately recognized that his initials on a gold or silver coin were a guarantee of its purity. Such Brasher marked money circulated freely and it is readily apparent that this service of Brasher's must have been of extraordinary benefit not only to the merchants, but to all the inhabitants of New York as well.

A few of the coins that Brasher thus marked are still in existence and are highly valued by collectors. But from the point of view of the numismatist, he has a still greater claim to fame. Until the present United States Constitution went into effect in 1789 and made coinage an exclusive prerogative of the central government, anyone could mint money. A few of the States did so after the Revolution, but their efforts were largely confined to the production of copper pieces. Also, a few individuals struck coins, among them being Brasher, who made a large gold piece now known as the "Brasher doubloon." This is the rarest and most sought for coin ever minted in this country. Quite possibly Brasher made the dies for it himself and probably the gold he used was obtained from old jewelry which he either bought or accepted in trade. The doubloon shows the arms of the United States on one side with the date 1787 below and, on the reverse, the sun rising over a mountain symbolizing the beginning of the new nation. The coins are stamped with the usual "E B." Two varieties are recognized by collectors, one with the mark on the breast of the eagle, the other with it on the eagle's wing.

Ephraim Brasher belonged to a Dutch family early settled in New York. His grandfather, Abraham Brasher, was a prominent supporter of Jacob Leisler and for his connection with the troubles of 1689-90 was sentenced to death, but was afterwards pardoned. The silversmith was born in 1744, his father being named Ephraim also. Little is known of his early life, but his marriage to Ann Gilbert in 1766 is recorded, at which time he had undoubtedly served his apprenticeship and was either working independently or possibly with his younger brother Abraham, also a silversmith, with whom he was from time to time in partnership. Ann Gilbert, as the name appears on the marriage records, was baptized in 1742 in the Reformed Dutch Church under the name of Adriaantie and she was a sister of W. W. Gilbert, another well-known New York silversmith. Incidentally, on the old Dutch records the name of Brasher appears in many forms. One of these variations is Brasier and this spelling was adopted permanently by at least one branch of the family. Thus, the silversmiths named Brazier were relatives of Ephraim.

Following the Revolution, Ephraim Brasher lived at 5 Cherry Street, a site now approximately occupied by one of the pillars of the approach to Brooklyn Bridge. When Washington became President, the house at 1 and 3 Cherry Street was selected for his residence. Thus he and Brasher were next door neighbors from April, 1789, to February, 1790, when Washington moved to Broadway. At the time Cherry Street was considered rather far uptown, but it was a reasonably fashionable district and it may be assumed the silversmith enjoyed a good position socially. Washington's household accounts disclose but one purchase of

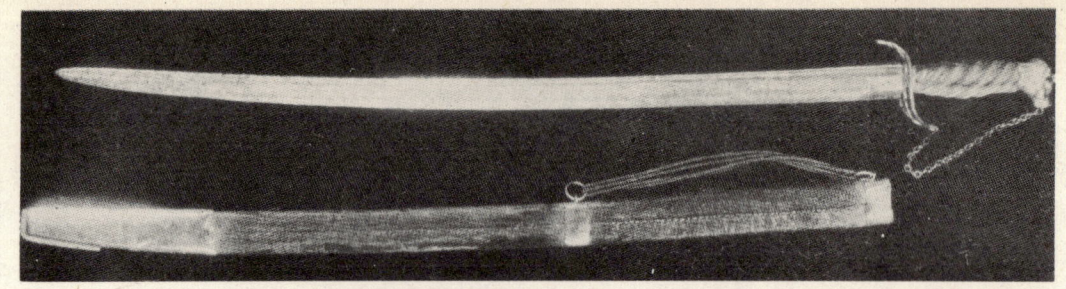

—Gallery of Fine Arts, Yale University

An Officer's Sword by Brasher
This originally belonged to Petrus Wynkoop, who in 1779 was an ensign in the First Ulster County Regiment.

—Metropolitan Museum of Art

A Brasher Coffee Pot
The form and decoration of this piece are typical of the fine craftsmanship of this New York silversmith.

—Museum of the City of New York

A Large Silver Bowl by Brasher
It is decorated with bright cut engraving of the period and bears the initials in script J C F for the unknown original owner. This bowl is 4-3/8 inches high and has a diameter of 9-3/4 inches at the rim.

silver during his residence in New York. Under date of April 17, 1790, an item appears in them reading, "Pd. E. Brasher for 4 Silver Skewers, 8-8-4." This entry is in New York currency in which the pound had a value of two and one-half dollars. Hence, the President paid approximately $21.00 for skewers. Judging from the price, these were probably large skewers which at that period were often used in place of carving forks. Undoubtedly they were quite handsome and appeared at Washington's formal Thursday dinners.

This purchase by Washington is significant, since it is well known he patronized only the leading merchants and craftsmen. And present-day judgment concurs in the opinion evidently held at the time that Brasher was a silversmith of high rank. His work is characterized by a purity of line and form that has few equals; and specimens of it, though not especially rare, are in good demand and widely appreciated.

Albany Was a Colonial Silvermaking Center
By Robert G. Wheeler
Assistant Curator of Local Arts and Crafts, Albany
(Illustrations Courtesy of the Albany Institute of History and Art)

AS THE Dutch settlers at Fort Orange, later Albany, established themselves on their new lands, a need for silversmiths became apparent, for the inland town was isolated from the seaboard centers with their craftsmen. Prominent among the early smiths to meet this local demand was Kiliaen Van Rensselaer, grandson of the first Van Rensselaer patroon.

In 1682, less than sixty years after the first Dutch settlers arrived at Fort Orange, Stephen Van Cortlandt could write to his daughter, Maria Van Rensselaer, "The man to whom I recommended your son Kiliaen at Boston hanged himself, so that Mr. Pattishall and Mr. Uscher have apprenticed him to one Mr. Jeremy Dumner."

Kiliaen served out at least part of his apprenticeship and then returned to Albany. In 1683 his mother wrote, "He is an able young man. I let him set up the silversmith's shop in the country. He does not waste his time. . . ." Thus Albany's silver tradition is almost as old as the city itself.

Though Fort Orange became Beverwyck and Beverwyck became Albany, the Dutch resisted the English influence from New York City and New England. Trade was brisk, for Albany, on the fringe of the western wilderness, was a port of entry. The thrifty burghers farmed their acres and grew more prosperous as they continued their trade in furs and lumber. Theirs was a simple, comfortable life.

As fortunes grew, the call for silversmiths increased. Every old Dutch family of any circumstance invested in tankards, in spoons, in tea services; silver intended to be handed down from generation to generation. Two Albany families of silversmiths, the Ten Eycks and Lansings took advantage of this demand. Related through marriage to every important family of the area, they had no lack of business.

In a recent excellent article on New York State silver, Dr. G. B. Cutten wrote at length concerning the Ten Eycks. These two paragraphs sum up his observations:

"Jacob Ten Eyck, born in Holland, moved to Fort Orange soon after 1660. Koenradt (1678-1753), his eldest son, was apprenticed to a silversmith, probably in New York City for his silver has a definite New York character. Members of his family married into that of the New York silversmith, Jacob Boelen. One of his trencher salts is among the earliest American salts.

"Koenradt's eldest son, Jacob (1705-1793), followed the new founded family tradition. With the exception of the time spent as an apprentice to Charles Le Roux in New York, he lived out his life in Albany. An expert engraver, he was perhaps the best of the Ten Eycks. Koenradt's fifth son, Barent (1714-1795) was apprenticed probably to either his father or brother. Little of his silver remains, for most of his work was probably used in the Indian trade."

During this period, the Lansings too were hard at work. In 1641, the Widow Lansing arrived at Albany with her four sons, who later became leading citizens of the early community. The silversmiths of the family learned the trade under the Ten Eycks, the Boelens and conceivably Jan Van Newkirke. Much confusion still surrounds the name of Jacob Lansing or Lansingh. This name and marks ascribed to it were probably used by a number of smiths of the family and passed down through several generations.

It was a Jacob Gerritse Lansingh, 1681-1767?, who made the rare silver teapot for Benjamin and Ann Egbert of Albany, circa 1760, that is illustrated. This pear-shaped, Queen Anne type piece stands 7½ inches in height. Octagonal sided, the spout

Teapot by Jacob Gerritse Lansingh
Long owned by successive generations of the Egbert family of Albany, it was made circa 1760 and bears on the bottom the initials of nine generations of the family

Tankard by Jan Van Newkirke
An heirloom of Lansing family and recently presented by Charles Lansing, this piece made circa 1700 is engraved with Lansing coat-of-arms. So fully documented, this piece raises the question, did its maker work in or near Albany during part of his career.

closely resembles the head of an abstract bird. The overall width of the piece is ten inches, the diameter of the base being 3⅜ inches and that of the top, 2⅞ inches.

Unique in its markings, it bears not only the initials of its original owners, but those of eight of their descendants who successively owned the pot. These included Isaac and Mary Lansing and Jeremiah and Helen Lansing Van Rensselaer. A similar teapot by Lansingh is also privately owned in the Albany area.

Until the acquisition by the Albany Institute of the Lansing family tankard by Jan Van Newkirke, this silversmith was considered solely as a New York City worker. However, other Van Newkirke tankards, privately owned in Albany and environs, hint strongly of activities in the Upper Hudson region by this artist.

Dating from the first decade after 1700, this tankard, one of the outstanding known early American tankards, bears on its front the floral coat of arms of the Lansing family. The initials "I L L" which appear on the bottom are repeated on the forehead of its richly decorated handle. On the cover, with its flanged edge and scalloped front, is an engraved V in the form of a cypher. This tankard stands 6¾ inches in overall height, tapering slightly from a five-inch base.

EARLY CREAM PITCHER

This silver pitcher bears the mark of Jacob Gerittse Lansing, of Albany, New York, and was made about 1760. The floral repoussè and shell motives over the three pad-footed cabriole legs are similar to pieces made by Bartholomew Le Roux of New York.

STANDISH BARRY,
BALTIMORE CRAFTSMAN

by Richmond Huntley

BARRY AT TIME HE WAS WORKING

SOME places have natural advantages that fore-ordain them as sites for prosperous communities. It would almost seem as if the first white men to settle Boston, New York, Philadelphia, and Baltimore must have sensed, even though dimly, that each was destined to become a rich center of commerce and so attract to itself skilled craftsmen to provide the household furnishings and accessories proper for such a standard of living.

Boston, New York, and Philadelphia did indeed make the most of their potentialities almost from the first but Baltimore lagged behind. Settled by a handful of Quakers from Lancaster County about the middle of the 17th Century, it was not organized as a town until 1729. As late as 1750 its population was barely 200. In fact it suffered from arrested development until the American Revolution was well under way.

However, once Baltimore Town sensed her destiny as a center of commercial importance, she lost no time. By 1790 she ranked third in the volume of commerce, being only outstripped by New York and Boston. She was the marvel of the day with an annual export trade of $2,000,000 which was a large sum in those days.

From an insignificant Pre-Revolutionary village much overshadowed by Annapolis, the seat of the provincial government, she had suddenly drawn to herself 13,758 inhabitants which had increased to 25,000 by 1798 when she was incorporated as a city.

Baltimore was also the home port of a fleet of 103 sailing vessels with a total of 13,564 tons of cargo space. Behind this was the staff of life. Wheat from the Maryland acres and the new West, flowed into Baltimore for shipment as grain, flour, or bread to Europe and the West Indies. Likewise Baltimore was an important port for the export of iron, lumber, and packing house products in return for raw sugar, more or less raw rum, and the many manufactured products still not made at home.

This is the explanation of why Baltimore, as far as her craftsmen are concerned, rose rapidly from an inconspicuous colonial town to an important American center during the last decade of the 18th and first two decades of the 19th Centuries. In furniture, glass making, and silversmithing, the craftsmen who worked there during those years, produced things of such beauty and individuality that they can be distinguished readily from the products of other craftsmen working in other places.

The craft of the silversmith achieved a high level of excellence here during these three decades

SUGAR TONGS SHOWING BARRY'S TOUCH

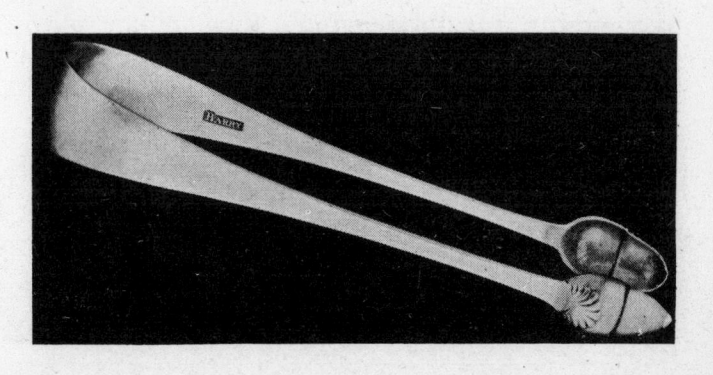

73

and the fact that in 1800 there were as many as 80 silversmiths listed as working in Baltimore, is itself an indication that this was no mean city as far as domestic silver was concerned.

Outstanding among these, was Standish Barry, a native son who after 25 years of leadership in his craft, suddenly turned grocer and sugar refiner and eventually retired, well-to-do we hope, to die, well-stricken in years, at Newport in Central New York. The curious thing about Barry, one that decidedly arouses interest, is that although he was a prominent personage and rose high in the citizen-soldiery, comparatively few pieces of his silver have come to light. Few examples bearing his mark are to be found in large collections and fewer still are included in important sales. Possibly the explanation is that the large proportion of surviving pieces are still the cherished heirlooms of the families for whom they were made.

In many ways Barry's life ran parallel with Baltimore's rise to importance. He was born there November 4, 1763. He was the son of Lavallin Barry of Dublin, Ireland, who migrated to the colonies and settled in Baltimore. The young boy, Standish, learned his trade from David Evans, a silversmith, watch and clockmaker, who came from Philadelphia to Baltimore in 1773 and continued working there some 20 years. His apprentice apparently first set up in business for himself the latter part of 1784 when he advertised in the Maryland Journal as a watch and clock maker and engraver with a shop on the north side of Market street, three doors below Calvert street. By 1785 he had taken as partner, Joseph Rice and moved to the northwest corner of Market and Calvert streets. This arrangement lasted but two years. The partnership was dissolved and Rice stayed on at the old address while the first Baltimore directory, that of 1796, lists Standish Barry as plying his craft at 92 Baltimore (Market) street.

COFFEE SERVICE TYPICAL OF BARRY'S WORK

There he stayed for four years. Then in 1800 he is listed as at 20 North Gay street. In 1810 he evidently decided to abandon his craft for thereafter he was listed first as a merchant, then as a grocer and sugar refiner until he finally retired from business in 1823. It is interesting that in his early years he advertised as a watch and clock maker as well as a worker in silver. This was not unusual with the early craftsmen of Baltimore and smacks of a town too small, even in the first years of his apprenticeship, to enable a man to live by one trade alone. Clockmaking and silversmithing often went hand in hand and in more than one case, the occupation of inn keeper was added as well.

In addition to being one of the leading silversmiths in Baltimore, Standish Barry had a long and honorable military career which began, when, as a boy, he volunteered in the local militia during the latter part of the Revolution and continued through the War of 1812. Here he became major of the Fifth Regiment Volunteer Infantry and later its colonel. He was described by one of his contemporaries as being "every inch a soldier."

In 1788 he married Agnes Thompson. According to the records of the First Presbyterian Church, six children were born to them, all of whom apparently lived to maturity. His son, Standish, Jr., with whom he spent his last days, became Assistant Treasurer of the United States.

In his day Standish Barry was a person of importance in the civic and military affairs of his native town but today his silver, and for the most part that made before 1800, is his real monument. His workmanship and design are fine as shown by the pieces that have come to light. He made at least some of the silver for Betsy Patterson who married Jerome Bonaparte in 1803, as evidenced by an oval sugar urn now in the Bonaparte Collection of the Maryland Historical Society. The Metropolitan Museum, New York, has a soup ladle which is part of the Clearwater Collection. This bears in addition to the Barry mark the stamp "No. 92," indicating that it was fashioned in the days when his shop was at that number on Market street.

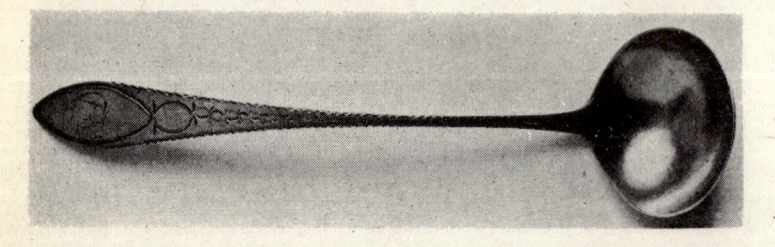

A BARRY LADLE

—*Metropolitan Museum*

AMERICAN SILVER

BALTIMORE 3 PENNY PIECE BY BARRY

A BARRY TOUCH

BARRY ALSO USED HIS INITIALS

There is also a standing patten in St. Peter's Church, Baltimore, which is the only piece of church silver from his hands that has yet come to light.

He was responsible in 1790 for a coined silver three pence which is now very scarce. It bears on one side a head with the inscription "Baltimore Town July 4 '90"; and on the other side, "Standish Barry,—Three Pence."

Like similar coins issued seven years earlier in Annapolis by the silversmith John Chalmers, it was probably used locally without consent or condemnation from the authorities. After all the state of national coinage was nil at that time; paper money was in a sad way and there was a shortage of small coin. What more natural than to devise a local medium of exchange?

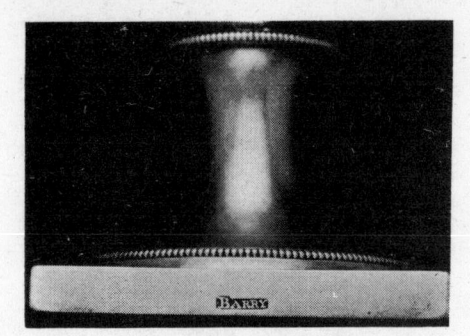

In 1824 Barry was elected Sheriff of Baltimore County for a three year term. This was apparently his last active service for his native town. After 1831 he moved to Newport, N. Y., where he died in 1844. During his life span a group of colonies had cast aside the protection of the mother country and emerged as a nation; his own little town of less than 1000 at the time of his birth, had grown to a thriving city of 80,000; and the number of his fellow craftsmen there had risen into the hundreds. Further, as the century entered its fourth decade individual craftsmanship was already entering the twilight of factory production.

Metropolitan Museum

EARLY NEW YORK SALTCELLARS

This pair of saltcellars was made by Charles Le Roux, probably for John and Anne Schuyler who were married in 1737.

Small But Useful American Silver

By Kurt M. Semon

—Museum of Fine Arts, Boston
Illustration I
Early Spout Cup
By Jeremiah Dummer, Boston, 1645-1718, this piece with two handles, nicely curved, spout and lid with finial is characteristic of the simplicity of 17th-Century American silver.

—Museum of Fine Arts, Boston
Illustration II
A 17th-Century Dram Cup
Made by John Hull and Robert Sanderson, the Boston silversmiths who became partners in 1652 when the former was appointed mintmaster of the Massachusetts Colony. Hull learned silversmithing in Boston; Sanderson was London trained.

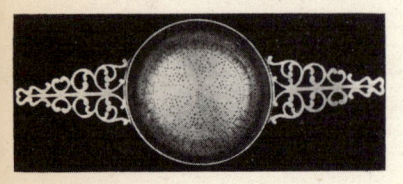

—Mabel Brady Garvan Collections, Yale Gallery of Fine Arts
Illustration III
Strainer Dated 1765
It was made by Jonathan Clarke, 1705-1770, who worked first in Newport and later in Providence. It has a perforated inscription reading, "Jabez Bowen, Providence, January 1765."

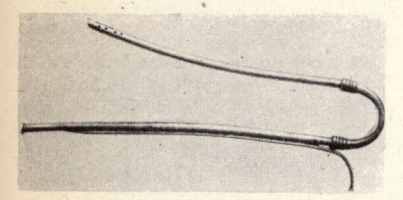

—Metropolitan Museum of Art
Illustration IV
Large Wine Syphon
Although it has not been possible to ascertain the maker's identity, it is probably an example of 18th-Century American silversmithing.

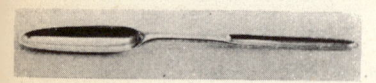

—Museum of the City of New York
Illustration V
A Rare American Marrow Scoop
Its maker was John Burt Lyng, a New York silversmith. As he was made a city freeman in 1761 and died in 1785, pieces bearing his touch-mark are mostly pre-Revolutionary.

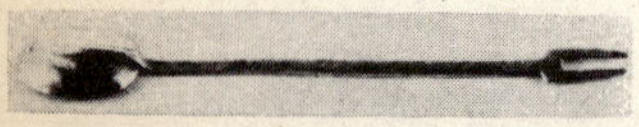

—Museum of the City of New York
Illustration VI
17th-Century Sucket Fork
With a two-tined fork at one end and a spoon bowl at the other, this piece bears the mark IK. The identity of this silversmith has not yet been established. He worked circa 1690-1700, probably in Albany.

"Stole at Flatbush on Long-Island, One Silver Tankerd, a piece of Money in the Led of King Charles II, and the Led all engraved, a Coat of Arms, before (in it Man on a Waggon with two Horses) mark'd on the Handle, L P A. One Silver Tankerd plain, with a Piece of Money in the Led, mark'd on the Handle A P or A L. One Cup with two twisted Ears chas'd with Skutchens, marked L P A. One Tumbler marked L P A. One Dutch Beker weighs about 28 Ounces, Engraved all around, marked L P A. All the above were made by Mr. Jacob Boele, Stamp'd IB. One large Cup with two cast Ears, with Heads upon them and a Coat of Arms, Engraved thereon. One Cup with two Ears, a small hole in the Bottom.... Whoever can inform Peter Lefferts of Flatbush on Long-Island, or Abraham Lefferts in New-York, so that it may be had again, shall have Fifteen Pounds Reward and no Question asked." *The New-York Gazette*, October 1-8, 1733.

THESE lines, similar to many other advertisements published during that period, give us a picture of the unsafety of the times. Silver, or plate as it was sometimes called, was a rare and desirable article, especially when the trade balance was adverse, as was mostly the case under the baneful influence of the English kings of the 18th Century. Their one-sided exploitation of the Colonies was a shortsighted policy comparable to that which caused the downfall of the Roman Empire.

As for the problem of theft, although there were no newspapers in 17th-Century America, various diaries, such as that of Judge Samuel Sewall, indicate that there were plenty of offenders even in those stern days. In fact, the owner of silver was in a difficult situation. If through astuteness and forceful business sense he was able to accumulate a quantity of silver in the form of coins, he had no bank or safe deposit vault to turn to. The early land banks were all failures and the day of the gilt-edge security was far in the future. So he called in the silversmith and commissioned him to make tankards, salvers, and other household pieces. These satisfied his pride, embellished his home with beautiful things, and afforded a measure of security since he had a better chance to recover such pieces, if they were stolen, than silver coins that could easily be spent in taverns and other places.

This advertisement in the *Gazette* is of more than passing local interest. Mr. Jacob Boele is of course the famous silversmith, Jacob Boelen, who arrived in New York in 1660. He was a distinguished burgher, assessor, and became alderman of the North Ward. His son, Henricus Boelen, continued the business after the death of Jacob in 1729 and was in turn succeeded by Jacob Boelen II. The name Lefferts is still in the memory of New Yorkers through the avenue by that name in Brooklyn. It is quite significant that the owner affirms no questions will be asked. His main interest was the safe return of his cherished pieces of silver rather than punishment of the thief.

Apparently the citizens of Philadelphia took a much sterner view of such offences if we are to judge by a news item from that city which appeared in the New York *Gazette* of April 27, 1752. It reads: "Friday last the trial of John Webster came on. When he was indicted and found guilty of breaking open the dwelling house of William Clemm of this city on the 24 of December 1750 in the night; and taking from thence a silver teapot and teaspoon; upon which he received the sentence of death."

But cities were not the only unsafe places. Further inland and in rural areas the lure of silver pushed people from the straight and narrow path. As late as 1845 a silversmith in Vermont was informed one day that several miles away there was a man lately returned from a successful business trip to the West Indies with not only a substantial letter of credit but a nice balance of silver coins. So the Vermont craftsman, looking for raw material that was hard to get, saddled his horse and with two saddle bags in front of him rode through the hilly and wooded country. But the silver rumor had spread, even to the lumbermen of the section, and when the silversmith came back through the woods after a successful trade transaction, there was a holdup. One of the lumbermen seized the reins and told him to get off the horse. But the rider was prepared. He drew an old flintlock pistol concealed behind one of the bags and with precise aim shot one finger from the hand that had seized the reins. No one ever molested him again. Somehow the rumor got about that here was a man who could and would shoot. He, for his part, never bothered to prosecute the erring lumberman. Besides it would have been hard to identify him since practically no lumberman had all ten fingers intact.

Although American silversmiths never indulged in mere copying of foreign pieces, the general style of their work follows the European pattern, changing from the simple and austere designs of the middle 17th Century to the brighter and more ornate ones of the William and Mary period; becoming more refined and reverting to simpler forms in the reign of Queen Anne; then swinging to the effervescence of the rococo which bridged the Atlantic and left its mark on different forms and decorations. Finally, with a changing Europe and the creation of our

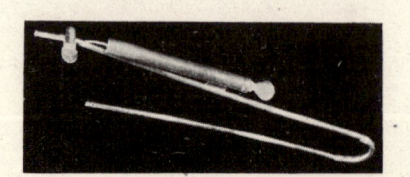

—H. F. duPont
Illustration VII
A Syphon with Pump
Made by Frederick Marquand, New York, circa 1820. An ivory knob forms the outer end of the pump plunger. Frederick, Isaac and Joseph P. Marquand were partners, first as Marquand Bros.; then Marquand & Co. Other partners were admitted and gradually the firm name was changed. Today it is Black, Starr & Frost-Gorham, Inc.

—Metropolitan Museum of Art
Illustration VIII
Early 19th-Century Pap Cup
William Thomson worked in New York as a silversmith until 1834. His touch-marks were frequently "W. Thomson" in script letters, "New York" in Roman capital letters, and the year the piece was made in Arabic numerals.

—Ginsburg & Levy, Inc.
Illustration IX
A Small, Early Brazier
Made by Adrian Bancker, a New York silversmith from before 1731 until 1772. Son of an early mayor of Albany, he came to New York, served his apprenticeship under Henricus Boelen, and in 1731 was made a freeman of the city.

independence, there came the chaste style which bore the name of the Brothers Adam and was an adaptation of Roman classic dignity.

The range of the objects in silver is not only large but furnishes proof of the versatility of American silversmiths as well as of the demands and domestic habits of their well-to-do clients. Apart from church silver, the more important and decorative pieces are linked to the habits of drinking and dining. Much to be admired are the early tankards, flat-topped and later dome-topped, the sturdy mugs, the caudle cups, the now very rare salvers, and the spoons of which large collections have been formed by discriminating collectors. But not so much is known about the smaller pieces. They may not compare in artistic importance but they are noteworthy as examples of our old domestic culture.

Therefore, we now mention, without any attempt at completeness, certain implements that had to do with eating and drinking — such as heating dishes, sugar tongs, pepperpots; articles made for style and vanity, like patchboxes, shoe buckles, spurs, and silver miniatures; also, jewelry, silver or silver gilt, very simple in form; and some rare pieces that seem to fall under the head of oddities.

SPOUT CUPS

These were primarily intended for use in case of illness. Shown here is an early two-handled one by Jeremiah Dummer, Boston, 1645-1718. Possibly the two handles in this example were made so that the patient could get a firm grip in sipping the hot contents or the bitter medicine given to him in the cup. But these little vessels, which measured from three to five and one-half inches in height, were also useful in the daily routine of domestic life and were made both with and without a cover (Illustration I).

DRAM CUPS

The word *dram* may have several meanings and is probably derived from the Greek, *drachme*. It may mean a small quantity. We also have an apothecary weight of that name equalling sixty grains or one-eighth part of an ounce. It may mean a small drink, such as could be swallowed in one gulp. This, together with the use of these dainty vessels for tasting wine or spirituous liquors, probably accounts for the name. In England they always figured as *tasters*. The one illustrated is very early and was made by John Hull and Robert Sanderson, Boston. This firm probably started about 1652 (Illustration II).

STRAINERS

These were used later for tea making but their earlier use was related to punch and kindred convivial drinks. The example shown here was made by Jonathan Clarke, Newport and Providence, Rhode Island, 1705-1770, and is quite remarkable. It has a perforated inscription, "Jabez Bowen, Providence, January 1765." Bowen was First Chief Justice of the Superior Court, Rhode Island, then Deputy Governor and member of the State Convention that adopted the Constitution in 1790 (Illustration III).

SYPHONS

As their name indicates, these were for transferring wines and stronger beverages from barrels, jugs, or demijohns to ordinary bottles or decanters. Of the two shown, the most remarkable is the one with the hand pump. There are also small syphons that were practically used as spouts if no spout cup was at hand (Illustrations IV and VII).

MARROW SCOOPS

Marrow, the paste inside the meat bone, was once considered a delicacy so the use of these little silver scoops is self-evident. However, marked American marrow scoops are quite rare. The one illustrated is by John Burt Lyng, New York, 1761-1785 (Illustration V).

SUCKET FORKS

Until the end of the 18th Century *sucket* was the every-day term for a sweetmeat in syrup. It comes from the French, *succade*, which in turn derives from the Spanish, *succada*, meaning sweet preserved fruit and possibly other sweet dishes. The end with the fork was used to pick up the sticky fruit and the spoon end served its legitimate purpose. The piece shown here has the mark IK, an unknown silversmith probably working 1690-1700 (Illustration VI).

PAP CUPS

They were chiefly used for feeding small children the needed liquid food. They always had soft edges so that if the infant grasped the cup no harm would be done. The one shown is of remarkable elegance of form and has a very fine decoration. It was made by William Thomson, 1810, New York silversmith (Illustration VIII).

BRAZIERS

The one illustrated is an early example by Adrian Bancker, 1703-1772. It is small and simple in form with original wooden handle. The chafing dish is descended from these early dishes for keeping food warm. Charcoal was used for heat (Illustration IX).

BUTTER TESTERS

Butter testers are proof of the shrewdness of our American merchants who dealt in farm products. They had to dig into the butter firkin to make sure that the quality beneath the surface was the same all through (Illustration X).

—*Mabel Brady Garvan Collections, Yale Gallery of Fine Arts*
Illustration XVI
Silver Book Clasp
By William Jones, Marblehead, Massachusetts, 1694-1730. This was probably attached as a hasp to the covers of a Bible.

—*Mabel Brady Garvan Collections, Yale Gallery of Fine Arts*
Illustration XV
18th-Century Patch Box
This is the work of Edward Webb, Boston silversmith. As he died in 1718, this piece is probably several years earlier. The lid is engraved with a circular decoration and initials.

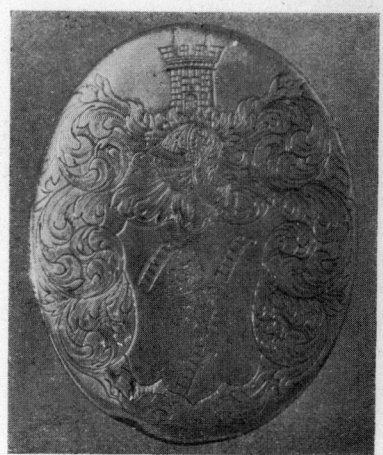

—*Mabel Brady Garvan Collections, Yale Gallery of Fine Arts*
Illustration XIV
Oval Tobacco Box
By John Coney, Boston, 1656-1722. The lid is finely engraved with Jeffries coat of arms. On the bottom is a Latin presentation inscription dated 1701.

—*Metropolitan Museum of Art*
Illustration X
Two Butter Testers
These were pushed into a tub of butter for a sample on which to grade it. The upper one bears the mark, TK, which was that of Thomas Kinney, Norwich, Connecticut, and the lower one by Thomas Hammersly, recorded to have been working as a silversmith in New York, circa 1756.

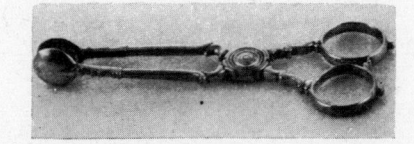

—*Museum of the City of New York*
Illustration XI
Sugar Tongs
Made by George Fielding, New York, circa 1731, these open and shut like a pair of scissors, which was an unusual design for such pieces.

—*Museum of Fine Arts, Boston*
Illustration XII
A Nutmeg Grater
By John Coburn, Boston, 1725-1803. With tight fitting cover and containing both grater and nutmeg, this was made to be carried in the owner's pocket.

—*Museum of Fine Arts, Boston*
Illustration XIII
An Early Pepper Pot
By Samuel Gray, 1684-1713, who worked in both Boston and New London. The design is similar to English ones of the same kind and period.

A TREASURY OF OLD SILVER

SUGAR TONGS

Sugar tongs were usually of the pincer type, but a few were made in the design of a pair of scissors. To the latter belong those shown here. They were made by George Fielding, New York silversmith, 1731, are very handsome, sturdy and functional without openwork or delicate detail (Illustration XI).

NUTMEG GRATERS

Nutmeg also came from the East Indies. Being a hard nut-like seed, it had to be grated when used for seasoning. American and European silversmiths made graters in box, cylindrical and other shapes which opened for use and had space for the nutmeg. Owners carried them much as cigarette lighters are carried today. The example here is by John Coburn, Boston, 1725-1803 (Illustration XII).

PEPPER POTS

Pepper, then as now, came from the East Indies. Until the 19th Century it was expensive. Hence, finely wrought pieces of table silver were made for this seasoning. The example shown here is very similar to contemporary English ones. It was made by Samuel Gray, Boston and New London, Connecticut, 1684-1713 (Illustration XIII).

TOBACCO BOXES

In Colonial America men of means prized tobacco containers of silver that would slip into a pocket. The box illustrated bears the touch-mark of John Coney and was made in 1701. Engraved with the Jeffries arms, it has a delicate rope edging and on the bottom are the words, "Donum R.G. 1701" (Illustration XIV).

PATCH BOXES

The patch box was a "must" in the days when the dear ladies added a special touch to their beauty with little round black patches. Probably this custom derived from France where it was in vogue during the reign of Louis XVI. The box shown bears the mark of Edward Webb of Boston who died in 1718 (Illustration XV).

DECORATIVE ACCESSORIES

A rare piece of silver is the book clasp by William Jones, Marblehead, Massachusetts, 1694-1730. It probably adorned a Bible given as a wedding present (Illustration XVI).

—Ginsburg & Levy, Inc.

American Silver Jewelry

Each piece bears the maker's touch-mark. At the top left, an engraved clasp by Joel Sayre, New York, 1778-1818; top center and right, four oval buttons with the I R mark of Joseph Richardson I, Philadelphia, 1711-1784. Center, chatelaine without chain by Samuel Richards, Philadelphia, died, 1796. At bottom, chatelaine with chain by Joseph Shoemaker, Philadelphia, 1795.

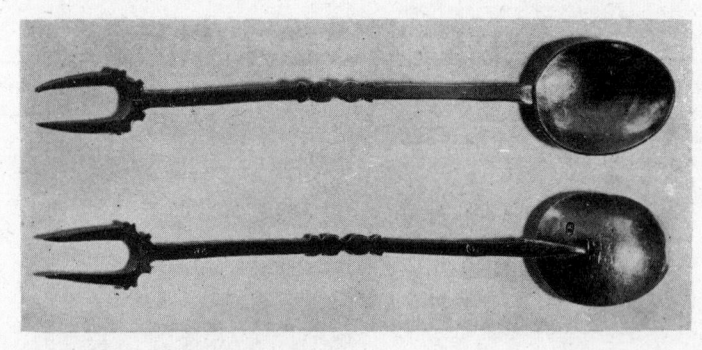

—Fogg Museum of Art

Pair of New England Sucket Forks

The design is characteristic of the 17th Century. They were made by William Rouse, Boston, 1639-1704, and are marked on the bowl and twice on the handle with his touch-mark, W R, in a round corner rectangle. They are loaned from the collection of Mrs. Julian L. Coolidge, a descendant of the maker.

—Edward E. Minor

Early Small Dram Cup

This was made by William Cowell I, Boston, 1682-1736. He had his own shop in 1707 and became an innkeeper shortly after his son completed his apprenticeship.

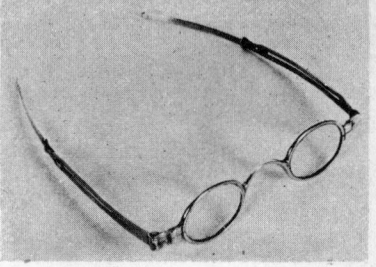

—Museum of the City of New York

Silver Spectacle Frame

The temples have sliding extensions that could be pushed back to about half their length when not in use and folded to go in the case. They bear the mark of Edmund Darrow, New York, working 1843-1861.

—Yale Gallery of Fine Arts

A Miniature Teapot

This bears the mark of Samuel Bartlett, circa 1750-1821, who worked as a silversmith in both Concord and Boston, Massachusetts.

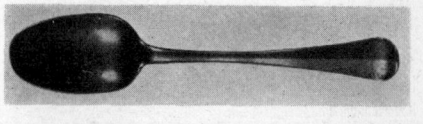

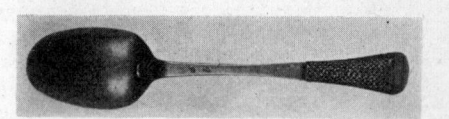

Spoon with Nutmeg Grater

Front and back views of a spoon by Ebenezer Chittenden, 1726-1812, who worked in New Haven and nearby Madison, Connecticut. The lower view shows the grater attached to the back of handle at the outer end.

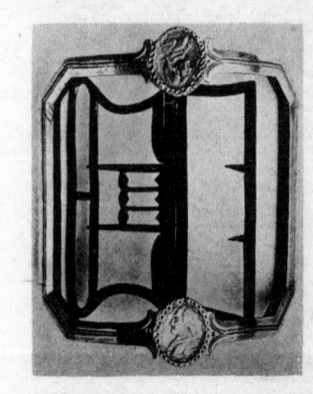

—Metropolitan Museum of Art

Pieces by Paul Revere, The Patriot

At the left, a silver spur; at the right, shoe buckle with silver frame bearing top and bottom profiles of General George Washington. This was probably made shortly after his death, when pieces decorated with his likeness were very popular as memorials.

Virginia Families and Their Silver

By Edward Morris Davis, III

Curator, Decorative Arts, Virginia Museum of Fine Arts
(Photographs, Virginia Museum of Fine Arts)

THE exhibition of silver owned by families of Virginia, made prior to 1800, recently held at the Virginia Museum of Fine Arts, Richmond, throws factual light on the silver owned by these families and provides a wealth of definite information for collectors.

The particular interest in arranging the exhibition was to bring to light and place on record those beautiful and important pieces owned and inherited by the citizens of this Commonwealth, thus forming a gallery of American origin and one of British origin.

These items of silver serve as an illustration of the mode of life in Virginia during the colonial and federal periods. Of the various classes of people in the Commonwealth, the wealthy plantation owners were the only persons able to afford fine things; they felt the ties with the mother country very strongly. Our investigations further substantiated the theory that these owners—keeping cash balances in England—bought their household articles, tables, chairs, draperies, silver, and so forth, direct from the mother country. Hence, we find the vast majority of inherited plate is of British origin.

Generally speaking, the silver, owned by inheritance, of pre-Revolutionary American make came into the Commonwealth through intermarriages of Virginians of a more recent date with persons of the Northern States. Undoubtedly, many pieces of the federal period were acquired by those Virginians who journeyed to Philadelphia and the North at the time of the Continental Congress and the early days of our republic.

In this latter group, we find a lovely oval teapot, where the curve of the wooden handle is very nicely carried through by that of the spout, marked I. Letellier, a Philadelphia "smith," and engraved L.D. for Lucy Daniel. Inherited in the same family is a circular coffeepot with beaded decoration and gallery, by Joseph Anthony, Jr., also of Philadelphia (1783-1844). Of great historical importance was a plain camp mug, bearing the crest of George Washington, made by Richard Humphreys of Philadelphia (adv. 1772). Christian Wiltberger (Philadelphia, 1770-1851) was the maker of an imposing coffee urn, fluted and with lions' heads, with rings for handles, which formerly graced the sideboard at Westover, the estate of the Byrd family. A typical, covered sugar urn, also marked C. Wiltberger, was exhibited. A descendant of the Hawes family of King William County, Virginia, exhibited an Adam style cream pitcher made by Daniel Dupuy (Philadelphia, circa 1790). The Cocke family exhibited a large stirrup cup (maker unknown), and a beautifully plain, large tankard, decorated with classical moldings, marked R. Green (Boston, 1707-1777). George Mason, the author of the *Bill of Rights*, was represented by a mug, marked C. A. Burnett of Alexandria, Virginia.

The most outstanding piece, which found its way to the Commonwealth in more recent years, was the covered butter dish with gracefully curved "keyhole" handles and feet, marked Revere, the mark of that famous horseman-patriot-silversmith, Paul Revere. This national hero was well represented by five other pieces: a porringer with keyhole handle, a circular teapot and a cream pitcher, both with beaded decoration, a beautiful gravy boat (incidently one of a set of four), and a graceful goblet (also one of four).

The two earliest pieces of American origin were the Davenport tankard by Jeremiah Dummer (Boston, 1645-1718), and the rattail spoon with trifid end, marked for John Coney (Boston, 1655-1722). The latter is initialed I.N. for John Norton, whose descendants also lent a pear-shaped can, marked Joseph Edwards (Boston, 1707-1777). A very majestic, Adam style coffeepot by John Aitken (Philadelphia, working 1785-1813), was part of a tea set which is still intact. A very interesting and unusual oval, covered sugar bowl with ring handles was the one marked W. G. Forbes (New York, circa 1773). Excelling in design was the oval tea set by Garret Schanck (New York, directory 1791), which was beautifully engraved (see Cover).

Few pieces of even possible Virginia origin were submitted. That there were silversmiths active in the Commonwealth in the 17th and 18th Centuries we know, mainly through their advertisements. Two of the pieces of hollow ware that came to light, and that have greatest possibilities of being authenticated, were an oval snuffbox with a large cabochon agate set in the top, engraved Mann Page, and with a maker's mark W.S.; and a small brandy warmer,

Virginia Silver of American Make

Left to right, top row: 18-Century stirrup cup—engraved, John Gilchrist to Philip Barraud—as inherited in the Cocke family; Paul Revere gravy boat; coffee urn by Christian Wiltberger, Philadelphia, 1770-1851, from Westover; Curtis family cream pitcher by Adam Lynn, Alexandria, 1796; tankard by R. Greene, Boston, 1707-1777, also from the Cocke family. Bottom row, left to right: Teapot, Joseph Anthony, Philadelphia, 1783-1814; covered butter dish, Paul Revere; teapot, also by Revere, Boston, 1735-1818.

Covered Sugar Bowl by W. G. Forbes

This piece, with ring handles, is most unusual. Forbes worked in New York City where, in 1773, he was made a freeman.

Washington and Randolph Cups

Left, camp mug with Washington's crest, by Richard Humphreys of Philadelphia; right, London beaker, 1752, by unidentified maker.

marked I.G., in an oval, which we hope to prove was the work of James Geddy of Williamsburg, Virginia. It may be well to note that this spelling of his name is now established by his own signature, receipting a bill rendered to Colonel Preston in 1772, which recently came to our attention. Unsigned, but unquestionably made in Virginia about 1760, was the bracelet of five miniatures set in gold, originally owned by Mrs. Gabriel Jones, the wife of that famous lawyer of the Valley of Virginia. Many spoons, buckles, and so forth, were exhibited, which we hope will become clues to the identity of the early Virginia "smiths."

As previously mentioned, the vast majority of plate owned by the 17th- and 18th-Century Virginians was of British origin. Some of these pieces are outstanding and of considerable importance. The frontal of the crown given, in 1677, by Charles II to the Queen of the Pamunkey Indians, in acknowledgment of their superiority over the Powhatans, is well known, being on exhibition at the John Marshall House in Richmond, Virginia. The diminutive hunting cup (circa 1680), given by the same royal personage to his close intimate, Sir William Temple, and brought to this country by the latter's nephew, Joseph Temple, who settled at Ayletts, King William County, Virginia, is not so well known but is of equal importance. This cup, which is only an inch and three-quarters in height, is engraved with an oak tree, three crowns and the motto of the Society of the Royal Oak, while about the rim appears—very worn—the lettering that surrounded the pound sterling during the reign of Charles II.

A flat, oval snuffbox, formerly owned by Benjamin Harrison of Wakefield, bears the London date-letter for 1677, while Nathaniel Harrison, of Brandon, Virginia, was represented by a tripod gravy boat with Vandyked rim (London, 1718). Another early piece was the plain cup (London, 1722, by William Sprockman) which was carried by the Reverend Emmanuel Jones, (Petsworth Parish, Gloucester County, Virginia) and used by him as a chalice from which he administered the wine of the Holy Communion to those of his parish who were sick. It was rather interesting to be able to exhibit two pieces of silver, formerly owned by the Huguenot, Edward Jaquelin (1668-1739), who settled in Jamestown in 1685; and, at the same time, exhibit not only his portrait but those of his wife and children (painted circa 1725). One piece was a coffeepot, the shape of a section of a cone with moldings at top and base and a scroll, wooden handle, bearing the London mark for 1732 (Joseph Smith having been the maker); the other was a *tazza*, engraved with a nag's head—the Jaquelin crest—bearing the London mark for 1723.

One of the most imposing pieces was the handsome monteith, bearing the arms and crest of the Garlick family, which showed

English Silver Owned in Virginia

Top row, left to right: Coffeepot, Joseph Smith, London, 1732; hunting cup given by Charles II to Sir William Temple, circa 1661; can, London, 1769, engraved with crest of John Randolph of Roanoke. Bottom row: Brandy warmer, probably by James Geddy, Williamsburg; gravy boat, London, 1718, originally owned by Nathaniel Harrison of Brandon.

medieval influence in the design of the crownlike, movable rim. Bearing the same crest, but at present owned by another descendant, was the lovely pear-shaped pitcher. Both were made in London by Fras Spilsburg, the former 1733, the latter 1734.

Three generations of John Tayloe's, of Mt. Airy, Richmond County, Virginia, and the Octagon House in the District of Columbia, were adequately represented. The earlier Colonel John (1687-1747), owned an interesting ladle with wooden handle (London, 1738, by George Jones). The outstanding pieces owned by his son John (1721-1779), were a large octagonal tea caddy (London, 1771, by Burrage Davenport) and a unique pie server of cutout scroll pattern (London, 1767). The grandson, Colonel John (1771-1828), who apparently only marked his silver with the crest instead of the coat of arms as had his father and grandfather, was represented by a fluted wine funnel (London, 1791) and a toddy warmer (London, 1793).

One of the most important pieces arrived too late to be included in the catalogue. It was the gold watch originally owned by that extremely wealthy Virginian, Robert "King" Carter of Corotoman, Lancaster County, Virginia. This handsomely engraved timepiece was made in 1711, by the so-called father of English clockmaking—Thomas Tompion of Fleet Street, London,—who, incidentally, is one of the two clockmakers to be accorded the distinction of burial in Westminster Abbey. A granddaughter, Anne Carter, of Cleve, King George County, owned the very handsome kettle-on-stand, made in London by William Grundy in 1749.

Inherited from Mrs. Nelson, mother of General Thomas Nelson of Yorktown, Virginia, was a typical George II repoussé teapot of inverted pear-shape, with an

Other English Silver

Top row: Monteith by Fras Spilsburg, London, 1733, with Garlick arms and crest. Bottom row: Two-handled cup, John Carter, London, 1774, with Custis crest and formerly at Mount Vernon; tea kettle-on-stand, William Grundy, London, 1749, inherited from Anne Carter of Cleve.

eagle-beak spout (London, 1751), and a very early tripod salt (London, 1739). A gold snuffbox was exhibited containing the miniature of Lord North, which was given to Thomas Nelson—who was a signer of the Declaration of Independence and a governor of this Commonwealth—in appreciation for saving the life of his lordship's son while Nelson was at school in England.

Among the pieces inherited through the Custis family was an extremely graceful, two-handled, covered cup on ball feet (London, 1774, by John Carter), engraved with the Custis arms and crest, and which formerly graced Mt. Vernon. Bearing the Fitzhugh arms was a lovely salt, with repoussé decoration of spiral fluting (London, 1764, by Robert and David Hennell), and a salver with shell-and-scroll border (London, 1763, by Thomas Harmann and Richard Mills).

A dignified punch bowl (London, 1786, by Edward Fennell) was engraved with the arms of Charles Carter of Shirley, Charles City County, Virginia, on one side and with his prized horse, Nestor, on the other. The same family exhibited an unusually large brandy saucepan with wooden handle (London, 1750) which attracted considerable admiration.

The only beaker in the exhibition bore the arms of the prominent Randolph family (London, 1752). A pear-shaped coffeepot, with gadroon decoration and an eagle-beak spout (London, 1765, by Thomas Whipman and Charles Wright) was engraved with the crest of the Byrd family. A covered sugar bowl (London, 1789) of inverted pear-shape and floral repoussé decoration and engraved with the Jennings arms, has the rare distinction of being an inherited piece that was made by the now very popular Hester Bateman.

An Important Silver Mug by Jacob Hurd

By Francis Waterhouse Bilodeau

JACOB HURD (1702-1758) has been called the most prolific of the 18th-Century New England silversmiths. Working in Boston during its commercial supremacy, this master craftsman and his two sons, Nathaniel and Benjamin, not only made pieces of outstanding merit for leading colonial dignitaries but more than one example of their work has been found in England. That Jacob Hurd himself produced a large quantity of silver during his working years is evidenced by the quantity that is still extant today, two centuries later. Representative exhibitions of New England silver do not lack for examples of his skill, and more pieces by him are still coming to light.

The silver mug shown here is an heirloom in the Dunlap-Gilman family of Brunswick, Maine, and is now owned by Miss Mary G. Gilman who lives in the old Gilman home there. This piece came into the possession of her great-grandfather, Captain John Dunlap, during the latter years of the 18th Century. It is referred to in his will as a "quart." Actually, it is of extraordinary size since it holds a full quart and three-fourths of a pint. It measures 13 inches around the top and 16½ inches about the base. It is 5¾ inches high and is signed by its maker both on the bottom and just below the rim at the left of the handle. On the latter are the initials of earlier owners of the mug. These, H^F S, are in the triangular arrangement so often used at that time; H and S being the first letters of the owners' first names and F that of their surname.

An interesting detail of the mug is a small hole at the base of the handle. It has often been suggested that this was intentionally introduced to provide a means for whistling for more when the contents of the mug had been drunk. Actually, there is a less romantic and more plausible explan-

—*Miss Mary G. Gilman*

The Dunlap-Gilman Mug

This bears the touch mark of Jacob Hurd and is a typical example of the work of this Boston silversmith.

ation. Hollis French, author of that excellent and recently published book, *Jacob Hurd and His Sons, Nathaniel and Benjamin, Silversmiths*, says, "You will find one on every hollow handle and it is for a vent which is necessary to allow the gases to escape in casting and brazing." That any sound can be produced is, it would seem, purely accidental.

The initials on the handle of the mug remain an intriguing and baffling mystery, as all efforts to determine who and what manner of people H and S F were have been without success. As already stated, Captain John Dunlap acquired this unusual piece sometime before 1800, or nearly forty years after the man who made it had passed to his reward.

Captain Dunlap was a prosperous merchant, at one time considered the wealthiest man in Maine. In 1789 he built the fine house which is still the home of his descendants. It was during that same year that he was chosen to superintend the construction of Massachusetts Hall, the first of the buildings of Bowdoin College. One of his sons, Robert L., was an early governor of Maine; another son, David, the ancestor of the Gilmans and next in line to own the "quart," married Alice McKeen, daughter of the Reverend Joseph McKeen, first president of Bowdoin College.

David Dunlap's portrait and that of his wife hang in the old Brunswick home along with other ancestral portraits for it was he who bought the title to the house. John and David both represented the District of Maine in the Massachusetts Legislature. Charles J. Gilman, of the distinguished Gilman family of Exeter, New Hampshire, who married Alice McKeen Dunlap, daughter of David, represented Maine in the 57th Congress and was for many years a leader in the political affairs of the state.

Thus the Hurd mug remains in the possession of a family distinguished for its public service, which is fitting and appropriate when one remembers that the list of Jacob Hurd's patrons included such names as Sir William Pepperell, hero of Louisburg; Thomas Clapp, president of Yale, 1740-1766; Spencer Phips, Lieutenant Governor of Massachusetts, 1732-1757; Captain Edward Tyng, commander of the American privateer, *Snow*; and Colonel Timothy Dwight, grandfather of Timothy 3rd, who was president of Yale, 1795-1817. Jacob Hurd also executed fine pieces of plate for Daniel Henchman of Boston, a prominent 18th-Century bookseller, whose daughter Lydia married Thomas Hancock.

History in American Silver

By H. Maxson Holloway
Curator of Decorative Arts,
The New-York Historical Society

—*Yale University Art Gallery*
1. Silver bowl, handsomely embossed with stylized flowers, given to Thomas Darling, tutor at Yale, by his students in 1745. Made by Cornelius Kirstede, of New York and New Haven.

From the early beginnings of our history the American people have shown their gratitude and appreciation for services rendered to their country in the performance of heroic deeds and successful military negotiations by presenting worthy citizens with beautiful pieces of silver plate appropriately inscribed. Silver, a metal known from ancient times because of its comparative scarcity, its brilliant grey-white color and its resistance to atmospheric oxidation, has long been used for articles of value such as coins, ceremonial ornaments and jewelry. Pieces of silver plate may originally have been chosen as suitable rewards because of the value of the metal and the artistic ability required of the silversmith in fashioning his object with meticulous and mechanical precision. Now, as then, such gifts are reckoned among the recipients' most prized possessions; they are handed down to descendants and many at last find permanent homes in museum collections. Thus we preserve for future generations memories of the works and deeds of our forefathers. Much of our glorious history is recorded in this manner on a bowl, a teapot, a cup, a salver or an urn.

The New-York Historical Society, 170 Central Park West, New York City, has chosen for its fall opening an exhibition of "American Presentation Silver" which covers a period of over 200 years and dates from the early 18th to the earthly 20th century. The exhibition is currently being shown in the Society's galleries where it will remain on view until January 12, 1947. Many leading museums, historical societies and private collectors have lent pieces from their collections for this comprehensive display—the first of its kind, it is believed, ever assembled in the United States.

Notable among the 18th century pieces is a two-handled covered cup wrought by Jacob Hurd, Boston silversmith (fig. 2), now a part of the Mabel Brady Garvan Collection at Yale. It is 15¼ inches high and its chastely simple design—an inverted bell-shaped body, molded cover with knob finial, and two scrolled handles—is a thing of real beauty. The inscription, engraved within a trophy of arms, reads: "To EDWARD TYNG Esq. Commander of ye SNOW Prince of Orange As an Acknowledgment of his good Service done the TRADE in Taking ye First French Privateer on this Coast the 24th of June 1744 This Plate is presented BY Several of ye Merchts: in Boston New England." In the *Collections of the Massachusetts Historical Society* for the year 1809 is an interesting paper by

—*Mabel Brady Garvan Collection, Yale*
2. Two-handled cup with cover, by Jacob Hurd, of Boston. Presented by the merchants of Boston to Edward Tyng for his capture of "ye first French Privateer on this Coast," 1744.

—*Historical Society of Pennsylvania*
3. Gorget made by Joseph Richardson, of Philadelphia. Presented to an Indian Chief before the Revolution for friendliness. It shows William Penn offering a winged pipe to an Indian.

82

AMERICAN SILVER

A discussion of distinguished examples of 18th century American presentation silver.

the Rev. Timothy Alden, Jr., entitled *Memoirs of Edward Tyng, Esquire*. The author states: "The subject of these memoirs received a commission from governour Belcher, dated 16 April, 1740, appointing him captain of his majesty's SOUTH AND NORTH BATTERIES AND FORTIFICATIONS IN BOSTON. When captain Cypnian Southhack resigned the command of THE PROVINCE SNOW, OR QUEEN'S GALLEY, PRINCE OF ORANGE, captain Tyng, who had left the sea and was settled in merchandise, was prevailed on to succeed him. In 1744, he acquired no small honour by attacking and capturing a French privateer, commanded by Monsieur De La Bra, of force superiour to that of the PRINCE OF ORANGE."

Another distinctive piece from the Yale University Art Gallery is a bowl which was wrought by Cornelius Kierstede who worked in New York and later in New Haven. This bowl was presented to Thomas Darling, Yale tutor, by his students in 1745 (fig. 1). It is without handles, handsomely embossed with tulips and other flower designs and with the inscription engraved around the rim of the bowl.

Ezra Stiles, later president of Yale College (1777-1795), was similarly rewarded by his students in 1755 upon resigning his tutorship at Yale. To him was given a tankard with tapering sides, molded base and rim, domed cover, bell-shaped finial and scrolled handle—the work of Samuel Casey of South Kingstown, Rhode Island. A contemporary biography of President Stiles, written by Abiel Holmes in 1798 pays him tribute in this eloquent manner: "At the Commencement in September, he resigned the tutorship, after having filled that office six years and a half, with singular usefulness and dignity, and with the highest respect and affection of his pupils. He had the tutorial care of five classes, four of which he conducted through a course of Mathematics and Natural Philosophy. The whole number of his immediate pupils was one hundred and ten. While a resident graduate and a tutor, together with his pursuit of the various branches of literature, and of theology, he paid particular attention to the study of philosophy and astronomy; and his experiments in the one science, with his

—*Mabel Brady Garvan Collection, Yale*

5. Paul Revere bowl, presented by the Springfield Militia to Gen. William Shepard for quelling Shay's Rebellion in 1786. Its uncommonly fine proportions make it an exceptional Revere piece.

—*New-York Historical Society*

4. Unique salver, made by Lewis Fueter, of N. Y. Presented in 1773 to Capt. Thomas Sowers, engineer, for repairing Manhattan's Battery.

—*Museum of Fine Arts, Boston*

6. Tapering tankard, by Benj. Burt, Boston, 1786. Given to Richard Devens for directing the engineering of the Charles River bridge.

7. Teaset by Paul Revere, given by grateful citizens of Boston in 1799 to Edmund Hartt, constructor of the frigate, Boston, at that time "one of the handsomest vessels ever floated." Among the best examples of Revere's federal period.

—Museum of Fine Arts, Boston

calculations in the other, compose a manuscript quarto volume. As a Tutor he was justly considered as one of the best qualified to execute that important trust." The tankard is also owned by the Garvan Collection.

American Indians, too, received silver presentation plate in the form of engraved gorgets and medals. Harrold E. Gillingham, who has probably done more research than any other person on Indian medals and has published several enlightening monographs on the subject, well expresses the early feeling of the white man toward the Indian in his article, *Early Indian Medals,* published by *Antiques* in December, 1924: ". . . to me the Indian medals have a particular fascination. There is something very personal in an article given to an individual for some deed performed, or in commemoration of some event, especially when that article is known to have been worn thereafter with great pride by the recipient. And the Indians did cherish their medals so highly that they passed them on to their children or to the succeeding chief of the tribe. In a few instances medals were buried with the owner... In early Colonial days, medals were given the red man as more or less official evidences of friendship. After the Revolutionary War, they were bestowed upon those Indian chiefs who made a visit to the 'Great White Father,' as our earlier presidents were called. A medal was also frequently given to the head chief upon the signing of a treaty. Hence such specimens are often called Indian peace medals."

In the collections at The New-York Historical Society there is an original copperplate engraved by Henry Dawkins of Philadelphia in 1770 for the certificates that accompanied the presentation of royal medals to the Indians by the Hon. Sir William Johnson. The reader will find the wording of this old certificate, herewith quoted in part, entertaining: ". . . Whereas I have received repeated proofs of your Attachment to his Britanic Majestys Interests and Zeal for his Service upon Sundry occasions, more particularly——I do therefore give you this public Testimonial thereof as a proof of his Majesty's Esteem & Approbation, Declaring you the said——to be a—— of Your——and recommending it to all his Majesty's Subjects and faithfull Indian Allies to Treat and Consider you upon all occasions agreeable to your Character, Station, and Services."

In the current exhibition of American presentation silver a section is devoted to medals and gorgets presented to peace-loving Indians by our government, with the addition of prints illustrating how the Indians wore these awards. The Historical Society of Pennsylvania owns one of the gems among these Indian pieces—a gorget made by Joseph Richardson, of Philadelphia (fig. 3). It is simply designed with a pictorial engraving of William Penn seated under an elm tree offering a winged pipe to an Indian seated on the ground near a smoking log fire, and the sun is portrayed smiling as it looks down upon the two figures before the fire. It is supposed that this gorget was issued by "The Friendly Association" in Philadelphia during the later part of the 18th century. Another gorget, a signed peace and worthy of mention, is one made by Barent Ten Eyck of Albany, little of whose silver remains. It, too, is simple in design, with an engraving of the British coat-of-arms below which is inscribed: "Danyel Cryn 1755." This piece and several other Indian items on display are the property of the Museum of the American Indian, Heye Foundation.

Among these peace medals a rare one owned by the Buffalo Historical Society is shown. It was presented by George Washington to Red Jacket, or Sa-go-ye-wat-ha, Chief of the Senecas at the time of the conference with the 50 chiefs of the Six Nations at Philadelphia in 1792. It is of oval design, the obverse showing a full-length figure of Washington in the uniform of a general, his right hand extended toward an Indian who is smoking a pipe of peace with a tomahawk on the ground at his feet. In the background is engraved a scene of a man plowing with a yoke of oxen; in the distance, low hills and a house are seen. The reverse shows the arms of the United States, the eagle holding in his beak a ribbon inscribed E PLURIBUS UNUM. The medal was valued and highly prized by Red Jacket and he wore it on all occasions. After his death it became the property of various descendants until it was acquired from one of them by the Buffalo Historical Society in 1898.

Probably one of the most important of all inscribed American pieces is the bowl made by Paul Revere, Boston patriot, which is known as the "Sons of Liberty" bowl and is now in the possession of Mr. Marsden J. Perry (see cover). It bears a lengthy inscription including the names of the 15 Sons of Liberty, who ordered the bowl, engraved in script encircling its rim. The history of this bowl may be summed up as follows: John Wilkes, in the 45th issue of his paper, the *North Briton,* attacked the royal policy of repressing self-government in the colonies. In 1763 the King issued an illegal warrant which took Wilkes to prison and permitted the search and seizure of his papers. As a member of Parliament he was considered the champion of the colonies and "No. 45" became a slogan for the patriots. In 1768 the Massachusetts House of

Representatives protested to the King against the repressive measures and sent a letter to the other colonies urging united action. They were ordered to rescind this letter but by a vote of 92 to 17 defied the order. These "Illustrious Ninety-two" became the toast of the patriot cause. The inscription on the bowl reads in part: "To the Memory of the glorious NINETY-TWO Members of the Honbl House of Representatives of the Massachusetts-Bay: who, undaunted by the insolent Menaces of Villains in Power, from a strict Regard to the Conscience and the LIBERTIES of their Constituents, on the 30th of June 1768 Voted NOT TO RESCIND." This was only the beginning of stirring incidents that eventually led to the American Revolution and finally to the birth of our republic.

Lewis Fueter, well known New York silversmith, is represented by a unique salver which he made as a presentation piece in 1772-1773 for Governor William Tryon and the General Assembly of the Province of New York (fig. 4). The salver was presented to Captain Thomas Sowers on March 13, 1773, by His Excellency Governor Tryon in recognition of his services in repairing the battery at the lower end of Manhattan Island. This salver is 21¾ inches in diameter with three claw feet and a scalloped border with a gadrooned edge. It is beautifully engraved with the arms of New York, encircled by the inscription: "This Piece of Plate is the Gift of His Excely. Govr. Tryon, the Genel. Assemy. of New-York, to Captn. Sowers Engineer. 13 Marh. 1773." Below the arms are engraved cannon, cannon balls, tools, fascines and other objects used in building fortifications, a compliment to the engineering achievement of the recipient.

In 1786, Richard Devens, Esquire, of Boston, was given a tankard with tapering sides, molded base and rim, domed cover with flame finial and scrolled thumbpiece (fig. 6). It was made by Benjamin Burt of Boston and is now in the M. and M. Karolik Collection at the Museum of Fine Arts, Boston. It is known that several gentlemen received presentation plate after the completion of the Charles River Bridge; it was considered one of the engineering feats of the day.

Devens was a special director of the work and one side of the tankard given to him shows a medallion with a view of the Charles River Bridge finely engraved. On the other side is a second medallion with the following laudatory inscription: "Presented to Richard Devens, Esqr: by the Proprietors of CHARLES RIVER BRIDGE, in Testimony of their entire Approbation of his faithful Services, as a special Director of that Work begun A.D. 1785, and perfected A.D. 1786." The two medallions are joined together by a decoration of floral festoons. *The Massachusetts Magazine,* several years later in the September issue of 1789, carried an interesting article on the bridge with a contemporary engraved view of the great engineering feat. Statistics show that the bridge had a length of 1,503 feet and a width of forty-two feet. It also had at each side a passage of six feet railed in for the safety of people on foot. When the bridge was opened it summoned from all parts about 20,000 spectators. Ceremonies were held at the State House and the members of the legislature as well as other dignitaries attended. A 13-cannon salute was accorded the momentous occasion.

Another important piece of historic silver made by Paul Revere shortly after the American Revolution is a bowl inscribed: "To GENERAL WILLIAM SHEPARD Presented by The MILITIA of Springfield as a Memorial of his Ability and Zeal in quelling SHAY'S REBELLION at Springfield Arsenal January 25th, 1787" (fig. 5). To recall to the reader the stirring incident of Shay's Rebellion: in 1786 Shepard was appointed major-general of militia for Hampshire County and was responsible for the defense of the federal arsenal and the protection of the federal court. His judgment in dealing with the insurgents and his skill in delaying them, as well as his decision to remove arms and ammunition from the arsenal without specific authority, were important in deciding the outcome of a difficult situation.

In 1799 grateful citizens of Boston presented Edmund Hartt with silver plate in appreciation of his work as constructor of the Frigate *Boston*. They chose a teaset (fig. 7), now in the possession of the Museum of Fine Arts, Boston, which is among the best examples of Paul Revere's federal period. In this set only the sugar basin is inscribed. It reads: "To Edmund Hartt Constructor of the Frigate BOSTON Presented by a number of his fellow citizens as a Memorial of their sense of his Ability, Zeal & Fidelity in the Completion of that Ornament of the AMERICAN NAVY 1799."

NEW YORK CANDLESTICK
One of a pair of silver candlesticks made by William Anderson, New York, a freeman in 1746.   *Museum of the City of New York*

MORE HISTORY IN AMERICAN SILVER: 19TH CENTURY PRESENTATION SILVER

HEROIC work at fires has resulted in a piece of silver being presented to many a hero, particularly if the fire was in a public building. In 1810 the Old South Church in Boston was saved from burning by Isaac Harris, a mast-maker whose shop was across the street. He was presented with a covered silver pitcher which was the work of Ebenezer Moulton, Boston silversmith, and is now owned by the Museum of Fine Arts, Boston. One side of the pitcher shows the burning church with Harris, mounted by a ladder to the roof, cutting away the blazing timbers with an axe; the other side bears the inscription: "To MR. ISAAC HARRIS For his intrepid and successful exertions on the roof of the Old South Church when on fire Dec. 29th, 1810 the Society present this token of their GRATITUDE Boston January 29th, 1811."

—*Historical Society of Pennsylvania*
2. *Cooler presented by Philadelphians to Stephen Decatur for his outstanding valour in the War of 1812.*

—*Oliver B. Jennings*
1. *Pitcher presented by New Yorkers to Capt. Samuel Reid for his gallantry at Fayal, 1814.*

At the close of the War of 1812, the nation paid its respects to its heroes through the presentation of silver plate. In the exhibition currently on view at the New-York Historical Society, silver is shown that was presented by the citizens of Baltimore and Philadelphia to Stephen Decatur (fig. 2); by the citizens of Albany to Isaac Hull and by the citizens of New York to Samuel C. Reid (fig. 1). Captain James Lawrence, who gave his life to the cause, was awarded a posthumous gift of plate which was received by his wife, Julia Lawrence. The city of Philadelphia gave a pitcher and soup tureen, appropriately inscribed and accompanied by the following letter, which is still preserved. "Philadelphia, 9th January, 1816. *Madam*, The death of your late gallant Husband Captain James Lawrence, has resolved upon us the honor of presenting to you in behalf of the Citizens of Philadelphia, two elegant pieces of plate of the manufacture of Mr. (Simon) Chaudron, intended to commemorate the Capture (during the recent contest with Great Britain) of the Sloop of war *Peacock*, by the American Sloop *Hornet* under Captain Lawrence's Command. You will receive them Madam as a respectful evidence of the high sense entertained of his Skill and Bravery on that occasion, which was rendered yet more conspicuous, by his humane and successful Exertions, in rescuing the vanquished Foe, from an untimely and watery grave. We have the honor to be With the utmost respect Madam, Your most Obedient Servants, George Harrison, Dane Wm. Coxe, Committee."

The City of New York also honored Lawrence in presenting

—*The New-York Historical Society*
3. *This pitcher and two fruit dishes were presented in 1819 by the City of New York in honor of Capt. James ("Don't give up the ship") Lawrence.*

86

Chamber of Commerce of the State of New York
4. *One of a pair of vases presented in 1825 to Gov. De Witt Clinton for linking the great waterways of New York with canals.*

Metropolitan Museum of Art
5. *Map case presented by the Governor of South Carolina to Lafayette on the occasion of his visit to that State in 1825.*

Hornet in the capture of the British Sloop of War *Peacock* on the 24th February, 1813." This silver was sent to Mrs. Lawrence with a laudatory letter from the committee on November 4, 1819. The next day Mrs. Lawrence replied: "*Sir*, I have the honor to acknowledge the receipt of your letter of the 4th inst. accompanying the Plate voted my late lamented husband Capt. James Lawrence, by the Hon. Corporation of this City whose liberality on a subsequent as well as on the present occasion, I feel proud to acknowledge.

"That his memory is cherished with affection and veneration by his fellow citizens will always be a source of consolation to myself—and as my Child advances in years, those public testimonies of respect and admiration of her Father's character will be incentives to nobleness of mind even in the breast of a *female*.

"Be pleased to communicate to the Committee my heartiest thanks, and accept for yourself the assurance of my sincere esteem. Your obedient, Julia Lawrence."

Today the Lawrence silver is a part of the Eugene H. Pool Collection in The New-York Historical Society.

In 1824 General Lafayette returned to America at the invitation of the United States Government. His tour was one series of ovations and receptions. In March 1825 he reached South Carolina and his visit to Columbia from March 11th to the 14th was an event that city still recalls. While he was there

The New York Historical Society
6. *Salver from the 400-piece dinner service given by the merchants of New York in 1855 to Perry for bringing Japan into the intercourse of nations.*

a large ball was given in his honor and Governor Manning addressed Lafayette in the presence of the people. As a lasting memento he was presented with a beautiful silver map case—with map (fig. 5)—which was simply and appropriately inscribed: "Presented by Richard J. Manning, Governor of South Carolina, To General Lafayette Whilst at Columbia in March 1925 In tracing your route through our Territory every inhabited spot will recall to your memory the devotion and affection of grateful people." This case, now belonging to the Metropolitan Museum of Art, is designed with great simplicity and was the work of Louis Boudo, Charleston silversmith. He engraved his signature in the lower right corner: "L. Boudo, Fecit Charleston, So Ca," and it is considered probably the most notable piece made by him.

In 1825 Governor De Witt Clinton was presented with two handsome covered-vases by the merchants of Pearl Street in the City of New York in testimony of their gratitude and respect for his public services (fig. 4). The merchants, being practical men, decided to have a competition for the design of the proposed pieces. A premium of $100 was offered for the best design of two vases which should be of the same outline but differ in ornament. Hardly six weeks had passed when the *New York Evening Post* for January 17, 1824, announced: "The premium of $100 for the design of the Clinton Vases, has been awarded to Messers Fletcher & Gardiner of Philadelphia." It does seem strange that the merchants selected an out-of-town silversmith when New York at that time had a goodly number of reputable silversmiths. Fletcher and Gardiner are known to have produced a considerable amount of presentation plate. In his famous diary, Philip Hone comments: "Fletcher & Co. are the artists who made the Clinton vases. Nobody in this 'world' of ours hereabouts can compete with them in their kind of work." The vases were copied from an antique vase found among the ruins of the Villa Adrian. The tablets and figures in bas relief are all different and show scenes of the Grand Canal or allegorical illustrations of the progress of art and science. Their form is circular, except that the lower part is slightly elliptical and the covers are surmounted by an eagle standing on a section of the globe. In one talon is borne the arms of the State and in the other a laurel wreath. The pedestals are square, with claw feet, three sides bearing decoration while the fourth shows the engraved inscription with the wording on each vase. One is inscribed: "TO THE HON. DE WITT CLINTON Who has developed the resources of the State of New York AND ENNOBLED HER CHARACTER The Merchants of Pearl Street offer this testimony of their GRATITUDE AND RESPECT." The other reads: "The Merchants of Pearl Street, New York, TO THE HON. DE WITT CLINTON Whose claim to the proud title of Public Benefactor is founded on those magnificent works, The Northern and Western CANALS." It is interesting to note here a contemporary newspaper article in the *New York Evening Post* for March 16, 1825, when the vases were on view for public inspection in the City Hotel:

"The Clinton Vases. The general wish of the ladies and gentlemen of this city to have a view of the beautiful Silver Vases, about to be presented by the merchants of Pearl-Street to his excellency De Witt Clinton, induced the patriotic subscribers to place them for exhibition in the Assembly room of the City Hotel.

"We looked in about one o'clock, but the ladies and gentlemen were so numerous, that we were only able to catch a glimpse of these splendidly beautiful, and highly finished specimens of taste, art and skill.... During the few moments we were in the room, ladies and gentlemen were entering continually, and the stair-way was thronged. The cost of the vases, we understand, was about $3500."

Today finds the permanent home of these historic vases in the Great Hall of the Chamber of Commerce of the State of New York in downtown Manhattan, which organization lent them for the exhibition of "American Presentation Silver."

Probably the largest silver service ever presented to an individual American was the dinner service given to Commodore Matthew Calbraith Perry, U. S. Navy, on December 28, 1855, by the Chamber of Commerce and merchants of New York in acknowledgement of his having successfully concluded a treaty with Japan in 1854. This service comprises nearly 400 pieces, including salver (fig. 6), tea and coffee sets, soup tureens, large and small dishes with covers, gravy boats, bonbon dishes, salt cellars and a great variety of flat silver. William Gale & Son, New York silversmiths, made the service at a cost of $6000, and the many pieces are handsomely engraved and chased with floral decorations. The salver is inscribed: "PRESENTED BY THE CHAMBER OF COMMERCE AND MERCHANTS OF New York TO COMMODORE Matthew Calbraith Perry, in acknowledgement of the signal services which he has rendered TO AMERICA and to the WORLD, by his able and successful negotiation of the TREATY WITH JAPAN."

The other pieces do not have such lengthy inscriptions. It is rather interesting to read the correspondence that took place at that time, especially today in our constantly changing world. The letter from the committee reads:

NEW-YORK, Friday, Dec. 28, 1855.
DEAR SIR: In behalf of the Chamber of Commerce and Merchants of New-York, we beg your acceptance of the service of plate which accompanies this, as a testimonial of the sense which they entertain of the important service which you have rendered to your country and the world, by your able and successful negotiations of the treaty with Japan.

To have brought this secluded Empire into the intercourse of nations, is an achievement which may be justly ranked among the great events of the age; reflecting honor upon our country; the more so, as it has been accomplished, not by bloodshed and the devastations of war, but by means of a frank, energetic, and determined course of negotiation.

It may require time to regulate satisfactorily the terms and mode of our future intercourse with Japan, and still more time to develop fully the commercial resources of that empire. But the great object is accomplished. Japan, once opened to the Western nations, will not be permitted by those nations to return to her former exclusive policy; and, located between the two great continents, that empire will hold a most important place in the future extending commerce of the world.

The spirit of enterprise which we witness in our day is but the beginning of the great onward movements which, aided and impelled by the advancing improvements in science and the arts, are destined materially to change the condition of the human family.

When this continent becomes densely peopled by the united American race, and China and Japan, with their teeming millions, become renovated by the light of Christianity and true science, the state of commerce and international intercourse will be such as we can now but faintly imagine. With these great results your name will be associated.

The merchants of New-York have ever felt a just pride in the navy of the United States, and in tendering to you this merited tribute of respect, they wish to express their admiration of the exploits of that arm of national strength, so ably represented by you; and their great esteem for the many distinguished officers who have contributed to its high reputation.

—*The New York Historical Society*
7. *Covered bowl presented in 1863 to Judge Anthon for his handling of the Civil War draft laws in New York.*

The Perry dinner service is today the property of The New-York Historical Society.

For the Civil War period, one piece of presentation silver worthy of mention is a covered bowl of simple, graceful lines with a finial in the form of an ancient Greek helmet (fig. 7). Made by Tiffany and Company, New York, it is now the property of The New-York Historical Society, the gift of Mr. Stuyvesant Fish. It is inscribed: "PRESENTED TO Judge Advocate General William Henry Anthon, BY THE Commissioners and Surgeons of Drafting in the CITY OF NEW YORK, AS A Testimonial of their appreciation of the eminent ability and unswerving integrity with which the proceedings preparatory to the draft were conducted. Dated New York, April 1863." The names of the committee—numbering five—are engraved below the inscription and include prominent military men and private citizens of the day.

American Art Association, Anderson Galleries, Inc., New York

SILVER TEA SERVICE MADE IN NEW YORK
Silver tea set consisting of teapot, creamer and covered sugar bowl, probably wrought by William Pelletreau, New York, 1786-1842.

Washington's Camp Silver, Pewter and Tin

By Stephen Decatur

Washington Camp Cup

This cup, one of a pair, with his crest, still remains in the possession of the Lee family. The cups were commented upon by Lossing in his early book on Mount Vernon. These were made by Richard Humphrey of Philadelphia.

IT HAS been said, and many times repeated, that George Washington, when Commander-in-Chief during the Revolution, lived simply and unostentatiously. This statement is undoubtedly true, although it must be accepted only in a relative sense. There was no more pomp and ceremony at headquarters than was strictly necessary and, certainly, he did not keep an elaborate table and cellar as was then the practice of European generals. But, except on occasions in camp when he wished to share the hardships of his men, he probably lived, as nearly as circumstances would permit, in the style and manner customary at hospitable Mount Vernon. Mrs. Washington was usually with him in winter quarters so that, with her and his military aides and secretaries, there were sometimes as many as eighteen persons in his official household.

In writing of Washington's life in camp, Benson J. Lossing in *Mount Vernon and its Associations*, first published about 1859, said, "Later in the war, Washington had a pair of plain silver goblets, with his crest engraven upon them, which he used in his tent. These were the only departure from that rigid economy which he exhibited in all his personal arrangements while in the army, not because he was parsimonious, but because he wanted to set an example of plainness and self-denial to all around him. These goblets are now used in the family of Colonel Lee at Arlington House."

Lossing was a faithful recorder, but it must be remembered that at the time he wrote this paragraph it was the fashion to depict Washington as a leading example of democratic simplicity. However, the statement does apply with accuracy to his conduct during the first month of the stay at Valley Forge, when the General, in order to inspire his suffering men, insisted upon living in a tent until huts had been provided for all of them; only then did he move into a house. But, of course, in the eight years he commanded the army, he actually spent a very small fraction of the time under canvas.

But Lossing, it appears, was in error in thinking that Washington had but two silver camp cups and that he did not obtain them until late in the war. In the possession of the United States Naval Museum at Annapolis is a bill of Edmund Milne, silversmith of Philadelphia, for twelve such cups made for the General in August, 1777. Washington, with his army, spent two weeks of that month in Germantown and Philadelphia while the British were preparing to attack the latter place from the south and, no doubt, obtained the cups then. Perhaps they were needed at the moment, since Lafayette and several other young French officers had just arrived and were much at headquarters. Two of these cups, bearing Milne's mark, are at the Valley Forge Museum. An inscription has been engraved on each one, giving its history,

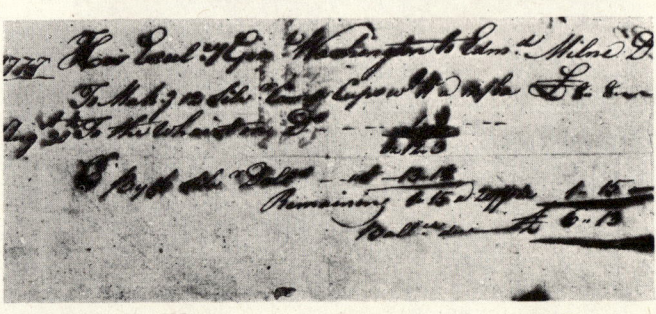

—Valley Forge Museum

—United States Naval Museum

Pair of Cups Made by Edmund Milne

These camp cups, bearing the initial "W" in scrip, were made by Edmund Milne, Philadelphia silversmith, in 1777, as the bill indicates. Originally, there were twelve of them.

but originally they were marked merely with Washington's final initial. The silversmith's bill shows the General gave him sixteen silver dollars from which to make them and Milne allowed one pound Continental currency per ounce troy for the metal they contained. It is further evident that a paper money pound was then worth, in silver coin, about one dollar and fifteen cents.

Cups of metal ware were, of course, a necessity with a moving camp and they would be used to hold whatever happened to be the drink of the moment. Colonel James McHenry, who became one of Washington's aides in 1778, and who was afterwards Secretary of War, left an account of an occasion at which the silver cups were surely used. He said that about two weeks after the Battle of Monmouth, when the army was in northern New Jersey, the General and his staff stopped on the march near the Falls of the Passaic. "After viewing these falls we seated ourselves under a large spreading oak within view of the spray and in hearing of the noise. A fine cool spring bubbled out most charmingly from the bottom of the tree. The traveling canteens were immediately emptied and a modest repast spread before us of cold ham, tongue and some biscuit. With the assistance of a little spirit we composed some excellent grog. We chatted away a very cheerful half hour and then took our leave of the friendly oak and its refreshing spring." Undoubtedly Washington shared the grog, although his preference was always for beer or wine at meals. He once wrote from Valley Forge that he had no

—United States Naval Museum

Later Pair of Washington Cups

These were made by Charles A. Burnett, silversmith, of Alexandria, at the close of the 18th Century. It is inferred that they date about 1798 when the European situation made it probable that Washington would have to resume command of the American Army. The inscription on these cups is of a later date and incorrect.

90

AMERICAN SILVER

wine or brandy to give his guests, but only "vile whiskey."

The United States Naval Museum has two silver camp cups which are practically identical with the pair at Valley Forge and which, until recently, were thought to have belonged to the same set. But instead of the mark of Milne, they bear that of Charles A. Burnett, a silversmith of Alexandria, Virginia. From available records, it appears that Burnett was not working before 1790; consequently, Washington could not have had them during the Revolution. One may guess they were obtained in 1798, when Washington again became Commander-in-Chief because of the threatened war with France and made his preparations to take the field. Perhaps he felt he needed more cups—or some of the old ones had been lost or given away—so he had the design duplicated. Burnett's name does not appear on any of the Mount Vernon accounts; but if the cups were purchased as part of the General's military outfit, their cost would have been a charge against the Government and so would not be entered in the private ledger. The whereabouts of the rest of the Milne cups seems to be unknown, but it is quite probable some are still in existence.

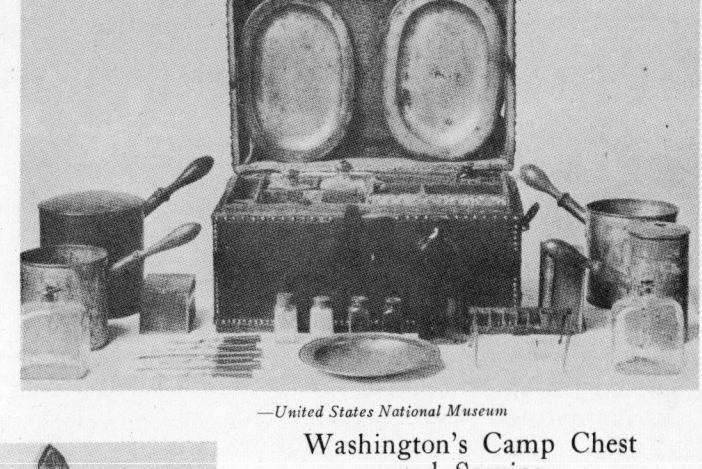

Incidentally, the two cups described by Lossing differ materially from the others. They bear the mark of Richard Humphrey, who is known to have been working in Philadelphia about the time the Revolution started. Available lists give no more information concerning him. Perhaps he died about that time. In any event, it seems certain he made the cups prior to the Declaration of Independence since they are engraved with Washington's crest, a device which he used very seldom, if at all, in public from that event until several years after the war. It is quite possible that Washington purchased them in June, 1775, when he was made Commander-in-Chief and was in Philadelphia, because he must have obtained some camp equipment at that time. He also bought a number of silver spoons, marked with his crest, from Humphreys and these, too, may have been part of his outfit. Lossing stated the cups were used in the family of Colonel Lee. This refers, of course, to General Robert E. Lee, whose wife was a great-granddaughter of Martha Washington. They are now owned by his descendants.

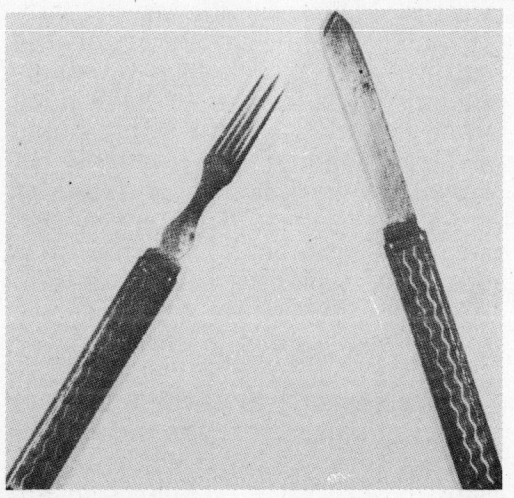

—United States National Museum

Washington's Camp Chest and Service

This is complete with cooking utensils, platters, plates, knives and forks, salt and pepper shakers, and two brandy bottles. The large pieces were made of tin.

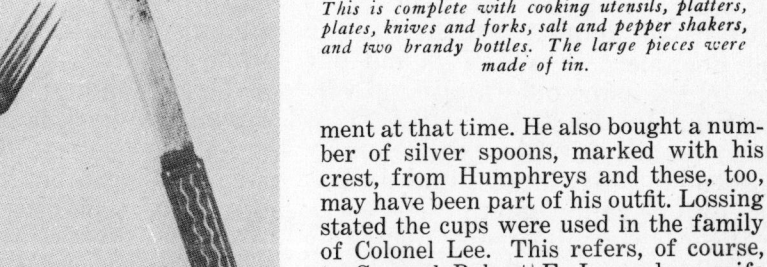

—Pennsylvania Historical Society

Camp Knife and Fork

This set, that fits together, was presented to General Washington by Charles Thomason, secretary to the Continental Congress. It was probably made at Sheffield, in England, the leading cutlery center.

During the Revolution, whenever the Commander-in-Chief occupied a house, he used the china and other tableware which it contained. But in camp, naturally, he had to furnish his own equipment and so, as was customary with all senior officers, he had a readily portable camp chest containing the articles for his mess. He may, of course, have had several such chests during the course of the war. In any event, one is now in the National Museum in Washington. The plates and other metallic utensils are described as being made of tin, and it may be remarked that the merits of tinplate were only then becoming appreciated. Another camp service, made of pewter, which seems to have a reasonably authentic claim to former ownership by Washington, was sold at the recent disposal of the collection of the late Mr. Erskine Hewitt. It comprises eleven large plates, twenty-eight medium-sized plates, and three bowls. It is understood to have been originally obtained by Washington from among General Braddock's effects after that officer was killed in 1755; and to have been given by Washington, during the Revolution, to Judge Hopper of New Jersey as a token of appreciation for the judge's frustration of a British raid in Bergen County. If at the time Washington had just acquired a much lighter and more easily portable service of tin, it seems logical to suppose he would readily have parted with the old, clumsier articles.

Besides its two cups, the Valley Forge Museum also owns a small set of bone-handled knives and forks which were once part of Washington's camp equipment. The Historical Society of Pennsylvania possesses a knife and fork given to the General during the Revolution by Charles Thomson, secretary to the Congress. They have a trick design; the prongs of the fork slide into the handle of the knife while the blade of the knife fits into the handle of the fork, thus forming one piece which can be carried in the pocket. The articles are too small to be really practicable and it seems improbable that Washington ever used them other than with humorous intent.

Unquestionably there are other articles still in existence which were once used on his camp table by General Washington, but it is almost impossible to prove their authenticity. From time to time objects, frequently of pewter, are brought forward with such a claim for them. Some may be what they purport to be, but it is rather difficult to picture the General going about the country shedding pewter plates.

—Parke-Bernet Galleries

Washington's Pewter Camp Service

This service, formerly in the collection of the late Erskine Hewitt, is recorded as having been given by General Washington to Judge Andrew Hopper of Bergen County, New Jersey. It consists of eleven chargers, twenty-eight medium-sized plates, and three small bowls. All but three pieces bear the touch of well-known London pewterers.

NICHOLAS SEVER'S PLATE RETURNS TO HARVARD

By W. Nicholas Dudley

A PIECE of marked 18th Century American silver accompanied by a document relating to it in the handwriting of the original owner is unusual enough, but an exhibit of 14 pieces all but one definitely mentioned in the document in which all but one are by the same outstanding silversmith, John Burt, and with 11 of them loaned for the exhibition by descendants of the original owner, is a unique achievement.

Such is the silver once owned by Nicholas Sever and now being shown in the Early American room at the Fogg Museum, Harvard University, Cambridge, Mass. All but one piece was the work of John Burt of Boston (1691-1745), whom many authorities on American silver rank second only to Edward Winslow and John Coney. These pieces are significant because they can be rigidly dated between 1715 and 1728, and on them are to be found fine specimens of three of the maker's four known marks. As a group they are invaluable for stylistic and signatory authenticity and all in all, furnish a chronological yardstick for other unmarked and undated silver of the period.

Of John Burt and his work we know that at his death in 1745 he left an estate of £6,460-4-9 and his tools inventoried at £238-7-6. Beside this he also had an extensive stock of bullion gold and silver and precious stones. Two of his sons, Samuel (1724-1754) and Benjamin (1729-1805) also were silversmiths. Burt, senior was a particularly prolific producer of the simpler pieces of hollow-ware, although he is known to have done some flat-ware and probably made a large amount of jewelry. In silver, his work is distinguished by simplicity, a sufficiency of restrained ornament, and no little degree of technical skill in design. All of these characteristics are exemplified in the Nicholas Sever exhibit.

Nicholas Sever, the original owner of this silver, was a Harvard College tutor and half of the pieces shown were gifts to him from his students. *Donum Pupillorum* or *Ex Dono Pupillorum* were the phrases used in marking such presents. How many other pieces of silver were presented to him we cannot know, but included in the exhibit at the Fogg Museum are a pair of chafing dishes or braziers, a pair of candlesticks and a small salver given to him in 1724, and a teapot and a cann, both presented four years later. From this one can judge that he was popular, to say the least, with the undergraduates and that some of them must have had liberal allowances, for the total weight of these seven pieces is 62 ounces, 15 pennyweight.

In the Spring of 1728 Nicholas Sever was preparing for some unknown reason to leave the Harvard faculty, although the fact that later in the year he married Sarah Warren Little of Kingston, landlady of the inn there where he later settled and became a local public figure, would seem to indicate it. But knowing that he was to leave Cambridge, Sever, being a methodical man, took stock of his plate and arranged for its safekeeping while he had no settled abode.

In his private ledger now owned by Major George F. Sever and shown by photostatic copy along with his silver, he made the following entries:

"1728

Apr:6: Ann invoice of my plate Vir:
A two Quart Tankard.
A Quart Tankard.
A pair of Chafing Dishes.
A pair of Candlesticks.
two Salvers A large & a Small one.
A pair of Canns.
two Porringers.
A Tea Pot.
two Salts. etc."

A little lower on the same page in the same handwriting is an entry of a few months later, just after Commencement Day, which fell on Friday, June 28, in that year. It concerns the safe keeping of this plate and reads:

SEVER'S SILVER INTACT AFTER TWO CENTURIES

All but the cann that has been converted into a pitcher are the work of John Burn, the 18th Century Boston Silversmith

—Fogg Art Museum

AMERICAN SILVER

"July 8th. Committed in trust
    to Deacon Cooledge
A quart silver tankard,
two porringers, two . . . ,
a large and a small salver
    All silver.
And to Steward Boardman, a large Tankard, a pair of chafing dishes, a pair of candlesticks, and a Tea Pot. All Silver."

Thus Nicholas Sever lacking present-day safe deposit vaults, endeavored to safeguard his plate until he would have further use for it such as by marriage at the ripe age of 48. We need not wait long, for further down on the same page four weeks later, he wrote: "Augst 9. Rec'd ye Plate from Mr. Boardman & Deacon Cooledge".

That was 204 years ago and yet today of the 14 pieces mentioned, only one, the two-quart tankard, had to be represented by another John Burt piece, and of the balance only the candlesticks are owned by other than Sever descendants. These sticks, however, were years ago presented to Harvard by the Rev. Winslow Warren Sever and stood on the mantel of the President's house during the administration of Charles W. Eliot. The rest is intact except that either one of the canns or the one quart tankard has disappeared. Otherwise the pieces are still in the possession of members of the Sever family and their cooperation in loaning them made this unique display possible.

—*Fogg Art Museum*

TWO-QUART TANKARD BY BURT
Made for the First Church Cambridge, it shows his craftsmanship and skill in handling the decorative detail

—*Fogg Art Museum*

ONE OF THE PAIR OF CANNS
Burt's vertical mark can be seen on the side near the handle

As the two-quart tankard could not be found the organizers of the display stepped across the street from Harvard Yard, so to speak, and borrowed one of the same size, also made by John Burt, from the First Church, Cambridge. This piece bears the mark *I.B* surmounted by a rude crown and inscribed in a shield. It was not unusual for American smiths to use the crown as if to imply a derived quality of royal patronage. The tankard is a plain, tapered, cylindrical form, with moulded base and lip, and a flat cover decorated with a straight gadrooned shoulder.

The scrolled thumb-piece and cast mask terminal of the handle were a detail just beginning to appear about 1724, a date which is borne out by the inscription on the front:
Belonging to the Church of Christ in Cambridge : 1724
and by the records of the church entered August 5, 1724: "Voted yt yr Should be a Tankard made of ye Silver money yt remains in Deacon Cooledges hands, for ye Communion table". It is quite proper to assume that Nicholas Sever's tankard was very similar to this one.

The pair of chafing dishes vary only slightly in height. Their other measurements are identical. They

TEAPOT DATED 1728

—Fogg Art Museum

It was given Sever by his students in that year according to the Latin inscription

bear the same crown and shield mark of John Burt as shown on the large tankard. The claw feet rest on wooden balls and they have the turned wooden handles and piercings typical of the period. On the base of each is *Donum Pupillorum 1724*. One has the initials *N S* for Nicholas Sever, and also, the inscription *E.P.S. to P.W.L.*, probably for Elizabeth Parsons Sever to Penelope Winslow (Sever) Lincoln. They were loaned by George F. Sever and Francis W. Sever.

With the candlesticks the crown and shield mark of John Burt occurs on the section of the base to the right of the inscription:

Donum Pupillorum
1724

The baluster stem and domed base are octagonal in section.

The quart tankard of the invoice has not been absolutely identified, so tankard or cann of that capacity is included. It is obvious at a glance that a spout has been added to this piece and that at a very late date. It does not follow the moulding of the rim, nor is the joining well done, nor the color of silver the same. It may be either the tankard or one of the canns mentioned in Sever's inventory. It has a bellied body with a hollow double scrolled handle and bears the mark of its maker, *W. Simkins*, in a cartouche to the left of the handle near the lip. This was for William Simpkins of Boston (1704-1780). It is the only piece in the collection believed to have been done by other than Burt, with whose work it suffers by comparison. It was loaned by James Warren Sever.

One of the pair of canns is shown, however, and from it we get a particularly fine, clear mark of the maker, *I. Burt* inscribed in a scrolled vertical cartouche. This may be seen to the left of the handle, near the lip. On the front of the bellied body is the inscription: *Ex Dono Pupillorum 1728* and on the bottom is a series of initials: *N. S., W. S., J. S., C. S.* and *C. W. S.*, standing for: Nicholas Sever, William Sever, John Sever, Charles Sever, and Charles William Sever, indicating that this piece passed from father to son in each generation. It is now owned by a daughter of *C. W. S.* and loaned by her.

The two porringers are almost identical. Another fine variant of the Burt mark in an oval, in which the first name spelled out is above the last, and occurs in the middle of the handles. On the solid portion of the keyhole pattern handle of one loaned by Dr. James Warren Sever are the initials *N. S. S.* for Nicholas and Sarah Sever. On the other are a series of initials and dates showing that like the cann this porringer passed from Nicholas through each generation to its present owner, Miss Jennie Seaton Harrison, who loaned it for this exhibit.

The teapot, typical of the finest design of the period, also has the inscription: *Ex Dono Pupillorum 1728*. The gracefully globular body has an octagonal spout, supported by a plain tongue. The rounded, fitted, hinged cover is surrounded by a delicately incised border with added scrolls at front and back. The apple-wood handle is riveted with silver sockets. There is no maker's mark visible. It was loaned by Miss Martha Sever.

There are also two very plain salvers. The large one has the inscription *Ex Dono Pupillorum* and while there is no maker's name, a close comparison with the smaller one which does bear John Burt's shield mark, and a consideration of such factors as provenance, tradition, and similarity of detail, leaves little or no doubt that both are by the same hand. The smaller salver is marked with the earlier inscription *Donum Pupillorum 1724* and

CHAFING DISH WITH BURT'S MARK

—Fogg Art Museum

The turned handle of wood and the claws holding wooden ball feet are good points

AMERICAN SILVER

on the top near the edge, appears the familiar shield mark of Burt. These were loaned by Robert Sever Hale and Richard Walden Hale, as were the last items of the invoice, the two salts. The latter are small and of the trencher type, oval in shape with plain moulded bands around top and base. The mark *I.B* enclosed in a shield, occurs in the concave top of each, although the shield has become obliterated in one and only the initials are visible.

So with the exception of the two-quart tankard, one of the canns or the quart tankard the various items on the inventory of Apr:6:1728 have come back for a time to the institution where their original owner once tutored the young men who showed their liking and appreciation for him in this concrete form.

NOTE: *For guidance and help, the author is indebted to Mr. Richard Walden Hale of Boston, Mr. Frederic Bruce Robinson, Assistant to the Directors of Fogg Museum, and to the thesis of a direct descendant of Nicholas Sever, Mr. Noel Sever O'Reilly.*

—Fogg Art Museum

THE SMALL SALVER
From this marked piece identification of the larger one as Burt's work is obvious

KITTERY'S RARELY SEEN COMMUNION PLATE

Seven fine pieces of old 18th century communion silver still owned by the parish of the First Church of Christ in Kittery, Maine. All pieces are the product of New England silversmiths and their possession by the church is easily explained by the prominence of their makers. (Top) Two-handled cup by Samuel Minott. (Second row, left) cup dated 1734 by William Whittemore; (center) Baptismal basin by Samuel Minott, dated 1759, and (right) another Whittemore cup. (Lower row, left) The Third Whittemore cup; (center) sprinkling font by Zachariah Bridgen, circa 1770, and (right) cup by John Burt, dated 1728.

Large Pieces of Lear Silver

In the center a cann by Daniel Roger, Newport; at the left a small unmarked American cup; at the right cream pitcher by Samuel Meriton, London, circa 1750; at right and left, footed salt dishes and pepper shakers by David and Robert Hennell, London, 1769, and by an unknown London maker with mark I.D-I.M in Swiss cross.

The Silver of Capt. Tobias Lear of Portsmouth

By Stephen Decatur

IT is a matter of general observation that in this country family possessions tend to become scattered in the course of a few generations. Division through inheritance and the normal rate of disposal and loss have their share in this rapid dispersion but more is due to the American habit of shifting domiciles with a frequency greater than in any other part of the world. Hence it is a rare event when more than a few pieces of furniture from the same estate remain together after 150 years unless, by some fortuitous chance, they have been kept in the house for which they were originally obtained.

This regrettable dissipation seems especially virulent with old silver. It is so easily portable; so readily convertible; and, once separated, seldom indeed are the various objects ever again brought together. Recently, however, a group of old silver was assembled where the pieces were not only interesting in themselves but had an unusual historic association since all had belonged to Captain Tobias Lear, the father of Colonel Tobias Lear, George Washington's private secretary and trusted friend. As the Captain died in 1781, it is really remarkable that so much of his plate could be brought together and, actually, the opportunity occurred almost by chance.

No other house in New England can boast of such a long and close connection with George and Martha Washington and their families as the old Lear home on Hunking street in Portsmouth, N. H. For practically 16 years Colonel Lear lived as a member of the Washington household, being regarded almost as an adopted son. Two of his wives were nieces of Martha Washington. Concurrently, an intimacy developed between the families which spanned three generations and extended 60 years. Two years ago the venerable house was on the point of collapse. Fortunately it was taken over by the present public-spirited owner, a man who is holding it until sufficient funds are secured for its acquisition by the Society for the Preservation of New England Antiquities. Meanwhile, it is open to visitors dur-

The Lear Coat of Arms

The crests on the silver were probably done from this rendering then owned by the Lear family.

ing the summer months and is gradually being restored to its original condition. Work on the interior has already been completed, so that it now presents much the same appearance it must have had when Washington made his famous call on Madam Mary Lear, his secretary's mother, in the autumn of 1789. Much care has been taken to secure the desired effect and fortunately many of the original furnishings could be located for study. In the course of these investigations, pieces of the Lear plate kept turning up and finally it was found possible to assemble and photograph them. In all, 19 pieces were located. Eight were early American and the balance old London silver.

Undoubtedly the small cream pitcher is the oldest piece. It bears English marks, but the date letter, unfortunately, is so worn away from repeated polishings as to be indecipherable. However, the maker's mark, S.M. in a rectangle, is readable and it is that of Samuel Meriton who was working in London in 1747. The unusual inverted pear form of the bottom of the pitcher, a design used only during the so-called transition period, seems to confirm the date of manufacture as close to 1750.

It is impossible to determine exactly to which Tobias Lear this creamer originally belonged, since the name was borne by father and eldest son for five successive generations, Washington's secretary being the fifth. The choice in this case is between the second and third of the name and most probably

96

it was obtained by the latter. The first Tobias Lear in this country died before 1700; the second, born about 1680, was hardly likely to be acquiring plate in 1750, considering his age, and the fourth (1737-1781) was a minor at that time. Tobias Lear the third, besides being a large landowner, was a sea captain and could well have purchased the creamer in England himself. He it was who built the house in Portsmouth about 1740, a splendid example of the hip-roofed style of the period. The family was socially prominent and, as his wife, Elizabeth Hall of Exeter, inherited a considerable fortune, he probably lived in a reasonably pretentious manner. The inventory of his estate, made after his death in 1751, shows he possessed a respectable amount of plate for his time.

The creamer was inherited by his son, Captain Tobias Lear the fourth (1737-1781) and unfortunately seems to be the only piece from the first three generations of the family to have survived. Quite possibly the other older pieces were turned in for more up-to-date and fashionable designs as was so frequently the case. It was the Captain who acquired the rest of the silver in the group. Like his father, he became a sea captain and between 1760 and 1770 made voyages to London in command of the ship *Panther*. Undoubtedly he purchased the other English pieces there himself in the course of his various trips. The six tablespoons, stamped with the London date letter for 1768, were probably obtained first. They bear the mark T.W in a rectangle, the touch of the well-known London silversmith, Thomas Wallis, and are unusually excellent examples of his work.

Next come the two round salt dishes with the date letter for 1769 and the mark of the London silversmiths, David and Robert Hennell, whose work is held in such high esteem. The tall pepper shakers have the London date letter for the following year. They are extremely fine and show every evidence of having been made by a mastercraftsman; yet apparently they are the work of an hitherto unrecorded firm of silversmiths, as the mark upon them, I.D.-I.M in a Swiss cross, does not appear on any of the available lists.

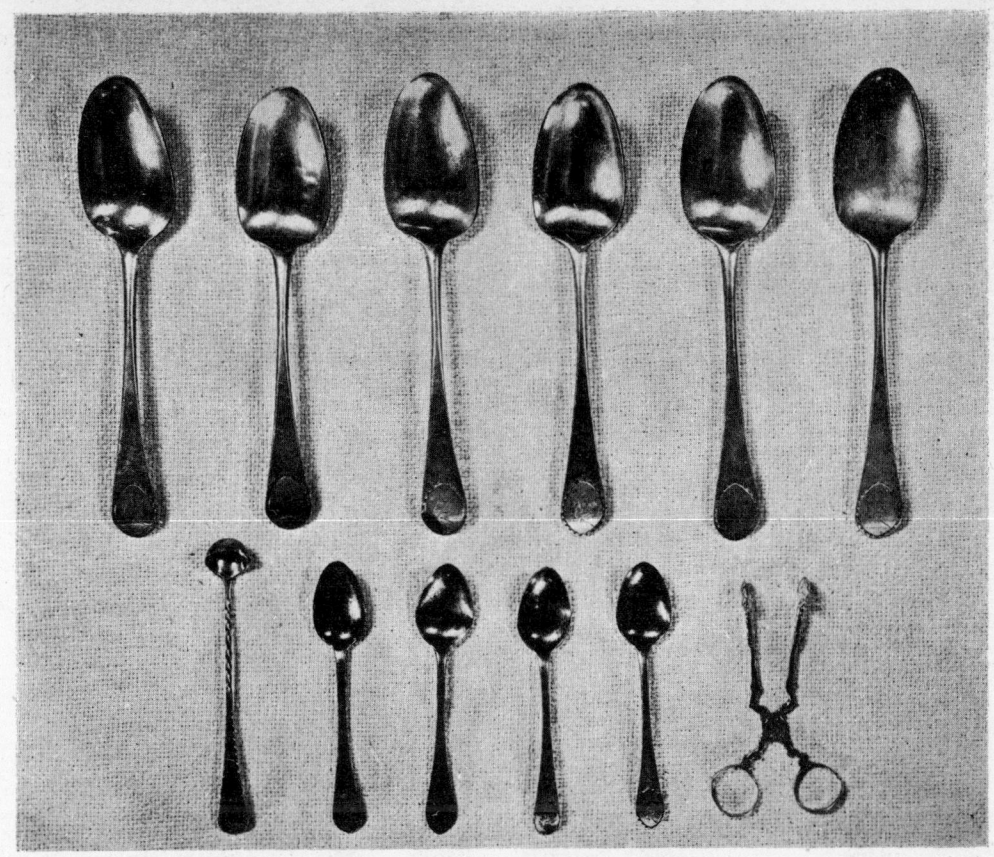

Smaller Pieces of Lear Silver

In the upper row are six tablespoons, London, 1768, by Thomas Wallis. Beneath are four teaspoons by Samuel Drowne of Portsmouth, N. H., and a conserve spoon and sugar tongs, both of which are unmarked American pieces.

The most interesting of the American pieces is the mug or cann, a very fine example of the work of Daniel Rogers (c.1745-1792), one of the best of the Newport, R. I., silversmiths. Beside it in the group is a little cup only two and one-quarter inches high. Unfortunately it bears no maker's mark, nor do the scissors-like sugar tongs and the conserve spoon with the delicate twisted handle. In the case of the latter two articles, the absence of a mark is probably due to lack of space.

The conserve spoon, however, is so similar in design and ornamentation to the four small teaspoons that it can confidently be attributed to the same maker. These spoons bear the mark of Samuel Drowne (1749-1815) of Portsmouth, N. H., and, as might be expected of this excellent craftsman, they are exceptionally graceful and nicely chased, even though they must have been made early in his career.

This American silver can be approximately dated as having been made between 1760 and 1775. Nearly all the pieces are engraved with the initials T.-M. L. for Tobias and Mary (Stillson) Lear and, as the couple were married in 1757, none of them can be earlier than this date. Nor is it probable that any of them can be later than 1775. From the beginning of the Revolution until his death in 1781, the Captain was in charge of the shipyard owned by his cousin, Governor John Langdon, where he supervised the building of the

The Lear House, Built Circa 1740.

From an oil painting about 1800, it shows the ell that has since been removed.

Continental frigate *Ranger*, Paul Jones' first command; the privateer *Portsmouth;* and the ship-of-the-line *America* which was presented by the government to France and which was the largest vessel to be constructed in this country up to that time. But the Captain received very little compensation for his work and that in Continental script; like nearly everybody he was hard pressed financially and he would hardly have purchased any plate during those years.

In addition to the initials, all the silver, with the exception of the sugar tongs where there is insufficient room, is marked with a unicorn's head erased— the crest of the Lears. This crest, as well as the entire coat-of-arms used by the Lear family, is identical with that borne by Sir Peter Lear of Linbridge in Devonshire who, emigrating about 1630 to the Barbadoes, amassed a fortune and, returning to England, was created a baronet in 1660. It seems quite certain that the first Tobias Lear in this country came from Devonshire about 1660 or slightly before. Relationship between him and the baronet has not been established, although it probably exists. In any event the arms were used by the family in America at a very early date and Captain Lear possessed a painting of them which is still in existence.

Besides his son, Colonel Tobias Lear the fifth, the Captain had a daughter. He bequeathed her one-third of his household goods and the balance to his widow. As the Colonel predeceased his mother, Madam Lear in turn left all her household furnishings to the daughter also. Eventually, therefore, she inherited all the plate and with one exception all the pieces in the group descended to her heirs. The little cup has a different history. Madam Lear had a great niece named for her, Mary Lear Blunt, born in 1798. On the occasion of the infant's baptism, consequently, Madam Lear gave her the cup suitably engraved, "M. Lear to M. L. Blunt," to commemorate the event.

Museum of the City of New York

SILVER CAUDLE CUP WITH VAN CORTLANDT COAT OF ARMS
This early New York cup was the work of Gerrit Onkelbag who was a freeman of New York City in 1698.

Old Canadian Silver

By Marius Barbeau

THE silver crosses discovered in the past hundred years in old Indian graves from Georgia to Wisconsin and Ontario are all of one type and bear such makers' marks as C A and R C. Puzzled archæologists at the time of their discovery presumed these initials to mean Cardinal Richelieu and Richelieu Cardinal, because these pieces of silver had been found where they seemed to have been lost during the régime of the French cardinal. One was in a grave mound in Georgia, traced back imaginatively to the De Soto expedition of 1540, and some of the others in the ancient Hurons' country in Ontario.

These amusingly faulty ascriptions would not have been offered had the archæologists known that among a host of Canadian 18th- and early 19th-Century silversmiths, two of them, Charles Arnoldi and Robert Cruickshank, had supplied the Montreal fur traders with large quantities of silver ornaments and trinkets. These were distributed from 1775 to 1840 along the trade routes to the west and the south. It must be granted that, until these last few decades, not the least attention had been paid to the long-sustained existence of a Canadian silvercraft covering two hundred and fifty years, and to the interesting evolution and features of this craft which are unique.

Canadian antique silver in small part goes back to France—at least two hundred pieces so far catalogued are actually old French silver; but it was predominantly French-Canadian made, as about one thousand such pieces have been recorded. This is only a part of what is still available. It was also derivative of British and other Continental prototypes, as shown by the few hundred recorded items made after 1770 in Montreal, Halifax, St. John, and Quebec by British, German, and Swiss craftsmen. Finally, it was strikingly original in the hundred of items made by native gold and silversmiths of the North Pacific Coast—the Tlingit of Alaska, and the Haida and Tsimsyan of the islands and the coast south of the Alaskan border.

The few samples of the gold and silver work here commented on merely suggest the diversity of early sources, the tendency of the Canadian craftsmen to adopt themselves to their surroundings, and to follow their own ways of working and designing under the New World influences. Canada in this respect should be considered as a part of the North American culture and studied for the important historical elements it furnished in the two or three hundred years of Continental penetration and semi-opened frontiers, when a New World culture was in formation.

The large silver reliquary at the Huron mission of Indian Lorette near Quebec (Illustration III), serves to represent the two hundred items of old French silver so far identified and still extant in eastern Canada. Known under the name of "Chemise de Notre-Dame," it was made by Thomas Mahon of Chartres and is dated 1676. It was presented to the Jesuits for their Huron mission. Well preserved, about twelve inches high and one and one-half inches in depth, it is a perfect example of French provincial craftsmanship. It is exquisitely engraved on both sides with pictures of the Virgin. It is not the only one of its kind possessed by the Indian missions of New France. Two splendid examples of Paris silver are the monstrances or *ostensoirs* of the Caughnawaga Iroquois mission near Montreal and that of Indian Lorette. An inscription in French around the rim of the base of one of these reads: "Claude Prévost, former alderman of Paris, and Elizabeth Legendre, his wife, have given me that I may serve at the Jesuit church of Three Rivers, in the year 1664."

A number of chalices, ciboria, sanctuary lamps bishops' crooks, reliquaries, crosses, statuettes, a large bust of the Jesuit martyr Father Brébeuf, ewers, and basins likewise of antique French provenance are still preserved in the religious communities and old churches and missions of Quebec and Montreal. These bear the marks of Paris and provincial towns and the touches of such noted craftsmen as Claude Ballin (1688), Guillaume Loir (1716), Pierre Hannier (1716), Eloi Guérin (1727), all of Paris, as well as Thomas Mahon, of Chartres.

Valuable as is the old French silver in Canada, it is less interesting in a way than the authentic French-Canadian work of the silver and goldsmiths in Quebec and Montreal, who worked from 1700 for al-

Illustration I
Ewers and Basin by Paul Lambert or Sieur Saint-Paul
This pair of ewers and basin were made by this Quebec silversmith circa 1725 for the Indian mission of Lorette. The basin is oval in shape. It is twelve inches long and nine inches wide.

Illustration II
By Françoise Ranvoyzé
This monstrance was made for the Quebec Ursulines about 1780 by this outstanding Quebec silversmith, whose dates were 1739-1819.

Illustration III
Reliquary Made at Chartres
Dated 1676, it was made there by Thomas Mahon for the Jesuit mission among the Hurons of Lorette. Beautifully engraved, it is representative of the early pieces of religious silver made in France and taken to Canada.

A TREASURY OF OLD SILVER

Illustration IV

By Michel Coton

This monstrance at the church of Sainte-Famille, Island of Orleans, was made by this Quebec silversmith about 1700.

most two centuries. The beauty and richness of their work and the continuity in style and decoration of the French tradition have long made the owners of such old Canadian silver believe that their treasures came from France in the early days. The author alone has recorded around one thousand pieces of silver and gold made by French-Canadians, whose ancestors had migrated to Canada before 1700, from Paris, Arras, Rouen and elsewhere and it is estimated that the total number of such pieces would be impressive.

Among the craftsmen of the French period (1690 to 1759), the leading masters were: Michel LeVasseur, at Quebec, who about 1705 took two apprentices—one of whom, Jacques Pagé dit Carcy, is known to us by his mark; and four others whose marks are represented in our repertory—François Landron, Jean-Baptiste Meson Basse, Michel Coton (Illustration IV), who were Quebec merchants as well as craftsmen, and Ignace-Francois Delezenne. Sieur Saint-Paul, whose work we know best because of thirty recorded pieces, was the most important of the French colonial period (Illustration I).

Paul Lambert or Sieur Saint-Paul, the son of Paul of the same name from Arras, France, used the mark of P L with a lily flower over it. His mark has already been found on both church and domestic silver. Among the pieces bearing his mark are three chalices, a bishop's crook, three ciboria, a sanctuary lamp, two pairs of ewers and basin, a holy-water pail, two altar flower vases, three piscines, two small boxes for sacred oils, two ampullas, two porringers, a cup or goblet with cover, a plate, and a ladle. These show the excellence of his art and his originality. His inspiration undoubtedly was traditional and may have followed models available in his time; yet we have not found elsewhere quite the same type of work, wherein gadroons are in low relief and stippled engraving is used extensively around the embossed designs. His style, as well as his ornamentation, have a charm that is akin to the best in folk handicrafts. It is distinctly hand work and sensitive, is a bit casual and does not in the least look stereotyped in any of its parts. He may be considered a leading silversmith of New France, and ranking only after the later craftsmen, François Ranvoyzé and Laurent Amiot.

The loosening of the ties with France after the British conquest, indeed, fostered the autonomous development in the craft—first, in Quebec and, later, in Montreal. Following the tracks of his predecessor, François Ranvoyzé (1739-1819) became the leader of the Quebec school, whose inspiration was traditional, yet whose personal skill, originality and industry, were outstanding (Illustrations II, VI and VII). His mark, so far, has been recorded on at least one hundred and seventy-seven pieces of church plate. Altogether two hundred and sixty pieces may be ascribed to him, covering a wide variety of forms from religious to domestic items. His working career covered nearly forty years. The style, decorative treatment—which was rich and heavily ornamental, repoussé and engraving, also incidental casting of figures —of Ranvoyzé was that of an artist rather than of a mere craftsman. A past master of his calling, he was a creative worker

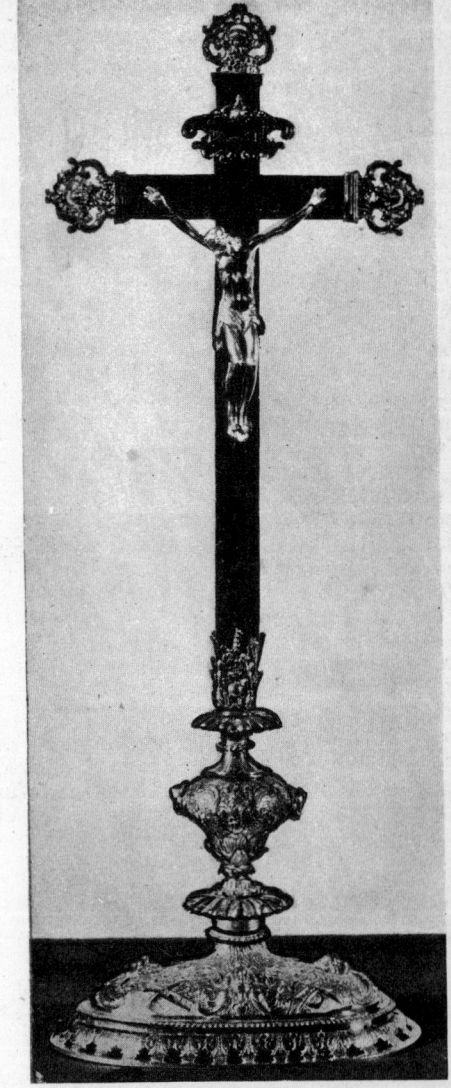

Illustration VI

Crucifix by François Ranvoyzé

This and the monstrance in Illustration II were made for the Quebec Ursulines about 1780, and are examples of fine religious silver made by this Quebec silversmith.

Illustration V

Ewers by Laurent Amiot of Quebec

Used as CHOCOLATIERES or AIGUIERES, that at the left bears a lengthy inscription stating that it was given as a tribute of gratitude to the people of Isle-aux-Coudres after the salvage in 1832 of the brig ROSALIND.

who decidedly left his mark in Canada. He also worked gold, as is shown by the fine church plate of the Islet church on the lower St. Lawrence.

His one-time apprentice, and then his competitor and rival, was Laurent Amiot (1764-1839), who followed in his footsteps; yet in some respects differed from him, as he went to Paris to complete his training in 1783. On his return he introduced a taste for current French forms and style as well as shop equipment. He was the only Canadian silversmith comparable to Ranvoyzé in quality of work and length of his active career, of more than fifty years. In quantity of production, he even surpassed his older master. We know three hundred and fifty-two pieces that either bear his mark LA or can be ascribed to him.

As the contemporary fashions from abroad were, after 1790, gaining ground in French Canada, Amiot readily adapted them when his clientele called for domestic silver (Illustration V), such as large ewers, tureens, teapots, cream jugs, and ladles. His silver of this sort might well be mistaken from French, British or American. Amiot's business in his Côte de la Montagne shop was so well established that at the time of manship of the 18th Century was largely a Quebec achievement, new developments took place at the end of that century —particularly in Montreal, which became a new and important center for silverwork in Canada. The growing British influence in Montreal, particularly because of work done by Robert Cruickshank for the Indian fur trade, did not materially interfere with the vitality of the French tradition in church silver. We find a few silversmiths there whose work compares well with their Quebec contemporaries, for instance: Pierre Huguet-Latour (circa 1749-1817), Salomon Marion (circa 1818-1832), and Paul Morand (circa 1819-1846).

Only a brief mention can be made here of the vast quantity of fine Canadian silver made by craftsmen of British and other origin in the eastern provinces of Nova Scotia, New Brunswick and Quebec. Like the French, the British residents in Montreal, Quebec, St. John, and Halifax were satisfied at first with importations. Some of the earliest jewelers, watchmakers and silversmiths in these centers were chiefly importers. They advertised the newest London creations received via the last ships. Yet John Langdon, who has recently made a study of the silversmiths of the Maritime Provinces, has listed no less than thirty craftsmen with British names, and a few others of Swiss, German, or French origin. His conclusion, as yet unpublished, is that, "sufficient data have been accumulated to show that silversmithing was an interesting and not altogether unimportant Maritime industry as late as 1850 and even a short while later." Its earliest pioneer, even prior to 1753, was Josiah Allen, of Halifax.

The outstanding British craftsman in Canada undoubtedly was Robert Cruickshank (circa 1775-1809), who may have had his training in London, migrated to Canada via the United States, and became an important silversmith and merchant in Montreal. And his influence, chiefly in domestic silver and ornamental silver for the Indian trade, seems to have been considerable.

A few Montreal silversmiths and jewelers, from the time of George Savage—that is, 1815— opened shops in Montreal and began to build up a clientele and a business that slowly progressed through the following hundred years. They found, locally, British, French-Canadian, Swiss and German craftsmen, whom, in several instances, they employed.

Illustration VIII

Silver Bracelets by a Tlingit Indian

Quebec and Montreal silversmiths numbered no less than one hundred and forty in all. Over eighty of them were French-speaking and over sixty English. The Maritime craftsmen totaled about forty; this means a grand total of Canadian craftsmen (excluding those of native extraction) of about one hundred and eighty, whose names are now on lists compiled by Mr. Langdon and me.

Far apart from the silversmiths of eastern Canada and also from their Indian imitators —there were many of these in the past century, principally among the Iroquoians—we find a group of native craftsmen on the North Pacific Coast who stand by themselves. This group consists of Haida, Tlingit and Tsimsyan silver and goldsmiths, of the islands and main coast immediately north and south of the Alaska frontier. The art of these craftsmen, purely decorative and ornamental, is quite original and remarkable. It is unique. Its features conform to those of the other varied crafts practiced by the same nations. It is the latest development in the recent growth of a native art that is nowhere else surpassed for individuality and refinement of stylization.

The characteristics of this native work, consisting of bracelets, brooches and head ornaments are both individual and derivative. They are individual in so far as they are restricted to ornamental objects which involve little or no embossing in hammering gold or silver coins into narrow convex bands, highly polished and rather thin, and into varied rounded and disklike surfaces with soldered pin attachment. As the engraving of ornamental patterns on the surface was customary, it called for great skill in the engraver, and drew upon the resources of other pictorial arts. Thus with slight transformation the current stylization of totemic or heraldic figures on totem poles, in house-front paintings and in all sorts of domestic and ceremonial objects was absorbed. In this, such silver was wholly derivative, yet original.

The decoration of the silver work among the Haidas, the Tlingit and the Coast Tsimsyans conformed to standards that were consistently carried out. The engravers used a stock of conventional patterns and symbols into which they injected new life and incessant variations. No two pieces, even of a pair, ever being quite alike. The first requirement was that the whole outer polished surface must be filled to the edge with design. Thus features and limbs

Illustration IX

Bracelet by Edenshaw

of the totemic animal were either enlarged in proportion with the rest, or boldly reduced or torn apart.

Technical devices, together with the tools used by these Indian silversmiths, were obviously borrowed from the white craftsmen who must also have helped in the first stages of the native craft. The early Russians at Sitka, who were versed in metal work, contributed much in this way. Indeed the earliest native imitators of the Russians were their close neighbors, the Tlingits, the most noted among them, Sitka Jack and his wife (Illustration VIII), about 1870 and 1880, and undoubtedly a number of others. Since 1880 the Haidas of Massett, on the Queen Charlotte Islands, have specialized in working in silver, where a few of them until recently have excelled; the most noted among them was Charles Edenshaw who, when he died a very old man in 1924, left a great deal of beautiful work after him (Illustration IX).

Illustration VII

Candleholder by Ranvoyzé

One of a set of twelve of varying sizes at the church of Saint-Augustin, Portneuf, Quebec. This one is twenty-one inches high.

his death it passed complete, with clientele and equipment, to his kinsman and associate, François Sasseville (1797-1864). From Sasseville it passed to another kinsman, Pierre Lespérance (1819-1882), who moved this workshop to Côte du Palais, Quebec. From Lespérance it again passed to Ambroise Lafrance. He was still working in 1905, when E. A. Jones, the British silver expert, visited his shop and had Lafrance's son, in training as a silversmith, make a cross and a cup for him. Some of the silver and drawings then collected by Mr. Jones are said to be now in the Mabel Brady Garvan Collection at the Yale Gallery of Fine Arts, New Haven, Connecticut.

If Canadian silver crafts-

Three Centuries of French Domestic Silver

A Review of the Unique 1938 Exhibition at the Metropolitan Museum

FOR the first time an American museum has assembled a loan exhibition that makes graphic the sweep of the work of the French silversmiths from early in the 16th Century to the close of the Empire period. This is *Three Centuries of French Domestic Silver* which opened at the Metropolitan Museum of Art, May 18, to continue for four months. When it closes on September 18 and the 850 pieces on display are returned to 23 private collectors and five European museums, it will probably be a generation before another such comprehensive exhibition is again attempted in this country. To borrow the needed pieces was indeed a feat.

Over a year has been spent by Preston Remington and other members of the museum staff in locating the pieces on display. In some instances remarkable examples of French silver were found in private collections outside of France that had been unknown even to the best informed French museum authorities. An example of this is the silver-gilt toilet service of 21 pieces from the collection of the late Duke of Devonshire. Made by Pierre Prevost, Paris, 1670-71, it is of unusual interest since it bears the arms and cipher of William of Orange and his wife Mary before they became King and Queen of England and best known to collectors for the period that was named for them.

Although the three centuries, of course, include the years when the House of Bourbon was at its height, only four or five examples of silver made for the French kings and nobles are on display in this truly representative exhibition. It is a mute reminder of the series of royal edicts which confiscated the plate of the wealthy to be melted and converted into coin to help finance the succession of wars in which France was involved during the 17th and 18th Centuries. To this purpose, the French kings also sacrificed their own plate. In fact, it was necessary to look outside of France for the few pieces on display which were found in England and Portugal and in the Museum's own collection. The latter includes the Orloff service that Catherine the Great of Russia presented to her favorite, Count Orloff, and repurchased from his heirs at his death. But for the golden jubilee that the King of Sweden is celebrating this year, some remarkable French silver that was presented to Gustavus III and is still the property of the Swedish crown would probably have been included in this exhibition.

Among the pieces of princely ownership are the very early pilgrim's bottle once owned by Henry III and given by him together with two basins to the Order of Saint Esprit; a soup tureen and platter and wine cooler made for Louis, Duc d'Orléans (1703-1752); and a sauce boat bearing the fleur-de-lis of France, made for Madame de Pompadour (1754-55). The pieces made for the Duc d'Orléans have remained in the possession of his descendants and were loaned to the exhibition from the collections of the present Ducs de Vendôme and de Nemours. If as elaborate and intricate pieces of silver were made for junior members of the Bourbon family and for the woman who exerted such an influence upon Louis XV, one can imagine how impressive must have been the plate that the French silversmiths executed on royal command. Certainly it must have matched the palaces.

After the passing of the House of Bourbon, Napoleon Bonaparte kept the silversmiths busy after he elevated himself to the rank of emperor, and the exhibition contains a number of pieces executed by his orders or for presentation to him. Among the examples of this period on display are a tureen, a coffeepot, and two candelabra from a silver-gilt table service said to have been given by Napoleon to his sister Pauline and her husband Prince Camillo Borghese of Italy; and the extraordinary tea and coffee service originally made for Prince Lubomyrski of Cracow, Poland.

If the Parisian silversmiths, 175 of whom are represented in this exhibition, played an important part in French silver history through the patronage they enjoyed of monarchs and noblemen at home and abroad, the Metropolitan Museum display also brings into full focus the work of the provincial craftsmen. There are 30 cities represented by some 230 examples of their work and in many instances one finds that the various provincial centers of the silversmithing craft had distinct characteristics based on the tastes of the particular clientele.

There were the silversmiths of Strasbourg who sold a large part of their output to Germans. Their customers were partial to silver-gilt pieces and so the majority of those shown at the Metropolitan are of this type. In a lesser degree this also held

—Lent by the Duke of Portland

A Classic Inkstand by Philibert Trouvé
Made in Paris in 1698, it was purchased in France by Matthew Prior, English poet and diplomat of the period.

—Lent by the Ducs de Vendome and de Nemours

Made for Louis, Duc d'Orléans
This elaborate soup tureen and platter was made in Paris, 1733-34, by Thomas Germain, considered the greatest silversmith of France.

—Lent by the Musée des Arts Décoratifs, Paris

Sauceboat for Madame de Pompadour
This ornate piece was made by François Joubert, Paris, 1754-55. Part of the design is fleur-de-lis of the Bourbon kings.

FRENCH SILVER

with the craftsmen of Metz. Similarly, silversmiths working in northern France catered somewhat to the trade of the Low Countries. Consequently, their pieces often have Dutch characteristics, and the masters of Toulouse wrought in a more ornate design to please the Spanish taste for which much of their work was destined.

While the French system of marking silver is involved, especially in its fine points, the fundamental procedure may be as readily understood as that of the English. First, the craftsman applied his own mark, most frequently his initials and some carefully chosen device. Sometimes, as in Strasbourg, the mark was the craftsman's name fully spelled out. Next, the piece was taken to the mint in Paris or one of its branches in the provincial cities where the amount of tax was ascertained and indicated by the mark known as *poinçon de charge*. This was followed by submitting the piece to the wardens of the guild to which the craftsman belonged. If it conformed to the standards imposed by regulation, the warden's mark was added and then the piece went back to the mint where, after the tax had been paid, the final mark, *poinçon de décharge*, was impressed and the piece was then ready for sale. It is by understanding these four marks and the various changes that took place in them through the years that enables one to identify the work of a craftsman and date the piece under consideration.

As a group, the 733 pieces of 18th and early 19th Century silver on display are particularly significant when one realizes that this was the period when the Gallic silversmiths supplied the inspiration and ideas that were copied all over the Continent and in England. It is true that some of the pieces are so elaborate and ornate as to be oppressive, but even with them the originals of design and execution which craftsmen in other countries followed directly or indirectly are apparent.

Further, while the French palace silver is over-ornate, the silver of the 16th and 17th Centuries, as made in France, possessed a simple dignity much akin to that made by the craftsmen of England and America. There is, for example, the two-handled silver-gilt cup made in Paris, 1620, which foretells the American caudle cup of almost a century later. Another example of this similarity of form is to be found in the dish warmer, Paris, 1719-20. It is very close to those made in this country at about the same time.

The porringer was an essential piece of silver in America and our craftsmen frequently lavished their best work on it. With the French its counterpart was the écuelle, a two-handled dish often with cover, used for serving individual portions of soup and other foods. A number of these are included in the exhibition and are particularly interesting since the shape and decoration of the handles bears a definite relation to the handles on American porringers. There is some doubt regarding the purpose served by our porringers. Is it not possible that the known use of these French equivalents may offer a clew?

The extremes to which French craftsmen went, especially when executing commissions for foreign kings, is aptly illustrated by a number of pieces made for the rulers of Portugal and loaned for the exhibition by the Museu Nacional de Arte Antiga at Lisbon. The high point of this extravagance seems to have been reached in a teakettle and stand done in the Chinese manner. The work of François Thomas Germain, Paris, 1756-62, it is almost a comic picture done in silver. The kettle itself is mellon-shaped with a spout in the form of a game cock's head, while the elaborate lid is a grotesque Chinese head surmounted by a typical flat hat of straw. Incongruous as it may seem, the stand and lamp for this tour de force in silver is restrained and classic in its design. This craftsman was, of course, the son of Thomas Germain, who is conceded to have been the greatest craftsman that France ever produced.

As is proper, the exhibition

—*Metropolitan Museum of Art*
Made for the Portuguese King
A coffee pot characteristically French in design and execution, by François Thomas Germain, Paris, 1756-57.

—*Lent by the Musée de Malmaison*
Presented to Napoleon
Part of the coronation gift from the City of Paris, this silver-gilt soup tureen and stand was made by Henry Auguste, Paris, 1804.

contains a number of specimens of the work of the elder Germain. These include the two pieces made for Louis, Duc d'Orléans, already referred to, and a silver-gilt teapot that bears the arms of William, Viscount Bateman. When Napoleon became Emperor of France his favorite silversmith was Martin Guillaume Biennais and the latter executed a wide range of silver for his imperial patron. The designs of many of these were by Percier and Fontaine who were Napoleon's architects. Some of the pieces by Biennais have classic restraint. Others are overpowering in size and ornamentation, a symbol in silver of the vanity that overtook Napoleon after he became emperor.

Considering the influence of Huguenot silversmiths on the craft both in England and America, it is unfortunate that lack of available data made it impossible to indicate in this exhibition which of the craftsmen represented belonged to this religious minority.

To have shown the type of work and design that these Protestant Frenchmen made in their native land would have made interesting comparisons possible with the work that they produced after the Revocation of the Edict of Nantes forced them to emigrate either across the Channel or the Atlantic. It might also have shown whether they were largely provincial craftsmen or whether some of them were Parisians.

Six silversmiths who followed their craft in La Rochelle are represented in the exhibition. It is reasonable to suppose that most, if not all, of these were Huguenots. But in any surmising as to what the silversmiths of this sect made in their native land one must look largely among the examples of the 17th Century. In this exhibition some 80 pieces of this period are on display. Characterized by simple form and restraint of decoration, they are a refreshing contrast to the over-ornate creations of the Napoleonic years.

—*Lent by Camille Plantevignes*
An Example of Classic Design
A plate and cover from the famous service given by Catherine the Great to her favorite, Orloff. By Jacques Nicolas Roettiers, Paris, 1771-72.

French Silversmiths Excelled but Germans More Prolific

By Seymour Wyler

THE earliest known French silver goes back to the Roman invasion when horse trappings were decorated with silver and gold. St. Eloi, 588 to 659, was the foremost of early smiths and did more to promote the industry than any other man of his time. He organized the first Guild and secured government permission so that it was its own law-making body with full privileges. Incidentally this was not only the first Guild to be organized in France, but probably the earliest anywhere. The French had a natural appreciation of art and preceded any country in Europe by several centuries in fully understanding and welcoming the art of precious metal work.

In St. Eloi's day the craft was practiced only by the priesthood. Not until the beginning of the 12th Century did the art of silversmithing become wholly secularized. The actual laws governing silver and goldsmithing in France up to the latter part of the 18th Century were:

1275—The first law was enacted requiring the use of a town mark.

1313—The first punch of guaranty was used. It was denoted by a fleur de lys in a lozenge.

1416—Usage of date letters was introduced.

Understanding what these laws constituted and their far-reaching effect on French silversmithing is most important for the collector. At first when the town mark was introduced and required it showed that a definite importance had been accorded to the industry. Within the next 40 years came the guaranty mark and with the date letter a century later, the first actual system of hall-marking silver was established in France. The mark of guaranty was very similar to that used in other countries to denote the actual fine silver content of a piece.

Under Louis XII a new office of Farmer of the Reserve was created. This person was required to impress his mark next to the maker's mark to show that duty had been charged. The law also required that he impress another mark to indicate that the duty had been paid and the piece was ready to be marketed. These peculiar punches were used until the duty was abolished. In 1797 the duty was reimposed but was levied at the time of the imposition of the first mark, so the discharge mark was abolished forever. The standard of the silver was also denoted by the same mark, so French silver from that date on only bore the maker's mark, the duty mark, and the town mark.

The luxury-loving French kings who were continually in debt or at war, caused France to suffer a greater loss than any country in the world as far as silver was concerned. Under the reign of Louis IV, all of the fine ecclesiastical plate was melted. In short, the extravagances of the Louis plus the Revolution sent all except carefully guarded pieces to the melting pot in wholesale manner.

The earliest piece of French silver still extant is dated about 1380.

—S. Wyler Inc.

16th Century French Wine Jug

German Rose Water Bowl

Made at Strassburg, 1682, by Johann George Burger

—S. Wyler Inc.

FRENCH AND GERMAN SILVER

Probably the most important is the famous and beautiful Cup of the Kings of France and England. Originally made in France and sent as a gift to the King of England, it was later returned to France, then sent to Spain, and finally to England again, where it may be seen today in the British Museum. Regarded as the finest piece of French silver in the world, it depicts the life of St. Agnes beautifully worked in relief.

The most outstanding name in later French silver history is that of Ociot, credited with being the creator of the style known as Empire. Rivalled in excellence only by the Brothers Adam in England, Ociot's designs spread like wildfire throughout Europe, and few styles in any period have enjoyed such lasting favor. Royalty all over Europe commissioned him to make services in this Empire style and much of his silver is in existence today.

However, the finest collections of French plate will not be found in France. The Kings and royal families of Europe and England were eager for these fine pieces and collected them carefully. Today the most outstanding collection of French silver in the world is in the possession of the English royal family.

—S. Wyler Inc.

Made in Dresden, 1751

—S. Wyler Inc.

French Cast Candlestick

One of a set of four. Made in Paris, circa 1790.

French silver is much sought after by collectors, and its value is great. The pieces are beautifully made, delicately designed, and finely proportioned. With the possible exception of Great Britain, perhaps no other country can point with so much pride to its silversmith's art.

Germany

No European country made a greater quantity of fine plate than the early Germans. Their natural love of things that would display their wealth and power especially fostered the silver trade.

There is a wealth of German ecclesiastical plate dating from the 12th Century to be seen today. Fine gold and silver objects were produced as early as the 5th Century, but few have survived. Among the earliest pieces of secular plate are the well-known ewer of Goslin, 1477, and the celebrated Luneberg horn of silver and ivory, made in 1486. These two historic pieces show beyond a doubt the characteristic traits of the working ways of the German silversmith. A wealth of detail work and almost an over-profusion of ornamentation are to be observed. Rarely, including the present-day German silver, are pieces worked with a definite note of simplicity. The influence of the Renaissance in Germany is apparent in the goldsmith's art earlier than in any other craft. It may be noticed as early as 1490. By 1520 it was firmly established.

No country in all the history of silversmithing produced so many drinking articles. This is only natural when one considers the life of the typical German of those days when wine and liquor were as important in the day's diet as the modern Englishman's cup of tea.

Augsberg and Nuremberg were the chief centers of silversmithing. Here the craft of the goldsmith was stimulated by the opulence of the patriots of these two international cities as well as by the patronage of ecclesiastics, princes and nobles. In Nuremberg one name stands out as the father of silversmithing. This is Wenzel Jamnitzer, often called the Cellini of Germany. He lived from 1508 to 1585. There is little doubt of his magnificent workings or inherent ability to create masterpieces. His name dominates the literature of goldsmithing in Nuremberg. Born in Vienna, he migrated to Germany in 1534. He was one of five children, each of whom was noted for his ability in art. He often produced pieces of

—S. Wyler Inc.

Bachelor Coffee Pot

Made by Weishaupt, Munich, 1843

beautiful enamelled and silver content and his work was quickly purchased by collectors all over the world.

In considering German silversmithing one must again mention the drinking objects produced, since they form an important part of silversmithing and helped no little in tracing the art history of the country. As early as the days of Caesar drinking from silver and gold-tipped horns was practiced. These were first made from the horns of the bison or ulus. Later many of the early ones were tipped with silver worked in beautiful detail, which made them the envy of many of the smiths of other countries.

Beakers were popular in Germany during the 16th, 17th and 18th Centuries. They were used as Guild cups and many are to be seen today depicting Scriptural and classical scenes in silver relief. Tankards were also made in great quantities, but mostly of another product combined with silver, such as serpentine, stoneware, amber and ivory. The fact that they were nearly always decorated with silver borders, proved the very definite flair for silver in the Reich.

Hunting cups were made in sets of from six to twenty, as well as double cups which were distinctly German and made nowhere else in Europe. Often referred to as bridal cups, they were a household object. The smaller top was reserved for the lady of the house while the master consumed his fill from the three-quarter bottom.

Nautilus shells and ostrich cups were also typical of the German smiths, and many beautiful examples may be seen today in the various museums of the world. In fact, every known type of silver object was made in Germany during the 17th and 18th Centuries. Many pieces were used in churches; others in the home; and many for purely decorative purposes. Pieces of tremendous proportion were also characteristic of the Germans. Animals were popular models, and it is not at all unusual to find today a life-size silver eagle of the 18th Century. Tea services, vases, massive candlesticks, were all made in profusion and exported in quantity to foreign lands.

The only great loss suffered by German art was during the Thirty Years' War, when hundreds of fine pieces were the target for the pillaging and plundering invaders.

Until 1884, the legislation regarding silver was enacted by each separate state of the Empire. It is almost impossible to study all of these ordinances as there were over a hundred German towns producing silver. As stated before, the two most important centers were Augsberg and Nuremberg. The town mark for Augsberg was always the same, a pineapple erect. Date letters were used and are most helpful in aiding the collector to make a chronological list of his pieces. The hall mark for the city of Nuremberg was the letter "N." First a capital Roman "N" was used and in the 19th Century a capital script "N" in a circle. After 1760 date letters were noted.

FRENCH TWO-HANDLED CUP
The maker of this silver cup in the Empire style was Jacques-Charles Mongendt, Paris, 1787.   *Museum of Fine Arts, Boston*

FRENCH SILVER
French silver wine flacon. Paris, circa 1790.
S. Wyler, Inc., New York

Fine Silver Was Made Everywhere in Northern Europe

By Seymour Wyler

AN intensive study of European silver reveals a striking fact common to nearly all the countries. Although silversmithing on the continent has been traced back to the 5th Century, very little early plate has survived. In this, social and economic conditions played major parts. Patriotism and dire need of money caused much secular plate to be melted for its metal value. That made for use in churches was often buried in the ground to preserve it from the ravaging hordes that scourged Europe during the Middle Ages. Sometimes centuries elapsed before these pieces again saw the light. Moreover, the amount found in this way is so small compared to the quantity that was buried, that one wonders how much more is still awaiting discovery. Town book records speak of large quantities of plate but comparatively little remains to be seen today.

Regarding the very early pieces very little data is available. Few records have survived and those few are usually in such a state of decay as to be practically unreadable. Yet early examples of plate still extant and now to be seen in museums, proclaim that they were the work of great artists and definitely prove that as early as the 8th Century, many magnificent pieces were wrought.

It must be remembered that in the days of early smithing, gold was used in a far greater quantity than silver. Therefore the study of early European plate, both sacred and secular, must include goldsmithing as well as silversmithing. Also, in order to gain a clear picture of the craft each country must be studied as an individual since few had the same governing laws for their Guilds or produced the same types of pieces.

BALTIC STATES

Silver is known to have been made since medieval times in the Baltic States. Not one piece has survived, however, and only a scattered few in museums remain as examples of a later period. Yet the centers of smithing are definitely established and a few prominent names are remembered.

Reval, capital of Estonia, had its Hans Ryssenbach, 1474, and Riga, capital of Latvia, had three outstanding smiths. The name of one has been lost though his work is remembered. The other two were Hans Urma and Thomas Smallde.

Such is the data on silversmithing in these provinces, once fiefs to the Swedish crown. Meagre as it is, it shows how widespread was the craft and how truly were the terms goldsmith and banker synonymous in the early days.

BELGIUM

In Belgium the 16th and 17th Centuries were a period of great commercial prosperity. Antwerp was the center of it and great artists flourished and produced a quantity of plate. Only one name was outstanding, however, in the field of silversmithing. It was

Coffee Pot Made at Mons 1771

—*Metropolitan Museum*

A TREASURY OF OLD SILVER

17th Century Flemish Casket

In silver-gilt by Vianen

—*Metropolitan Museum*

Hans of Antwerp. Yet his maker's mark has never been definitely identified and so no actual piece can be pointed out as actually made by this great master.

In fact, with all of Antwerp's prosperity, the most important center of artistic activity was Bruges. Here Flemish art reached its zenith under Charles the Bold. It is an irreparable loss that none of the splendid secular plate wrought by the Flemish artists remains today. This is probably due to the great depression which engulfed Belgium at the end of the 17th Century. Then as now it took a heavy toll, causing securities which were of plate rather than paper to be literally liquidated via the melting pot in order that their owners might have bread.

Ecclesiastical plate fared better and there are a number of pieces still extant. Probably the most famous is the magnificent gold and enamel reliquary, made in 1466 by Gerard Layet, now to be seen in Liege Cathedral.

Although there was no definite legislation for silver until 1814, many of the early makers used date letters. This has been an invaluable aid in tracing the exact year in which a particular piece was made. As many fine objects were executed as pieces of commemoration, the importance of date letters is obvious.

The earliest known Guild in Belgium had been organized by the 15th Century at Ghent. The outstanding master here was Corneille de Bont, who worked in 1471.

Many of the early Flemish pictures depicted silver objects, but so few of the latter are to be seen today that but little knowledge can be gained from their pictured likeness. In the National Gallery in London there is Gonzales Cozues' canvas, "Taste," done in 1618. Here is depicted a cylindrical castor, definitely proving that this style of muffineer was known in Flanders earlier than in England.

It will be noticed that many cities in Belgium produced silver and gold at an early date. The names of Mons, Liege and Tournai must also be listed as centers of silversmithing.

Silver in Belgium was made in two qualities, that of 900 fine being shown by the block letter A in an irregular shield; and that of 800 fine being recognized by the same letter in a square shield. The various town marks by which the early Flemish silver can be recognized, are as follows:

Antwerp—"An open hand erect beneath a crown, resembling electoral bonnet in spade shaped outline, point upwards." (Only two makers' marks known from here.)

Bruges — (Two town marks were used). "A lion's head couped, surmounted by a crown." "A small block letter 'b' passing through a crown."

Brussels—"Capital Roman B in plain oblong, and a lion rampant, contourne, in ellipse," and the letter "o" in a shaped shield.

Ghent—No known hall marks.

CZECHOSLAVAKIA

In Bohemia, now known as Czechoslavakia, the city of Prague was outstanding as the center of art. Under the encouragement of Premysl Otakar II, the "Golden King of the 13th Century," silver and goldsmithing flourished to a high degree. Fortunately many pieces have been preserved which are recognized as the work of masters and from which many later craftsmen of continental Europe copied their designs. On the other hand, the silversmiths of Prague were in their turn influenced by other workers in foreign lands and the French style of the First Empire penetrated into their ateliers as in other European capitals.

Silver Tankard about 1812

Made by Isack Andersen Feldthus

—*Metropolitan Museum*

NORTH EUROPEAN SILVER

In Prague, also, beautiful ornaments were fashioned from pieces of semi-precious stones, cut and carved and surmounted by bands of magnificiently chased silver and gold. These are to be seen in museums and only by viewing them can one get a true idea of the delicate quality of their work.

The other center of smithing was Olomone, known today as Olmutz. Pieces have been traced from here as early as 1575 from workers who registered their marks and many smiths are known to have wrought even earlier, though no definite marks or pieces are available.

DENMARK

No Scandinavian silver dating before the 13th Century has survived although pieces are known to have been made some 500 years earlier. This was due to many wars and much economic strife. Also the demand for costly pieces was not great and consequently craftsmen from other countries did not settle in Denmark in any such numbers as in other parts of Europe. However, quite a little data is available from the records and one notes the unusual fact that as early as 1685 the first ordinances governing the manufacture of silver were introduced.

Perhaps the most definitely Danish article was the drinking horn, that earliest known drinking vessel ever made by man. Originally made in Iceland by the settlers, they were brought into Denmark by fur traders and those coming there for winter supplies. They were made of whalebone or similar hardy substance. The Danish silversmiths mounted them with plain silver bandings and what had heretofore been purely useful, became ornamental as well.

During the 30 Years War, vast quantities of plate were buried in the earth for protection against the invading enemies. Only recently have many pieces been found, thus making the present day collections of early Danish silver more comprehensive.

Shortly after horns and other silver drinking vessels had been introduced, there was a demand for a more florid style and Danish smiths executed pieces of a heavily embossed nature. Flat chasing was rarely used, as they did not possess the skill to do fine work. Therefore when one finds a piece of Danish silver prior to 1700 with the contemporary chasing, it is most valuable.

Perhaps 90 per cent of all silver made in Denmark was in the form of drinking vessels. It is quite understandable when one considers the people. The flair for extravagant ornaments had no place in their life, and as they were among the hardiest and most serious drinkers in all Europe, the smiths worked to please the local trade.

From Iceland came great quantities of bone and ivory. These were used for tankards and later surmounted by silver. One name in particular, that of Magnus Berg, stands out as the man who gained greatest recognition in his special field of beautifully carved ivory pieces.

Copenhagen was the center of most of the Danish silversmithing. The town mark was "In an ellipse, 3 towers or minarets above the date." The outstanding names among the early silversmiths with the years of their workings are: Steen Peterson, 1620; Dietrich Skillings, 1707; Jacob Hoffman, 1723; and J. N. Randers, 1733.

The only other registered town in Denmark at all recognized as important in silversmithing was Odense, which bore the town mark of "A fleur de lys, joined to 2 spreading leaves in an ellipse."

—*Metropolitan Museum*

Danish Standing Cup

Made by Niels Jonsen, Copenhagen, 1705-31

16th Century Chalice from Antwerp

—*Metropolitan Museum*

Italy, Spain and Portugal Made Elaborate Silver

By Seymour Wyler

No country in all of Europe was richer in ecclesiastical plate than Italy, but in direct contrast it suffered the greatest losses in secular pieces. This was not due so much to conflict and invasion as to the practice of melting existing plate to be remade by other artists. Florence was the world center of art and students came there from all over the country. After they had served their apprenticeship they had to submit a finished piece as an example of their skill. If it was accepted, they were known as full-fledged masters.

The inherent love of art in all its phases raised the craft of goldsmithing to a higher standard than had ever been known before. The most beautiful silver and gold work in the world was produced in Italy. From this country all the royalty of Europe ordered marvelous services and as time was not an important element, the most magnificent things in art were achieved.

The patronage of the arts really started under the pontificate of Nicholas V, 1447-1455. Unfortunately nothing remains of the workings of this period. The decided flair for further improvement on the original pieces caused them to be destroyed, so that the precious metal might be used again. As early as 1314, Florence had legislation covering goldsmithing and from the records we know that many of the world-famous painters and sculptors were also goldsmiths, though nothing remains today of their efforts.

The quantity of secular plate made in the 16th Century far exceeded that made for the churches. Italian love of luxury and of living in the best of taste had created a demand for beautiful pieces to grace the homes of those so well able to afford them. Much work in the combination of gold and crystal was done. The most noted of these workers was Valerio Belli, 1468-1546.

The most famous goldsmith, of course, was Benvenuto Cellini, whose story is familiar to all students of the arts and of history. It is enough to say that his few remaining pieces fetch higher prices from collectors than any other silver in the world, regardless of date.

The first goldsmith's association in Italy has been recorded as early as 1035. Prior to the consolidation of the several small Italian states, each section used its own particular markings on silver and gold objects. The general laws passed to legalize the production of silver were not introduced and adopted until 1873. The town marks of the main silver producing centers were:

Naples: "NAP" beneath a crown in octagon.

Rome: In the 18th and 19th Centuries the gold hall mark was "Two keys in saltire, beneath a tiara in small ellipse." The silver hall mark was "Two keys in saltire, beneath a mitre in outline." Later the mark was changed to "Two keys in saltire, beneath a pavillion d'Eglise."

Venice: A winged lion's head affronte.

Spain

Her conquests in the New World brought vast wealth to Spain and under Philip II, 1556-1590, the material prosperity of the country was further increased. Philip, who was one of the chief monarchs of Christendom, adorned the great Escorial with vast quantities of plate and finely jewelled objects. These were executed not only by Spanish workers, but by leading silversmiths of other countries. Never had patronage of the goldsmith in Spain reached the heights it did then. Serious losses in plate were to occur a little more than two centuries later, however, when the fine pieces in the Escorial would be thrown into the melting pot for coin to finance the armies of the Civil Wars of 1833-1840.

Of the early part of the 16th Century no secular plate remains. That most brilliant era in Spanish history when the court of Ferdinand and Isabella flourished, has left no traces of the magnificent

—*Metropolitan Museum of Art*

Italian Candle Snuffer
Roman work of the late 17th Century

work created during that time. The works of art for the great cathedrals were undisturbed, however, and so ecclesiastical silver of the early days may be seen today in the many museums of Spain.

In the study of Spanish silver notice must be taken of the huge monstrances decorated with beautifully executed silver and gold statuettes and known as custodias. Many of importance are still extant. Enrique D'Arphe was responsible for the great custodia of Cordova in 1513, as well as the Antonio, under the influence of the Renaissance style, made one at Santiago in 1544. The finest

SILVER OF THE LATIN COUNTRIES

known example in the world today, however, was made by Enrique's grandson, Juan de Arphe. The latter was the best known of this family of illustrious silversmiths and his masterpiece was fashioned at Valladalid.

From the 15th to the 17th Centuries, Spanish silver was prone to over-elaboration. The public demanded it and the smiths naturally worked to please them. Perhaps no vessel of domestic and ornamental use was made in greater quantity during the 16th Century than the rosewater dish and ewer. The few remaining pieces prove beyond a doubt the flair for pieces in the more ornate manner. Also peculiar to Spanish silver history was a shallow dish with a short foot that derived its shape from early Valencian pottery. Few examples remain today.

The defeat of the Armada in 1588 was a body blow to material prosperity. Literary art improved, but that of the goldsmith declined. Then came the reign of Philip III and the waning power of Spain. Along with this was a noticeable decline in the arts in general, which continued and reached its lowest point in the reign of Philip IV.

During the 18th Century, although Spanish silversmiths were influenced by French artistic efforts, demand for pieces in the English style was so great that many typically English table pieces, such as cruets, inkstands, and candelabra were fashioned.

The habit of looting treasures of a country by invading armies is evidenced by the amount of Spanish plate found in France and England today. Most of it was taken either during or after the wars between those two countries and Spain.

As early as the 13th Century silversmiths were working at Toledo, Seville, and Burgos, and in the 14th Century work is to be noted at Valencia, Valladalid Guadaloupe, Genoa, and several smaller towns. The most important center of silversmithing was Madrid with Barcelona not far behind in the quality and quantity of pieces produced. The filigree work in silver so peculiar to many of the Spanish smiths, was started in Barcelona. Later, work in this design was done at Cordova and Salamanca.

Very little is known of early Spanish hall marks and only through existing book records can pieces be actually dated.

—Metropolitan Museum of Art

Ornate Portuguese Basin and Ewer
Made at Oporto, circa 1750

Portugal

The rise of Portugal to the foremost colonizing power in Europe during the 15th Century, caused a marked development in the taste of the people for objects of luxury. The churches also benefitted from this upgrading of culture and became filled with beautiful pieces fashioned from precious metals.

There was no natural metal to be mined in Portugal. Consequently the only means of getting gold and silver for making plate was from the mines of South America and Asia where Portugal already had political influence. During the reign of Emanuel I, demand for plate grew in proportion to steadily increasing wealth and some of the most magnificent plate in all Europe was produced by Portuguese smiths. Shortly after this, however, a blight fell on the style of these silversmiths as a type of architecture known as the Arte Manuelina permeated the country and cast its shadow on other forms of art. It had practically no artistic merit and the pieces of plate fashioned under its influence suffered

—Metropolitan Museum of Art

Spanish Candlesticks
Made at Saragossa about 1750

accordingly.

The 16th Century was the golden age of silversmithing in Portugal and under the Empire, 1499-1580, social life in Lisbon was said to equal that of Rome. Certainly appreciation of the fine arts was quickened to a height never again reached in the history of the country.

Portuguese plate at this period, like the Spanish, was prone to over-ornamentation and resembled that of its neighboring country to such a degree that it was impossible to distinguish between the two in the absence of marks. In early silver French and other foreign influences on the craft were noted while from 1703 on, the date of the Methuan treaty with England, the styles of English silversmiths were reproduced almost entirely. In the two main silver centers, Lisbon and Oporto, demand for English styles progressed to such a degree that certain unprincipled smiths even punched English hall marks on their wares.

In 1721 began the serious destruction of plate when the extravagant tastes of John V, 1706-1750, caused wholesale melting of early pieces to get funds to pay for his indulgences. In 1755 the great earthquake "of Lisbon town" and resulting fires completed it. Most of the fine specimens were lost forever.

Several cities in Portugal were recognized as silver centers, such as Beja, Broga, Lisbon, Oporto, Setubal, and Evara. The first legislation for silver in Lisbon was noted in 1460 and in Oporto there is the mention of assayers as early as 1570. A complete system of hall-marking was not established in Portugal until the 18th Century.

The Portuguese hall mark for silver and gold wares was a capital Roman P beneath a pellet in arched outline. Lisbon, itself had a capital Roman L beneath crown in irregular outline.

—Metropolitan Museum of Art

A Perfume Burner

Made at Lisbon late in the 18th Century

—Metropolitan Museum of Art

A Spanish Standish or Inkstand

Made at Salamanca 1775-1800